Ancient Colonizations

Ancient Colonizations

ANALOGY, SIMILARITY AND DIFFERENCE

Edited by

Henry Hurst and Sara Owen

Duckworth

First published in 2005 by
Gerald Duckworth & Co. Ltd.
90-93 Cowcross Street, London EC1M 6BF
Tel: 020 7490 7300
Fax: 020 7490 0080
inquiries@duckworth-publishers.co.uk

www.bloomsbury.com

A catalogue record for this book is available
from the British Library

ISBN 0 7156 3298 1

Typeset by Ray Davies

Contents

Contents

Contributors

Carla Antonaccio is Professor of Classical Studies, Wesleyan University, USA.

Henry Hurst is Reader in Classical Archaeology, University of Cambridge.

Elizabeth DeMarrais is University Lecturer, Department of Archaeology, University of Cambridge.

Sara Owen is Research Associate on the Greek Colonization and the Archaeology of European Development project, Faculty of Classics, University of Cambridge, and Fellow and Director of Studies in Classics, Fitzwilliam College, Cambridge.

Nicholas Purcell is Fellow and Tutor in Ancient History, St John's College, Oxford.

Gillian Shepherd is Lecturer in Classical Archaeology, Institute of Archaeology and Antiquity, University of Birmingham.

Anthony Snodgrass is Emeritus Professor of Classical Archaeology, University of Cambridge.

Nicola Terrenato is Professor, Department of Classics, University of North Carolina at Chapel Hill.

Illustrations

Introduction

Henry Hurst

When the seminar series which gave rise to this book was being devised,[1] Sara and I (as organizers) had slightly different objectives. This might perhaps be expected from our different specializations in Greek and Roman archaeology, but we also differed in ambition. Mine, the lower ambition, was simply to have those with Greek and Roman expertise speak and listen to each other in the same forum on the topic of colonization, problematizing it in terms of their special field of study and setting out their terms of reference. As I had learnt from being a Roman archaeologist with an interest in this area within a Faculty of Classics, there was almost no dialogue between Greek and Roman specialists on this topic:[2] the two fields of study started from a different type of textual base within the Classics; they had different traditions of scholarship and points of reference; and, as the chapters in this volume will show, the non-scholarly manipulations of these areas of knowledge have also differed significantly over the last century and a half, with an impact in shaping the two areas of scholarship. Yet, if one moves from these edifices into the archaeological evidence, say, for Mediterranean settlements where there was an interaction between different material cultures, and thinks especially about the type of evidence retrieved and the types of more purely archaeological approaches which have been prevalent over the last generation or so, it seems obvious that Greek and Roman archaeologists should have a great deal to say to each other on this topic, as, indeed, we take for granted that they have in more newly defined fields such as landscape archaeology.

Sara's higher ambition, eloquently set out in her own chapter, and central to the character of this book as a whole, was to look critically at the whole question of 'colonization' in the ancient world and unpack – or at least poke vigorously into – the cultural baggage we carry as modern Westerners in thinking about this topic, focussing especially on the intellectual tool of analogy, which is usable both for clarification and for obfuscation, but which, as she and other authors argue, has tended more towards the latter role on this topic. This is a Greek concern more than a Roman one in the first instance – Romanists have tended to expend more of their energy on the related but different topic of Romanization – but it is the starting point for the closer communication between subdisciplines that I was looking for.

The chapters in this volume, then, respond to this more ambitious agenda and in so doing also, I believe, go a considerable way in outlining a way forward for Greek and Roman colonization archaeology in tandem, outlining shared and wider issues while acknowledging concerns peculiar to each. Each one of the seven chapters is more than capable of standing on its own, so that any attempt to place them into some sort of logical 'order' will be liable to do them an injustice by selective emphasis of part of their contents, but all the same a sort of logic can be made to present itself without, I hope, undue distortion. Two ends of this seem to be represented by Sara's 'Analogy, Archaeology and Archaic Greek Colonization' and Nicholas Purcell's 'Colonization and Mediterranean History', in that the first of these is – predominantly – a broad exposure of the 'problematique', while the second is – predominantly – an experiment in thinking outside the problematized traditional categories. The qualification is to stress that these characterizations only partly apply and to re-emphasize that the other five contributions again fit at most only broadly within these bounds.

Three of the five – Gillian Shepherd's 'The Advance of the Greek: Greece, Great Britain and Archaeological Empires', Anthony Snodgrass's ' "Lesser Breeds": the History of a False Analogy' and Nicola Terrenato's 'The Deceptive Archetype: Roman Colonialism in Italy and Postcolonial Thought' – could be characterized as substantially historical and partly geographical in their approach, which is to explain how thinking and the terms of reference for the history and archaeology of Greek colonization and the Roman Empire came to take the forms it took over the last century and more. But none of these three pieces is purely historiographic: Snodgrass sets out his prescription for the direction in which he would like to see study go in future and articulates how his historical survey is of leanings he would like to see corrected; Shepherd and Terrenato likewise both link their surveys to 'new thinking' sections – Shepherd illustrates how Sicilian architecture of the Archaic period can be talked about outside the traditional framework, while Terrenato in a section entitled 'Prospective' looks forward to a new way of looking at the cultural and social frameworks of the Roman Empire.

The other two chapters concentrate more on dealing with problems of colonization studies as we face them today. Elizabeth DeMarrais generously responded to our invitation to broaden the scope with 'A View from the Americas: "Internal Colonization", Material Culture and Power in the Inka Empire', in which she not only provides a succinct account of the present state of Inka colonization archaeology (with a strikingly different sense of what colonizing entailed) but addresses issues familiar from the ancient world like the role of elites and a central authority in material displays and the question of whether there was a phenomenon which could be called 'Inkaization'. Where her study has most to offer as a contribution to our concern with analogy is perhaps in the methodology and thinking of Inka archaeologists about their data set. Carla Antonaccio's 'Excavating Colonization' addresses today's concerns in Greek colonization archaeology and argues for (and against) certain conceptual approaches, working these arguments out in the context especially of ancient Sicily. From a Roman archaeology perspective, thinking of the discussions of the idea of acculturation in that field, it is interesting to see how the concept of hybridity is being used (and the variations of emphasis upon it in different chapters) within Greek settlement archaeology. Perhaps following that observation a comment might be added about a general preponderance of Greek over Roman content in the chapters, or rather two comments: the first is that this was partly intended in view of the recent wealth of books dealing with theoretical issues in Roman provincial archaeology;[3] the second is that, apart from Terrenato's chapter explicitly on the Roman Empire, Roman matters are treated in Purcell's chapter and approaches in Roman archaeology are points of reference for discussions in several chapters. This is not a book just for Greek archaeologists.

Differences of emphasis and views of course do emerge from a careful reading of the chapters, but these are by and large insignificant in comparison with major areas of what seem to be common ground among all contributors, and in any case the differences are revealing about debated areas. From the common ground one gains the sense of a subject that has largely shed an imprisoning conceptual framework, for which new targets for study are being defined with a view to moving forward and being less isolated from the rest of archaeology (and, for that matter, history). If this book contributes towards these ends, it will have served its purpose.

Notes

1. In the summer and autumn of 2000; the seminars were given in the Lent term 2001 in the Faculty of Classics at Cambridge.

2. I am aware of efforts to make precisely the bridge referred to here, as for example the 1998 conference in London on 'Parallels and Contrasts in Greek and Roman Colonization: origins, ideologies and interactions', but the papers of this conference had not been published when this book was in preparation.

3. For example Brandt and Slofstra 1983, Millett 1990, Metzler et al. 1995, Mattingly 1997, Woolf 1998, Keay and Terrenato 2001, and successive Proceedings of the Theoretical Roman Archaeology Conference, which has taken place annually since 1991.

1

Analogy, Archaeology and Archaic Greek Colonization[1]

Sara Owen

Introduction

The study of Archaic Greek colonization has undergone tremendous change in the past two decades. One of the main changes has been the ever greater use of archaeological approaches. Whilst archaeological evidence has had a prominent place in the standard studies of the last half-century (e.g. Graham 1978; Boardman 1964; Dunbabin 1948), some of the more recent archaeological approaches have looked more carefully at long-term processes and social interactions within the colonies themselves (e.g. Carter 1998; Shepherd 1995). Theoretical concepts derived from anthropology (such as core-periphery) have stimulated studies of how populations were actually using 'foreign' material culture (Frankenstein and Rowlands 1978; Cunliffe 1988; Dietler 1995, 1999). Other scholars have begun to focus more upon the agency of local populations (see e.g. Gosden 2004).

In particular, the comparatively recent interest in the relationships between Greek colonies and the local populations (see e.g. the papers in Descoeudres 1990) has shown that Greek colonization should no longer be seen as a uniform phenomenon with the same processes and interactions occurring wherever the Greek colony may be. These changes of approach make the study of Greek colonization one of the most vibrant fields in Classical archaeology. However, whilst some centrally important areas within the topic have received much recent discussion, such as the relationship between texts and archaeology and the issue of ethnicity (see e.g. Osborne 1998; Morgan 1999; Lomas 2004; Antonaccio, this volume), the full extent of the problem caused by the analogies used to elucidate the evidence has received little critical analysis.[2]

This is not to imply that scholars have failed to point out the prevalence of the analogy with modern European colonization and imperialism – far from it. In fact it has become something of a truism to state that past studies of Greek 'colonization' have been influenced by, or even based upon, the colonial experience of Britain and other Western European nations from the sixteenth to the mid-twentieth centuries AD (as Shepherd, Snodgrass and Antonaccio illustrate from different viewpoints in this volume; see also Dietler 1995; Shepherd 1993, 1995; Osborne 1998; De Angelis 1998; Lyons & Papadopoulos (eds) 2002). The central concern of scholars, however, has generally been the type of interactions that this analogy has bestowed upon the subject, rather than the analogy itself.

I will attempt to show here that despite the advances in the study of Greek colonization to which I have referred, the underlying assumptions of what colonization is, and many of the anthropologically-inspired theoretical models which have so advanced the study of cultural interactions in these contexts, are still based upon the analogy with modern European colonialism – an analogy which has not been fully analysed or justified. Rather it exists as a set of assumptions of what colonialism is. Whilst many of the problems arising from the analogy have been addressed by scholars, the assumption that asymmetrical power relationships, drawn along ethnic lines, existed in all 'colonized' areas from the Late Geometric and Archaic periods onwards is one which still pervades much of the literature. My intention, then, is to set out these problems, relating them to other theoretical approaches in the study of ancient colonization (as, for example, the debated topics of Hellenization and Romanization), and, in a brief concluding section using my own research area of Thrace, illustrate an approach which I believe would overcome many of the difficulties outlined.

Traditional approaches

A traditional, but still widely held, view of Greek colonization might go as follows: first, the movement is very much an organized process, whether organized by an individual or a state. It is for specific ends – the attainment of land, or trade. The local populations of the area settled are conquered or beguiled into handing over territory, and are at a disadvantage due to the military and cultural superiority of the Greeks. In fact they often attempt to take on Greek cultural identity through the use of Greek material culture and styles. Whilst intermarriage is often posited, it takes the form of Greek males marrying local women, and is often therefore portrayed as symbolic of this asymmetrical relationship (see e.g. Dougherty 1993a).

This is an admittedly stereotypical, but nonetheless accurate, characterization of a widespread narrative of Greek colonization. Although this narrative has begun to be attacked in recent years, it still remains very influential.[3] It derives its strength from certain key features of the study of this subject: the types of evidence that are normally privileged, the approach generally taken to questions of ethnicity and the analogies used to elucidate the motivations for, and processes of, Greek settlement.

The first of these issues has been addressed particularly well by Osborne (1998). Greek colonization is perceived to be a fully historical subject, and therefore suffers from the privileging of literary sources over archaeological evidence. The literary evidence is often seen as explicit, and so more able to answer the questions asked of it than archaeological evidence (Graham 1982). Indeed, Purcell has rightly pointed out that the current interpretative model 'is as complete a subordination of archaeology to the slavery of text-based history as one could imagine' (Purcell 1997: 501).

This privileging of texts has produced some real problems for the ways in which archaeology is used. The attempts to combine archaeological and textual evidence have often resulted in trying to make archaeology confirm events described in textual sources rather than looking at social or long-term processes. One problem with this method is that of time scales. Whilst in recent years archaeological focus has again passed to smaller temporal scales of analysis, with agency theory, this has not taken the form of discussions of specific individuals. In fact Archaic Greek archaeological resources are unable to provide a date range more refined than a twenty-year span. This may seem to be a purely negative point from the historian's point of view. However, it is arguable not only that our literary and archaeological sources are often illuminating different parts of the same world, but that they are often incapable of being *straightforwardly* correlated because they often work on such completely different time scales. Indeed, the archaeologist may be in a position to identify social trends which are impossible for an actor in a single period to recognize. Thus, whilst it is possible that on occasion the foundation of a Greek colony may have been a single event, trying to find such single events in the archaeological record is unproductive and gets us no further than merely trying to confirm literary sources. The focus upon this aspect means that we miss out on studying the broader and longer-term social processes which led up to such events. The concept of colonization as a single event has thus tied the hands of archaeologists studying the first periods of Greek settlement, since the establishment of foundation dates has been more important to scholars than looking for patterns in the pre-settlement period and studying evidence for first contacts and interactions.

The literary texts themselves have their own problems as sources of evidence. One example of the problems stemming from simplistic readings of the texts is the presentation of Archaic Greek colonization as a uniform phenomenon, a state enterprise from the first. As Osborne has pointed out, whilst there is evidence to support the view that Greek colonization could be a state enterprise by the Classical period, there are great differences between the Classical and the Late Geometric foundations (Osborne 1998). Rarely, if ever, is there reliable evidence of such early state-organized movements of populations. The archaeological evidence from the Greek colonies in the West generally indicates a 'mixed archaeological record and failure to mimic the material culture of a single Greek mainland city' (Osborne 1998: 264). Similar mixed material has been noted in the North Aegean and Black Sea areas too (Owen 2000a, 2003; Archibald 1998; Isaac 1986; Solovyov 1999). Those scholars who have suggested that the literary evidence occasionally supports the existence of state-sponsored colonization in the eighth and seventh centuries BC have not taken into account the contexts of the literary traditions – that is their roles in the Classical recreations of pasts for the settlements concerned (Osborne 1998, quoting Graham 1964). Few have taken into account the complexity of the contemporary contexts of these sources, in terms of the relationship between the foundation stories from which we glean much of this data and the contemporary living colonies in which they are created. This is further complicated by the fact that many scholars have noted changes in ideology which occur in fifth-century BC Greek sources concerning Greekness and the distance between Greeks and other peoples (e.g. Cartledge 1993; Hall 1989; Hall 1997; Dougherty 1993a; Gosden 2004). This insight has however not affected the confidence with which archaeologists have used them as evidence for a single event which is unproblematically to be found in the material record, and even for the relations between Greeks and native populations in the Archaic period.

This leads into a second important issue within this subject: ethnicity. This is a complex subject, and only a brief discussion can be presented here. Greek colonies are sites in which the identification of race in the archaeological record becomes a central problem. We want to be able to identify and distinguish between the Greeks and the local populations in the archaeology – their burials, settlements and ritual sites. However, it has become increasingly clear that the material record does not provide a simple means for such identifications (Jones 1997; Hall 1997; Morgan 1999). Race is not identifiable in the material record. Indeed, the belief that simple distinctions between peoples can be made from archaeological remains stems from the basic classificatory system that we still use to describe 'coincidental distributions of material traits': that of archaeological cultures (Morgan 1999: 93). As Morgan points out, we need such classificatory tools. A problem arises only when the descriptive classification is assumed to have social or racial significance (Morgan 1999). Ethnicity, as a self-conscious affiliation, is one of several social identities, along with gender, age and status, which may be actively played up or down according to local needs. This is important to us because many studies of Greek colonization see the spread of Greek styles and objects as indicative of a spread of Greek identity (see below). However, the material culture of others may be used not as an indication of ethnic affiliation, but as exotic and prestigious (cf. Helms 1988, 1993). Such an insight has a great impact upon our attempts to understand interactions between Greeks and local populations (see e.g. Dietler 1995, 1999; Gosden 2004; Owen 2000a).

Analogy and archaeology

The third, and perhaps even more important, factor that has led to the production of the traditional account of Greek colonization has been the analogy used to elucidate and amplify the source materials – that of modern European imperialism.

All archaeological inference is based upon analogy, whatever our theoretical background. At the simplest, and most mundane, level, when we call a particular vessel shape a bowl or a storage vessel, that is an analogical name – a name arising from our understanding of how such a shape is likely to have been used based upon our experience of similar shapes. Such inference is not foolproof, as has been acknowledged for many years, and we need to be careful to gather as much evidence as possible of how such items were actually used by the people under study. Indeed, the more links that we can make between the material record and our experience – the bowl may be found in an area associated with food preparation (which we label a kitchen), it may even contain remains of food – the more confident we become in our interpretation.

Given that analogical reasoning is at the heart of archaeological interpretation, its correct use has become the subject of much debate. A central issue has been how one moves from archaeological evidence to the understanding of past societies. At question is the set of assumptions that allows us to move from static archaeological data to discussing past social dynamics. These assumptions are often banal and seemingly trivial and thus often not formalized, but implicit. Much of the archaeological discussion about this issue has therefore been involved with making such assumptions explicit. This means being clear about the assumptions and comparisons we use (the analogies) to attempt to understand past societies from material remains.

Wylie (2002) and Hodder (1982) have distinguished between two forms of analogy – formal and relational. Formal analogies draw parallels between unrelated contexts and hold that if there are some points of similarity between the two, then there are likely to be others too. This form of analogy is weak, and the observed similarities may merely be coincidental (Hodder 1982: 16). Relational analogies, by contrast, attempt to identify a link between two contexts that is often cultural or directly historical. In such analogies it is argued that the 'similarities between past and present situations are relevant to the unknowns that are being interpreted' (Hodder 1982: 19).

Among the greatest dangers of analogical reasoning, however, are not only the risk that we succumb to social evolutionary ideas (Johnson 1999: 52) but also the possibility that we ignore crucial differences between the archaeological record and our chosen analogy. Indeed, as Lloyd has stressed, contrast can be one of the most informative aspects of analogical reasoning (Lloyd 2004). There is also another, related danger. As Wylie has noted, 'analogical arguments are, by definition, "ampliative"; because the conclusions of these arguments claim more extensive similarities than their premises establish, they are always liable to error' (Wylie 2002: 143).

The study of Greek colonization has until recently, however, been led more by the trends in text based subjects than by those in archaeology. Ancient history has grappled with the issue of analogy in a rather different way from archaeology. The issue of how we understand the ancient world and interpret the evidence we have has indeed been addressed with reference to modern analogies. The worries about whether analogies are acceptable at all have not really been in evidence. To take one example, the great modernist/primitivist debate about the ancient economy was ultimately based, not upon *whether* modern comparisons were appropriate to the ancient context, but upon which period of modern economic development was most appropriate as a comparison.[4] However, there has developed in the past four decades a theoretically more sophisticated comparative history in which contrast has been as important as similarity (e.g. Finley 1973, 1975; Cartledge 1985b, 1998; Lloyd 2004). This is beginning to have some influence upon the debates within Greek colonization studies (see e.g. Lyons and Papadopoulos (eds) 2002).

The modernist/primitivist debate in particular has been very influential in Greek colonization studies. For instance, the motivations debate, which is still ongoing, began as a discussion of the relative merits of the idea of 'trade before the flag' (Blakeway 1932-3, 1935) and the primitivist conception that Archaic trade was very small scale and that land was thus the main motivation – the 'aim of colonization was not *commercial* but *imperial*' (Hasebroek 1933: 110). One positive development in the study of Greek colonization has been the evolution of this debate from one merely about the scale of trade to one more explicitly about the nature and location of the ancient economy, and therefore whether modern or anthropological comparisons are more suitable. The latter, substantivist, position has now been suggested for a variety of areas (e.g. Dietler 1995, 1999; Owen 2000a, 2003). If the exchange of objects is primarily a social phenomenon – if the circulation of 'foreign' material is governed not by 'rational' economics or the profit motive, but by the power that their links with the world outside evokes – this has far-reaching implications for the study of culture contact in general and Greek colonization in particular.

Analogy and Greek colonization

Until relatively recently, modern European colonialism was used as an explicit analogy for Archaic Greek colonization. Blakeway's (1932-3; 1935) conception of 'trade before the flag' had clear parallels with the British experience in India, and in particular is a direct analogy with the East India Trading Company prior to British colonization. Dunbabin (1948) and

Woodhead (1962) both made explicit use of the comparison. The latter even quoted Stanley Baldwin's idealization of British colonization as the heading quotation in his *The Greeks in the West* (1962: 17).[5] Woodhead continues: 'Stanley Baldwin spoke of British colonization, but his words could as readily refer to the Greeks who left their Aegean cities to found new homes and farm new lands in Sicily, and along those coasts of southern Italy later to acquire the name of *Megale Hellas* or *Magna Graecia*' (1962: 17).

There have been many recent attempts to show that this analogy is unfounded and damaging (see e.g. Shepherd 1993, 1995; Osborne 1998; De Angelis 1998). What has primarily been focussed upon, however, is the way in which British colonialism is portrayed in the comparison as a noble and civilizing venture. The analogy has not yet been entirely dispensed with. Indeed, some modern analyses have reinforced the comparison. For example, one recent comparative approach has attempted to show how the literary sources for colonization may be read 'as a kind of discourse that organises its story in familiar and culturally significant ways' (Dougherty 1993a: 6). Dougherty's work uses the analogy of European settlement in America, and specifically the essays published by settlers justifying their actions in occupying a foreign land, claiming that 'Greek stories about colonising Sicily or the Black Sea in the seventh century BC are no more transparent, no less culturally constructed than the nineteenth century British tales of empire in India; they are every bit as much about power, language, and cultural appropriation' (1993: 4). This is an exciting new and more subtle reading of the textual sources, but her attempts to disentangle the metaphors employed in the narratives tend to make assumptions about the nature of Greek colonization. Thus the metaphor of marriage is interpreted less as a symbol of integration than as according to the violence of the act of founding a city on foreign territory (1993a: 67).

Dougherty's study does represent a welcome move away from dogmatic adherence to the letter of the text, but to interpret her material she has used an accepted historiographical tradition (which sees colonization as the violent seizure of territory) derived from imperialist readings of the very texts for which she is attempting to produce a more subtle reading. This historiographical tradition is subject not only to the vagaries of the ancient sources in which, from the fifth century 'historical, literary, mythical and legendary material are combined as needed to represent and legitimate action' (Dougherty 1993a: 5; cf. Turner 1981: 149-53), but also to scholars' preoccupations which are still deeply steeped in our colonial past.

The problem for modern scholars lies in the fact that this is not merely a convenient and disposable analogy used as an explanatory tool. Rather, there is a complex history of cross-referencing in which European colonialism drew upon perceived ancient models and was then used as a tool with which to understand these ancient 'models'.[6] As one commentator has put it, 'it is no accident that the symbols of empire associated with modern

European colonialism, and indeed the institutions and language of domination, often resembled those of the ancient Mediterranean states: the latter served as models for modern practice and as a reservoir of symbolic raw material manipulated in the invention of traditions of cultural ancestry and the construction of the discourse of domination for the colonial powers' (Dietler 1995: 91). Greek colonization is therefore 'intimately implicated in the phenomenology of modern European colonialism' (Dietler 1995: 91).

It is not enough, therefore, simply to point out the extent to which the ideas of modern colonialism and the easy analogy it affords to the modern scholar has affected the study of Archaic Greek colonization. The web of influences is a complex one. The strength of the model (the association) resides in the extent to which imperialist readings of Greek sources were used as a model and justification for modern colonial practice, which was then used as a good analogy for interpreting the ancient phenomenon. The seductive closeness of the words and concepts used to describe the two phenomena, 'word magic' as Finley called it (1976: 174), has tangled scholars to the extent that even those who have rejected the imperialist model still apply some of its central assumptions, such as the existence of asymmetrical power relationships in the Archaic period (e.g. De Angelis 1994).

All this indicates that the analogy was not one that was necessarily chosen primarily for its ability to elucidate the ancient material nor one that was initially systematically applied in an academically reasoned way. Rather it developed organically and piecemeal as part of the imperialist process in the eighteenth and nineteenth centuries, and served contemporary imperialist ends. Currently, it exists as a set of assumptions about what colonization is rather than a rigorously used analogy. The ideology of Hellenism has, however, led scholars to treat the analogy as somehow relational – based upon the idea that there is indeed a direct historical and cultural link between ancient Greece and modern Western Europe. In fact, however, it is a weak formal analogy (in so far as it can be categorized at all) based upon very few points of contact between the ancient and modern contexts (see e.g. Snodgrass, this volume; Wylie 2002).

Despite the long-running anxieties about analogy within archaeological work outlined above, Greek colonization studies have only recently taken active notice of the detrimental effects this particular analogy has had upon the study of the subject (see e.g. Lyons and Papadopoulos (eds) 2002; Shepherd 1995, this volume; cf. Gosden 2004). The most central of these is the fact that this analogy has led some scholars to ignore the role that local populations had to play in the process of Greek settlement, with attention mainly paid to Greek motivations for 'colonizing'. Assumptions have also been made about the nature of Greek colonies themselves. For example, although there is little (and late) literary evidence for the subjection of local populations by Greek colonists, this aspect of Greek colonization has been assumed by many to have been a central part of the process even in the earliest periods of Greek settlement. This is the case even in areas in which Greek colonies are known to have had to pay tribute to local powers such as the Odrysian Kingdom in Thrace (Archibald 1998). The assumption is made that a power relationship existed between Greeks and local populations which put the latter at a disadvantage from the beginning. Finally, the culture of the Greeks has been assumed to be overwhelmingly superior to that of the local populations. A central concept which has developed out of the analogy with modern colonialism, and which still underlies many studies of the subject, is that of Hellenization.

Hellenization has been seen by many as a natural and obvious process. The widespread adoption of Greek styles and use of Greek objects in many local contexts have been used to demonstrate the natural attractiveness of Greek material culture and, indeed, its cultural superiority (e.g. Boardman 1980: 200, now repeated in a new edition, 1999: 200). But Hellenization implies much more than mere adoption of Greek material culture. The concept implies a one-way influence in which Greeks have 'nothing to learn, much to teach' (Boardman 1999: 190). More specifically it has at its heart the assumption that the use of Greek styles and objects in some way indicates the adoption of a Greek identity: that the styles used by people are necessarily related to their ethnic or cultural identity.[7] This is an essentialist assumption that sits uneasily with more recent ideas about the relationship between ethnic identity and material culture (see above p. 8; also Jones 1997; Hall 1997).

The concept of Hellenization also has links with modern colonialism. It is based upon the concept of acculturation – a concept developed in the early twentieth-century anthropology and sociology 'within a common framework of thought derived from the colonial era and a widespread interest in the assimilation and modernization of non-western societies' (Jones 1997: 33) i.e. 'civilizing the natives'. Indeed, as Jones (1997: 33) and Hingley (1996: 39) have pointed out, the related term 'Romanization' was embedded in imperial politics (particularly with reference to India) and linked to nineteenth and early twentieth-century concepts of 'progress' and 'development'. The derivation of this concept led to the process of Hellenization (and Romanization) being viewed as a deliberate ploy, part of an imperial agenda (see e.g. Dominguez 2002 for a more recent expression of this view).

Romanization has been widely questioned as a legitimate concept for discussing the complex ways in which Roman material culture and styles were used within the Roman Empire (e.g. Webster and Cooper 1996; Woolf 1989, 1998; Jones 1997; Hingley 1996; Terrenato, this volume). Scholars of Greek colonization have only recently followed in the Romanists' footsteps in questioning both the explanatory power and the implications of this concept. In some ways, however, the tardiness of the Hellenists is understandable, as Hellenization is a rather stronger ideological concept than Romanization. It is extremely strong in many countries with Greek remains on their shores, partly due to the culture-historical methodologies which dominate archaeological thought in many of these countries. However, perhaps even more important to the strength of this model is the importance of Hellenization within the national (and nationalist) ideologies of many countries in Europe. Local identities have been fed by the concept that, through colonization and subsequent Hellenization, ancient Greece forms the basis of European civilization. Indeed some studies of Greek colonization have emphasized this as a reason for the importance of their particular area of study (Tsetskhlazde and De Angelis 1994: ix). Thus the barbarian versus civilized paradigm (the Hellenization by Greek colonies of local 'Barbarians') is used ultimately to account for the emergence of European civilization (Wailes and Zoll 1996: 23).

There have been many attempts to move away from the Greek-centred explanatory framework inherent in concepts such as Hellenization. Many scholars have rightly been put off by the attitudes towards the colonized which pervade such models of culture contact. One tactic has been to suggest that the analogy has been with the wrong period of European colonization (e.g. Snodgrass, this volume). The argument goes that there are very few analogical points of contact between Greek settlement overseas and the vast machinery that was nineteenth- and early twentieth-century European Imperialism; that indeed it is the attitudes of this period towards other races which have pervaded the subject and affected scholars' attitudes to the local populations encountered by the Greeks. However, it is argued, the earlier period of first contact can provide us with interesting analogical material. As Snodgrass (this volume, p. 49) points out, this is not new. Indeed Boardman's much-quoted assertion that '[the Etruscans] gave the Greeks the metal they wanted in return for what was often hardly more than the bright beads with which merchants are usually supposed to dazzle natives' (Boardman 1999: 200) is in fact using the earliest periods of European contact and colonization as a referent. It can be legitimately argued that this early period of contacts forms a better analogy for Greek colonization than does the heyday of the British Empire, with its strict racial legislation and economic power. Indeed, it is precisely this period of 'first contact' that more successful anthropological and postcolonial approaches have adopted as a good referent (e.g. Antonaccio 2004, this volume; Lyons & Papadopoulos (eds) 2002; Thomas 1991; see below).

Another attempt to compare this earlier period can be seen in the archaeological approach which was pioneered by Frankenstein and Rowlands (1978) for the relationship between Central Europe and the Mediterranean in the Archaic and Classical periods: the core-periphery model. This model was applied to explain the emergence of a highly ranked society in the Early Iron Age of France and Germany. Frankenstein and Rowlands argued that local chiefs managed to gain control over the supply of prestige goods from the Mediterranean. The trade which supplied these goods was instigated by Greeks who were in need of raw materials. Not only, however, did the control over these foreign goods lead to greater prestige for the chiefs, but in accordance with dependency theory (McGuire 1992: 136), the goods themselves became crucial to internal exchange, being 'wealth objects needed in social transactions and the payment of social debts' (Frankenstein and Rowlands 1978: 76). This led to greater hierarchy and dependence upon an external system over which the society had limited practical control. This model has in recent years been widened to the entire Mediterranean and the Black Sea (Pare 1993; Taylor 1989).

This model is based upon Wallerstein's 'world systems theory': an historical model for the rise of capitalism (1974, 1980, 1991), which draws on the ideas of Mandel, the *Annales* school of history and Marxist dependency theory (McGuire 1992: 47-8). The theory offers an interpretation of the expansion of Europe and the growth of capitalism from the sixteenth century AD onwards. Wallerstein describes the development of a world system in which a European core exploited 'peripheral' territories, by extracting raw materials and cheap labour in return for manufactured goods (cf. Woolf 1989; Champion 1989). This injection of prestige goods gave rise to a local economy based upon the competitive giving of gifts. The prestige goods eventually became necessary for social transactions, thus giving rise to dependence in the Third (or Developing) World.

The model of core-periphery (and prestige goods exchange) employed by archaeologists is based specifically upon the relationship of dependency that Wallerstein sees developing in his economic world system, in which the core is not a large coherent political power (world-empires) but a group of states. This situation has been used as a parallel for the ancient Mediterranean in which Greek and 'barbarian' worlds have been argued to have been, from as early as the end of the seventh century BC, 'inextricably bound together in a network of economic interdependence' (Cunliffe1988: 193).

This model therefore comprises a direct comparison with the effects of European imperialism. Indeed, central to whether such a concept can be used to discuss the Archaic Mediterranean is the debate about the ancient economy. Frank and Gills (1993, 2000) for example, argue for a five thousand-year world system in which differences in economic scale are acknowledged, but differences in kind between the pre- and post-Columbian world are denied. My own, substantivist, position is that such studies impose modern Capitalist economic frameworks upon the pre-Capitalist past (see also Gosden 2004). In addition, the fact that the model implies dependence on the core by the periphery reinforces the concept of a power relationship between Greek 'colonies' and the native populations which is, here, economic in character. Related to this is the problem that if we accept this overarching framework of explanation, and see all regions with Greek colonies on their shores as peripheries, we obscure the variability and the role of these societies in determining prehistoric developments (McGuire 1992: ch. 5). Therefore, despite the fact that this model does attempt to place more emphasis on the local context, it may legitimately be questioned whether the referent here – the development of Capitalism – is helpful for explaining the ancient economic and social patterns.

Another tactic for moving on from Hellenocentric approaches has been to suggest that the problems with the analogy stem from the type of interpretation of modern imperialism which has been foisted upon the past; that is an interpretation of the nineteenth and early twentieth centuries, which is overwhelmingly pro-imperialist and filled with negative attitudes about the colonized. An interesting route of interpretation has therefore recently begun which introduces postcolonial approaches to explore the mixed and murky aspects of Greek colonization. These approaches have been based upon, in particular, the work of scholars such as Stoler (1989) and Thomas (1991, 1994) who have emphasized the importance of looking at the specific historical, geographical and cultural contexts of modern colonial situations. They have stressed the importance of recognizing divisions of, for instance, class and gender as well as ethnicity, and stressed that these may well have produced divides in the local situation which cut across the poles of colonizer/colonized. Thomas, especially, emphasizes the cultural biography of objects and 'the mutability of things in recontextualization' (Thomas 1991: 28). It is this element of recent postcolonial research which has been seen as most useful for the study of ancient culture contact (see e.g. Antonaccio 2004, this volume). Dietler (1995, 1999) in particular has produced sensitive discussions of the choices exercised by different groups in Southern France, emphasizing the ways in which Greek and Etruscan objects and consumables were chosen to fit into existing patterns of behaviour and customs.

In many of these studies, the concept of hybridization has been used. This concept explores how 'the effect of colonial power' can be seen as 'the production of hybridization rather than the noisy command of colonialist authority or the silent repression of native traditions' (Bhabha 1994: 112). Hybridity has been seen as a space for negotiation between colonizer and colonized: a middle ground (Antonaccio, this volume, pp. 100-1; White 1991; Malkin 1998, 2001). In material culture terms, it has been applied to explain the appearance of mixed styles in colonial contexts (see e.g. Antonaccio, this volume). This approach has produced some exciting new ideas which have warned us that identities might not have been clear cut in colonial situations. However, the concept of hybridization is not a neutral one. It assumes that the material culture retains at least some of its old meanings in recontextualization (that it would be seen by the people using it as a hybrid of two distinct and 'ethnic-indicating' styles). Moreover, it explains how the colonized creatively subverted elements of the colonizers' material culture, and therefore carries with it the assumption that there was a dominant culture to be subverted: an assumption that needs substantiation in this context.

Despite these changes in emphasis, one element remains comparatively constant in the study of Greek colonization – the assumption that from the outset there was an asymmetrical power relationship between Greeks and local populations that put the latter at a disadvantage. Indeed, one recent study of the influence of Greek styles in Spain claimed that the very penetration of Greek styles was evidence of a deliberate and active colonialist programme on the part of the Greeks (Dominguez 2002).

What unites all these studies, and leads to this assumption of asymmetrical power relationships, is the maintenance of the analogy with modern colonialism. In fact the postcolonial approach has the effect of further emphasizing this comparison, and in particular the assumption that conquest and asymmetrical power relations were an integral part of Greek settlement (see e.g. Rowlands 1998; Lyons and Papadopoulos (eds) 2002; cf. Van Dommelen 1997). Whether the analogy is useful at all is not questioned. Snodgrass (this volume) has eloquently demonstrated that there are few points of contact between Greek colonization and modern European imperialism, and there is therefore no need for me to repeat them all here. To list but a couple of disanalogies: there was no nation-state (the main mover in modern colonialism) in Archaic Greece; only rarely could an ancient Greek mother-city lay claim to possession of a colony. Indeed, following Finley (1976) and more recently Osborne (1998), the word 'colony', when applied to the Archaic Greek world, should be recognized as a misnomer. Not only does the semantic cluster around the word generate strong and misleading ideas about what these settlements were like, but, according to Finley's typology, the fact that the Greek settlements were from the start independent *poleis* cannot be reconciled with the complete agreement of our modern European sources (sixteenth to nineteenth centuries AD) that a colony was a dependency of the country from which the emigration was initiated (1976: 171). Thus, despite the emphasis some scholars have placed upon close links between Greek 'colonies' and their mother-cities (e.g. Graham 1964), we can be clear that the Greek settlements of the Archaic period 'were from the start, independent city states, not colonies' (Finley 1976: 174; cf. Cartledge 1998b: 47). In fact the only real point of correspondence between the two contexts is the fact that there were movements and settlements of people. The paucity of points of contact between the two contexts indicates that this is therefore a very weak formal analogy for which, as yet, inadequate argument has been made.

That is not to say that it is impossible for a coherent argument to be made that some aspects of the analogy may be helpful. Indeed some of the understandings of the ways in which cultures interrelate gleaned from some postcolonial studies of first contact situations have been very useful for undermining some of the more traditional assumptions of how different ethnic groups might interact and how material culture could be used and manipulated in this process (see e.g. Thomas 1991; cf. Antonaccio, this volume). Even more helpful may be the kinds of contrast pioneered in comparative history (Rowlands 1998). The problem is a more general one – that in some ways the analogy has worked the wrong way round. Rather than elucidating a given context – the specific historical context of Archaic Greek colonization – the analogy has set the agenda and questions. The over-extension of the analogy – its ampliative effect – has the effect of denying the historical specificity. In fact we have prejudged the answer to some of the most important questions: what were the processes of interaction and settlement in the different areas? What were the social processes which led to Greek settlement? How did various Greeks and local peoples interrelate? *Were* there unequal power relationships? If so, of what type? Did ethnic awareness develop? What kind of awareness – Greek versus local population or local city-state?

The argument here is therefore a simple one. We need to tackle the question as far as possible without the prejudices which the comparison with modern European imperialism has produced. That analogy has led to only one side of the story being fully explored. This is due to the assumptions made about the nature of the power relations between the Greeks and local populations and the overwhelming focus upon the motivations of the Greeks. The argument is not anti-analogy. Indeed, analogy is a staple of archaeological inference. However, there is an important distinction between the imposition of specific historical models (such as the many explanatory models of modern colonialism) on the pre-Capitalist past and the use of anthropological insights (often gained under colonialism) to broaden our understandings of the ranges of human behaviour and experience (cf. Gosden 1999).

Thrace and Greek colonization

It remains, then, to sketch what sort of approach might be taken in this light. In the final section, I want to outline how an alternative long-term approach might be used to discuss the Greek colonization of Thrace.

The Greek colonization of Thrace has long been studied with the analogy of modern imperialism in mind. The model of violent conquest and asymmetrical power relationships is strong despite archaeological evidence which shows mixed Archaic levels in many colonies (see e.g. Danov 1990; Archibald 1998; Isaac 1986; Owen 2000a). The model of Hellenization has been used by Bulgarian archaeologists and politicians alike to claim a place for Bulgaria in the heart of Europe's Hellenic heritage (Zhivkova 1986; see Owen 2000a: ch. 3). This model effectively denies any agency on the part of the Thracians.

The model of violence and eventual civilizing of the local Thracians has also remained strong due to the existence of a contemporary literary source – the fragmentary poetry of Archilochos, and the later biography of the poet which was concocted from his verses (see Owen 2003). Some of these verses mention fighting with Thracians, others show some familiarity with Thracian areas and customs, and one even implies diplomacy but none of it is conclusive (see Graham 1978). Yet, this poetry, despite its satirical flavour, has been used to indicate that relations between Greeks and Thracians were universally bad. One fragment, taken from an inscription, was even restored (by a 1930s scholar) to have Archilochos call the Thracians 'dogs', when there is no justification for this strong (and rather modern sounding) reading on the stone (see Owen 2003).[8]

The Classical period has often been the main focus of archaeological research within Bulgaria and Greece; however, some interesting patterns appear when Thracian material also is studied. My approach has been to look at the area of Thrace over the long term, looking at the social contexts into which the Greek settlers came. A study of the Thracian Early Iron Age identifies a complex model of social change which results, finally, in the drawing in of Greeks (among others) into social networks of exchange. The burial evidence in particular indicates a change during the ninth and eighth centuries BC from small kin-based societies to societies in which certain individuals and/or lines distinguish themselves (or are distinguished) (Owen 2000a).

I have suggested elsewhere that the ninth and eighth centuries saw the emergence of an elite in Thrace, based upon the appropriation of iron (Owen 2000a). During the course of the eighth century BC foreign materials and objects begin to join iron in 'rich' burial contexts, and finally oust it as an important status indicator. This prestige use of imports can also be distinguished in the final phase of the cemetery at the Thracian settlement at Kastri on Thasos (Owen 2000a, ch. 10; Koukouli-Chrysanthaki 1996). The patterns visible in this area fit well with the anthropological ideas of Helms concerning the importance of imports as tangible evidence of knowledge of the world outside society (Helms 1988, 1993). It is important to note that these imports are not just Greek: the first wave of imports in the eighth century includes Scythian, Baltic and Levantine as well as Greek objects (Owen 2000a, ch. 7). These general trends in Thracian material culture indicate that social changes within Thrace were responsible for an increasing outward-looking tendency and the initiation of contacts with other peoples. This contrasts markedly with the assumption that is normally made: i.e. that contact with Greeks leads to social change.

The evidence from Thasos town shows an evolution of these same trends.[9] The earliest levels so far excavated have revealed evidence of an apsidal house with mixed Thracian and Aeolian Greek ceramics and with possible evidence of iron working.[10] The earliest levels of the Artemision reveal the same mixed ceramic deposits.[11] The existence of Greek material has been used by some to suggest that this house and the first levels of the

Artemision are Greek – indeed Parian Greek.[12] This suggestion is based upon the literary dating of the Parian settlement, and I concur with Graham that there is no evidence of Parian settlement until the mid-seventh century BC (Graham 1978). The mixed material is, however, interesting. I would not suggest that the presence of Aeolian material necessarily implies the presence of Aeolians. However, the use of this imported material – as everyday tableware – is in striking contrast to the prestige use of some of the same type of imported ceramic in Kastri a few years earlier.[13] This suggests that a high level of cultural interaction with some Greeks was attained before the Parian settlement, and that some 'Greek' material culture was no longer viewed as exotic imports, but as normal everyday crockery.

However, of particular interest to me has been the extent to which the first evidence of Greek settlers integrates into the existing landscape of Thasos. This is clearest in the ritual sphere in which evidence of the reuse and/or continuing use of Thracian ritual places is growing. In particular the Artemision[14] and the Herakleion[15] show evidence of pre-Greek-settlement Thracian ritual activity – the former in terms of Thracian offerings, the latter in terms of physical remains. The study of landscape offers archaeologists an insight into how people structured their lives in physical terms, how they viewed their world. In particular, the ways in which new settlers absorbed, reused and/or restructured the existing landscape and existing monuments are crucial to an understanding of how they viewed their new home, how they incorporated its past. This past may have been one to be wiped out, restructured, or reused, reinterpreted and incorporated into new traditions. The study of the ways in which Greek settlers integrated into existing landscapes, or created new ones, must therefore offer a fertile area for future studies of Greek settlements 'abroad'.[16]

Much still needs to be done, and the archaeological record of early Thasos town is scanty. However, I hope that such approaches may begin to indicate (what we must always have suspected) that cultural interactions between Greeks and Thracians in the seventh century were rather more complex than the emphasis upon Archilochos allowed us to believe. The archaeological evidence indicates first that the Greek contacts with Thrace in general were part of a more general opening up of that society to foreign contacts: indeed, that changes within Thracian society were *responsible* for the opening up of contacts with Greeks, among others. Second, the interactions between Thracian Thasians and some Greeks were intensive prior to Parian settlement. Lastly, the evidence from ritual sites seems to indicate that there was at least some Greek integration into existing ritual landscapes. The complexity of the archaeological record of early Thasos therefore stands in stark contrast to the simple monolithic oppositions between Greeks and Thracians of the accepted literary model.

*

The thrust of this chapter has been that a particular historical analogy has restricted our range of explanations of the material record, and restricted what has been studied under the umbrella of 'Greek colonization studies'. As the case study indicates, approaches which concentrate only upon the Greek side of the equation, and only on the period after Greek settlement, are missing a crucial part of the process: the long-term processes that only archaeology is in a position to explore. The role of analogy could be to expand our ideas of the ranges of human behaviour rather than restrict us to familiar Western models.

Notes

1. This piece expands upon some of the arguments I first explored in my PhD thesis (Owen 2000a). It was written while I was a Research Fellow at Magdalene College, Cambridge. I would like to thank the audience of the Cambridge Philological Society for their constructive responses to a presentation of this paper in January 2004. I would also like to thank Henry Hurst, Martin Millett, Laura Preston, Robin Osborne and Anthony Snodgrass for reading a draft of this paper and making helpful comments.

2. Gosden 2004 has most recently emphasized the differences between pre- and post-Columbian colonialism. He has not, however, discussed the problem of analogy between modern colonialism and Greek colonization in full. This is an important book, which has unfortunately arrived too late for me to take full account of its arguments here.

3. For recent arguments against this version, see Antonaccio 2004 and this volume, Lyons and Papadopoulos (eds) 2002.

4. Thus primitivist and substantivist interpretations, often confused (see Morris 1994b: 351-3; Chapter 4 below), should be distinguished. Primitivists argued that Greece was a household economy. Substantivism grew out of Weber's critique of the primitivist/modernist debate, and held that production and exchange were embedded in other institutions. See also Cartledge 1998a: 6-7: 'The most serious misunderstandings can arise when the debate about the level and quantity of Greek economic life becomes confused with the argument over its politico-social location.'

5. 'They went forth, urged by the love of adventure, by the passion for discovery, by the desire for a freer life in new countries. Wherever they went, they carried with them the traditions, the habits, the ideals of their Mother Country. Wherever they settled they planted a new homeland. And, though mountains and the waste of seas divided them, they never lost that golden thread of the spirit which drew their thoughts back to the land of their birth.'

6. As Jenkyns (1980: ch. 13) has pointed out, it was a commonplace to say that the British Empire was really two empires, one of which involved the settlement of colonies with a population of largely British origin, the second of which consisted of subject peoples governed more or less despotically. Adderley, in 1869, described these as 'Grecian' and 'Roman' elements respectively (quoted in Jenkyns 1980: 333-4). See e.g. Cramb 1915; Bryce 1914; Lucas 1912; Cromer 1910: 11.

7. Interestingly, the Orientalizing phenomenon is not assumed to mean the adoption of Eastern ethnic identities by Greeks.

8. Hiller von Gaertringen 1934-6; a new reading has just been published by Tsantsanoglou of 'phusi' ('Thracian by nature') rather than the accepted 'kusi' ('Thracian dogs'). I thank Tsantsanoglou for kindly sending me a copy of this article (2003).

9. Much of this material has been published in Owen 2003. See also Owen 2000a.

10. The most accessible discussion of this sondage and the apsidal house is Graham 1978. See AR 2003 for a discussion of the most recent excavations of this sondage.

11. See Weill 1985.

12. Greek: Bernard 1964, Weill 1985; Thracian: Graham 1978, Graham 2001, Grandjean 1988; Unsure: Koukouli-Chrysanthaki in *AAA* 3 (1970) 215 (Greek), but in *AAA* 6 (1973) 240 (Thracian); Mixed?: Pouilloux 1964.

13. Bernard 1964. I refer here to G2-3 ware. Grey bucchero is also present as imports and locally produced copies. See Owen 2000a: 157-9.

14. For the Artemision, see Weill 1985. She concurs with Bernard 1964 that the sanctuary was a Parian foundation, despite the lack of Parian ceramics (see partic. p. 210). Grandjean 1988: 436-41 suggests that a Thracian cult on this site was taken over by the Parians. My identification of eighth- and early seventh-century Thracian fibulae amongst the unpublished finds from the earliest levels of the Artemision must strengthen his case. For illustration and argument, see Owen 2000a: 160 and fig. 10.3.

15. Pre-Greek cult has long been suspected in the Herakleion, in the form of a Phoenician sanctuary. No archaeological evidence backs this up (see Graham 1978: 88-92 for the full argument and references). However, the rock altar bears a striking resemblance to sacrificial stones – an element of the Early Iron Age 'megalithic culture' of Southern Thrace (see Owen 2000a: 162, ch. 5). In addition Graham has suggested that the so-called bothroi (or post-holes) around the altar are of Thracian origin. They have been persuasively interpreted as basins – another component of the Thracian megalithic culture – by Najdenova 1990: 88. See Graham 2001: 379-84 for a detailed discussion. I have dated these aspects of Thracian material culture to the eighth and seventh centuries BC (see Owen 2000a: ch. 5). See also Owen 2000b on the fourth-century reuse of a Thracian rock-cut tomb on the Thasian acropolis as the 'cave of Pan'.

16. A project, based in the Faculty of Classics, Cambridge University, and funded by the Leverhulme Trust, exploring this very aspect began in August 2004.

2

The Advance of the Greek: Greece, Great Britain and Archaeological Empires[1]

Gillian Shepherd

Under the entry for the word 'colony', the ninth edition of the *Encyclopaedia Britannica* (1877) makes the following note:

> It is the English speaking race that has shown an unexampled energy and capacity for colonisation.

For its time, the comment was not inappropriate and it was to become increasingly apposite as the nineteenth century wore on and Britain entered her age of high empire between *c.* 1880 and 1914. Over the course of this period, large portions of the globe not already under the control of one European state or another came under their sway, with Britain being one of the more aggressive in the pursuit of colonial expansion (Hall 2000: 9). By the time the twentieth century dawned, Britain had painted perhaps one-third of the world map red, a policy both reflected in and no doubt fuelled by views such as those expressed by John Ruskin, Slade Professor of Fine Art at Oxford, in his inaugural lecture of 1870:

> There is a destiny now possible to us – the highest ever set before a nation to be accepted or refused. We are still undegenerate in race; a race mingled of the best northern blood. We are not dissolute in temper, but still have the firmness to govern and the grace to obey. We have been taught a religion of pure mercy ...
>
> This is what [England] must do or perish. She must found colonies as fast and far as she is able, formed of her most energetic and worthiest men, seizing every piece of fruitful waste ground she can set her foot on, and teaching these colonists that their chief virtue is to be fidelity to their country and that their first aim is to be to advance the power of England by land and sea: and that, though they live on a distant plot of ground, they are no more to consider themselves therefore disenfranchised from their native land than the sailors of her fleet do, because they float on distant waves. So that literally, these colonies must be fastened fleets ...
>
> Ruskin 1870: 27-30

The 'most energetic and worthiest men' were, by and large, also Oxford men. Cambridge appears to have had less success in grooming young men to serve the Empire and Imperial posts were most often filled with Oxford products (Symonds 1991: 20). A number of these had read Modern History, but still more were Classicists: armed with Thucydides and other ancient texts, they employed ancient Greece and Rome in the service of the Empire through recourse to Classical precedents (Symonds 1991: 31-5; Jenkyns 1980: ch. XIII). The analogies did not operate in one direction only, however: if the activities of the ancients beyond their homelands supplied a pattern for the Imperial cause, so too could the British Empire provide a last upon which antiquity could be modelled and the two accordingly brought still closer together. Already very familiar with the Athenian and Roman empires, historians now turned their attention to a new area: the Greek settlement of the West, namely Sicily and Italy, in the Archaic period.

By the later nineteenth century, relatively little had been written, in English at least, on the subject of the ancient Greek settlement of Italy and Sicily. Travellers had provided some general descriptions, such as Captain W. Smyth's account of 1824, *Memoir descriptive ... of Sicily* (Smyth 1824). The great ruined temples of Paestum, Agrigento and Selinunte had since the days of the Grand Tour provided architectural inspiration, but archaeological exploration of such sites was otherwise in its infancy and if the Western Greek states made an appearance in history books, it was usually in the context of the activities of mainland Greek cities, such as that of Athens in the ill-fated Sicilian Expedition described by Thucydides (Books VI-VII). As the British Empire entered its apogee, however, Sicily and Magna Graecia became the subjects of specific study and the ideas expressed by Ruskin – arguably prevalent in Victorian and later Britain – were put to good use.

The first of these is the concept of race and with it racial purity ('we are still undegenerate in race'). The appeal which categorization and classification held for the Victorians is well documented and race was a newly recognized category in the British colonial experience (Hall 2000: 19; cf. also Snodgrass, this volume; Collingham 2001). In the study of ancient 'colonies' the concept of race is clearly manifested in the distinctions applied to indigenous populations and competing groups such as Phoenicians, with religion (in the absence of the great Victorian distinguisher, colour) an important marker ('we have ... a religion of pure mercy').

Ruskin's second concept, expressed in the phrase 'best northern blood', is that of hierarchy. This was the natural progression from classifications by race: for the Victorians, the opportunity not just to distinguish different categories but to rank them as well was irresistible and operated against the background of social Darwinism inspired by Charles Darwin's theories of evolution (Hall 2000: 19). In the contemporary world, this meant a ladder on which white Anglo-Saxons sat firmly at the top; in the ancient world, this position was occupied by either the Greeks or the Romans, depending upon the period under discussion. For the colonizing movements of the Archaic period, this meant specifically the Greeks of Old Greece: Greeks in the 'colonies' came second. Analogy between the two hierarchies was inevitable and resulted in correlations between the glory that was Greece and the glory that was Victorian Britain and her Empire. The latter was cast as the direct successor of the former and studies of the ancient world applied the model of the British Empire to antiquity and in doing so contributed to its reinforcement in contemporary thought.[2]

The third concept central to Ruskin's exhortation is that of the colonists' 'fidelity to their country', in which the 'country' is not their new abode, but the motherland. One way in which such fidelity could be demonstrated was by constant reference to the mother country as the superior and guiding entity: this applied of course politically as well as culturally to the various parts of the British Empire, but was less readily apparent in the case of the early Greek 'colonies' which were – unavoidably – politically independent. Nevertheless, as the amount of archaeological material increased, the cultural arena supplied rich pickings by which to demonstrate the inferior achievements of the Western Greeks and their dependence, combined with often inept imitation, upon the models provided by the mother country.

One of the earliest and most significant of these studies of the Greek West was E.A. Freeman's *A History of Sicily*, published in four volumes between 1891 and 1894 (Freeman 1891-4). Freeman was Regius Professor of Modern History at Oxford between 1884 and 1892 and while much of his work concerned the history of the Normans he also delved into antiquity with the full force of the imperial model at his disposal. Other briefer studies published in the later nineteenth century show the imprint of Ruskin-esque ideas[3] – and it is perhaps no coincidence that many of these and later studies of aspects of the Greek West were made by scholars with Oxford connections – but Freeman was overt in his use of the ideals of high empire and the notions of race, hierarchy and fidelity combined with modern analogy appear prominently in his work.

This is particularly true of the first volume of *A History of Sicily* (1891), in which Freeman sets out what may be described as his theoretical approach. He reviews the various inhabitants of Sicily and establishes distinctions of race which are reinforced by religion. For Freeman, this is primarily the distinction between Greek and Phoenician or, in his own telling terms, between the European Aryan and the Semitic. Here the interference of nineteenth-century anti-Semitism may also be detected: Freeman regards the clashes of the Greeks and Phoenicians in Sicily as prefiguring the later strife between Christianity and Islam and appears so implicitly convinced that modern Europe is the direct successor of ancient Greece that he parallels Greek religion and Christianity on the one hand and Phoenician religion and Islam on the other. The result is the concept of religious war and the language of the crusades and Christianity applied to the ancient Greeks, their paganism conveniently suppressed:

> ... before Aryan Europe had adopted that Semitic faith which the Semitic man himself despised, the creed of Aryan Europe was already worth fighting for, and well was it fought for on Sicilian soil. In days when no purer light had already been given, it was already a crusade to strike a blow for Apollôn by the shore of Naxos, for Athênê on the island of Ortygia, against the foul and bloody rites of Moloch and Ashtoreth ... it was before all the Greeks of Sicily to whom it fell to be champion of Europe, to be in the second struggle more than the champion of Europe, to be the champion of Christendom.
>
> Freeman 1891-4, I: 11

This passage should be placed in the context of Freeman's own rampant anti-Semitism and racism which he expressed trenchantly elsewhere,[4] but while these were extreme they were by no means atypical for his time. Freeman did, however, encounter a stumbling block in the undeniably significant cultural achievements of the Phoenicians which he concedes to be of merit, yet nevertheless manages to class as inferior. This is made most clear when he speculates upon what might have happened had the Phoenicians gained full control of Sicily in the early period: he is sure that the island could never have become the Sicily 'which holds so brilliant a place in the world's history ... The true Sicily is the hellenic Sicily and no other' (Freeman 1891-4, I: 10).

Here we also see the hierarchies beginning to crystallize. Having discussed the distinction between Greek and inferior Phoenician, Freeman moves on to consider what he calls 'different classes of barbarians' (Freeman 1891-4, I: 21) and in so doing sets up a ranking of different populations in the West. Apart from the Phoenicians, another sophisticated group he identifies comprises the inhabitants of central Italy on the grounds that neither Greeks nor Phoenicians were able to make much impact in this area: the Italians were 'capable of receiving a large measure of Greek culture as something foreign ... They had reached far too high a stage of native progress to become adopted children of the Hellenic family' (Freeman 1891-4, I: 20). The Italians, however, were far more acceptable than the Phoenicians by virtue of their European origins:

> Still the Italian foes of the Greeks of Italy were after all kinsmen. They were European; they were Aryan; they were, however little they deemed of it, members of a common household, sharers in a common heritage. The Greeks of Sicily had, as we have seen, to wage a deadlier fight with utter aliens.
>
> Freeman 1891-4, I: 21

These 'utter aliens' ('lesser breeds without the law'? Cf. Snodgrass, this volume) were of course the Phoenicians, not the indigenous inhabitants of Sicily. The Sikels did not, in Freeman's view, present a problem and are placed further down on the rungs of the social ladder:

> The Sikel in short I hold to be an undeveloped Latin. He had lagged far behind his kinsfolk in Italy, because his land had drawn to itself foreign

> settlers from the beginning ... When the Sikel's day of progress came, it took the shape of assimilation to the Greek, of gradual adoption into the Greek body.
>
> Freeman 1891-4, I: 20

The Sikel then too is at least a European, if an inferior one. Furthermore, unlike the Italians, the Sikel is regarded by Freeman as a viable object of another activity favoured by Victorian imperialists, namely civilizing the natives: the Sikels could receive the full benefit of the superior Greek culture through complete Hellenization. Given the relative lack of archaeological evidence at the time for Greek-Sikel interaction, such opinion appears all the more influenced by the aims and priorities of its time, but it was to be reinforced rather than adjusted by subsequent discoveries and research in which the strength of Hellenization and the view that cultural influence travelled in one direction only are prominent features. In a further discussion of the various groups in Sicily – Sikans and Elymians as well as Sikels – Freeman once again betrays his times with the attribution to the ancients of like-minded Victorian concepts of social hierarchy:

> It might have amazed Thucydides if had seen any of these races put into the same class, however wide that class, with the Greeks. Yet for our purposes we must put the Greeks and Sikels together as sharers in the common heritage of Aryan Europe, however much the one people may have outstripped the other. The Sikels admitted of full hellenisation: they could be made into artificial Greeks.
>
> Freeman 1891-4, I: 308

Now that the ranking is established, the field is clear for the insertion of modern colonial analogies as Freeman presses his point (labours it even), with a comparison between Greek Sicily and the colonization of America and also the English settlement of Britain, although the latter he regards as more migration than colonization proper (Freeman 1891-4, I: 318). The analogy works both ways: in paralleling Greeks and the English Freeman aims not only to strengthen his case for Greek superiority but perhaps also to reinforce modern hierarchies:

> ... the advance of the Greek over the Sikel was in every way the advance of the higher over the lower man. The English advance in America was so far more strongly. For the advance of the Greek against the Sikel was after all only the advance of European against European; it was the advance of kinsmen to whom the lamp had first been handed against kinsmen who had lagged behind them in the race. That is to say, if the Sikel was not as the Briton, still less was he as the Red Indian ... The Sikel could become a Greek yet more thoroughly than the Briton could become an Englishman.
>
> Freeman 1891-4, I: 319-20

Nevertheless, the ranking is not quite complete. At the top of the tree sit the Greeks, and below them the Italians followed by the Sikels (and

Sikans and Elymians) with the Phoenicians somewhere out on a lower limb, but the Greeks themselves have yet to be divided into two groups, one higher and one lower. This means of course the distinction between Greeks in Greece and the 'colonials' in the West. However successful it may be, a colony will never match up to its mother-city and must be to some degree subservient – and here Ruskin's concept of 'fidelity' makes its appearance in the assertion that 'each [colony] owed to its special mother city the reverence of a child' (Freeman 1891-4, I: 15). As with the Phoenicians, Freeman encountered a problem in the palpable success, prosperity and power of the Western Greek states, which at times throughout history had manifested themselves at the expense of mainland Greece, most notably in the Sicilian Expedition when on the evidence of no less an authority than Thucydides the Athenians were 'utterly and entirely defeated' at Syracuse (VII, 87, 6). His solution was to distinguish between true greatness and a lesser 'colonial greatness' (Freeman 1891-4, I: 6):

> At Syracuse ... we see the highest point to which the Greek colony could rise. The greatness of Syracuse is essentially of the colonial kind. It is a greatness which could for a while outstrip the cities of old Greece in prosperity and splendour, but which was still a greatness essentially inferior in kind and less lasting in duration.
>
> Freeman 1891-4, I: 328

Once more modern analogies are available for support and Freeman again picks upon America. As a general comparison, his choice of America is perhaps not without some validity: although he does not state his reasons at length (cf. Freeman 1891-4, I: 329), they are conceivably because the colonization of America by the British was not, at least in its initial stages, part of the creation of an empire and that, by the time Freeman was writing, America was like the Greek colonies fully independent, although he avoids the fact that this independence was acquired through revolution. A further point of comparison might have been the presence of other powerful competing groups in the early European settlement of America such as the French and Spanish (Europeans, at least, unlike the Phoenicians). Freeman could also draw upon the nineteenth-century British attitude towards America as culturally inferior, an attitude he seems to have shared, despite the flourishing cities complete with neo-classical architecture of the United States.[5] Whatever successes America had had were, according to Freeman, due to the English – he appropriates them for the English by the conspicuous absence of the word 'American' – but are still of this lesser, colonial type of greatness:

> ... we may say that North America has become the greatest home of the English folk [but] it is the greatest home only in the sense in which for a while Sicily contained the greatest power of Hellas.
>
> Freeman, 1891-4, I: 7-8

And thus the hierarchy is complete, with the Greeks of Old Greece comfortably at the top and providing a mirror image for the modern world where the English (perhaps a more accurate term than 'the British') were confident in the belief of their own supremacy and in addition could bask in the reflected glory of Greece. With Freeman's *magnum opus*, the notions of the superiority of the Greeks over every other group in the West and of the superiority of the mother-city over the colony were firmly established in anglophone scholarship of the late nineteenth century, Britain's own period of high empire. If the model of the contemporary British Empire was not explicitly used – and it is interesting that it was not, given both Freeman's time and the extensive use made of such a model by his successors – its attendant social attitudes make their impact clearly felt. Freeman's more extreme and racist views regarding modern politics do not seem to have been generally accepted – *The Oxford Magazine* in 1883 (p. 162) ribbed him with the comment that 'the only people to whom he is distinctly unkind are the negroes, the Irish, the Chinese and Mr Oscar Wilde' – but nevertheless his work on ancient Sicily established a general conception of Greek activity in the West from which there was to be little deviation for nearly a century.

In the course of the next fifty years, relatively little was written in English about the Greek West in general and Sicily in particular. One important study which did appear was Aubrey Gwynn's 1918 essay 'The Character of Greek Colonisation' (Gwynn 1918), which treated Greek foundations more generally. Gwynn's approach was somewhat different in that he used analogy with modern colonization as much to point out the differences as the similarities with ancient colonization, and on issues such as intermarriage and other relations between Greeks and natives he was relatively open-minded. Nevertheless, signs of late imperial thought creep into his text: Gwynn seems to regard intermarriage as a more common feature of remote colonies and the consequence of isolation rather than choice, since in these places 'intercourse with the rest of the Greek world was rare and difficult' (Gwynn 1918: 109), and here too the concepts of race (including racial proximity to Europeans) and hierarchy contribute to the formulation of his thesis:

> ... in every sphere of their colonising activity, the Greeks met with races which, though socially and intellectually their inferiors, were still, in feature and colour, of the same general type. Even the Libyan tribes, of which we have been speaking were ... not negroes, but Berbers.
>
> Gwynn 1918: 109

Elsewhere fidelity appears, in Gwynn's admiration for the Greeks' tenacious adherence to their inherited traditions in the new *poleis* abroad, while in a reference perhaps to America (and even the newly federated Australia?) he bemoans the lack of such fidelity in some modern colonies and the resulting deleterious effects:

> The relations of French Canada to France resemble, perhaps, more closely the relations of a Greek colony to its μητρόπολις than do the more progressive Anglo-Saxon colonies, where progress has often been achieved at the cost of respect for tradition, and of much else that is beautiful.
>
> Gwynn 1918: 122

Further advances in the field were made in the 1930s by Alan Blakeway in his pioneering work on the archaeological evidence for Hellenization and famous 'trade before the flag' argument (Blakeway 1932-3 and 1935). As archaeological evidence began to emerge in Italy and Sicily in the late nineteenth century, Blakeway commenced the exercise of demonstrating Greek superiority through material evidence which would be more fully explored by Thomas Dunbabin (see below). In his classifications of Greek and Greek-style pottery found in Italy, Blakeway's conclusions betray a Freeman-like ranking of Greeks and indigenous populations: Etruscan art 'enjoyed the benefit of Greek influence', while Etruscan craftsmen were 'more quick to learn [than Sicilian potters]' (Blakeway 1935: 130, 133). Pottery made by Greeks at Cumae, meanwhile, is 'provincial' and 'inferior in everyway to the best products of Corinth ... but none the less characteristically Greek' (Blakeway 1935: 145).[6]

In 1948 Blakeway's student Thomas Dunbabin produced *The Western Greeks*.[7] Dunbabin's work differs significantly from Freeman's in one respect in particular: while Freeman's work was more strictly a history, Dunbabin was able to incorporate the vast amount of archaeological material which had appeared in the intervening half-century, much of it revealed by the father of Sicilian archaeology, Paolo Orsi. He modestly denied any innovation in this regard, claiming that Freeman had already taken this approach by using what archaeological sources were available before 1890 (Dunbabin 1948: viii), but in fact material evidence scarcely makes an appearance in Freeman's text and in any case there was very little available even if he had felt inclined to use it. Dunbabin's work constitutes the first major attempt in English to study Sicily and Southern Italy through a combination of historical and archaeological material and indeed he claims the latter had revealed 'a completely new picture' (Dunbabin 1948: viii) of these areas. As regards the historical sources, however, Dunbabin takes the view that 'Freeman's history stands the test of time' (Dunbabin 1948: viii) and in fact although their respective works are very different there are nevertheless significant points of comparison between the two, including the use of analogy with modern colonization.

In the first place, although Dunbabin did not construct complex hierarchies and racial oppositions in the overt manner in which Freeman did – he is in fact less concerned with the various other groups in Sicily and in accordance with his title concentrates upon the Greeks – nevertheless these features of imperial thought are scattered throughout his text. They appear most obviously in Dunbabin's attitude to the Sikels and other indigenous groups, whom he regards, like Freeman, as both culturally inferior but of 'similar stock' (Dunbabin 1948: 42) to the Greeks and predisposed to soak up the 'superior' Greek culture like sponges: the inhabitants of Southern Italy had 'little to contribute to Greek civilisation' (Dunbabin 1948: 186), while the Sikels' 'capability for civilisation' (Dunbabin 1948: 43) is underlined. Equally, the stress on distinctions of race set up by Freeman also re-appears in the assertion of self-imposed isolation from the natives on the part of the Greeks:

> I am inclined to stress the purity of Greek culture in the colonial cities, and find little to suggest that the Greeks mixed much with Sikel or Italian peoples, or learnt much from them.
>
> Dunbabin 1948: vi

Instead, he argues, in the Archaic period these peoples had 'no place' (Dunbabin 1948: 47) in the Greek settlements and 'in most cases the Greeks kept the Sikels at arms length ... even when they lived in Sikel territory' (Dunbabin 1948: 192). The Greeks, according to Dunbabin, held the Sikels in aversion at least until they had acquired some trappings of Greek culture: 'so long as the Sikel remained Sikel the Greek regarded him as an inferior being and was proud of his own descent' (Dunbabin 1948: 193). The Western Greeks themselves, however, also again occupy an inferior position vis-à-vis the mainland Greeks with regard to their cultural achievements: in these respects they are dependent upon Old Greece, especially Corinth ('it is long before any of the arts produced work which had not Corinthian models', Dunbabin 1948: vii). At times they are also unable to keep up, lagging behind the achievements of the motherland (for example, in architecture: see below) or simply incapable of living up to her standards. For example, the perceived dearth of what Dunbabin regards as good quality early red-figure vases in Sicilian graves is explained not by differing funerary customs and rates of wealth disposal, but instead by the claim that 'rather than poverty the Sicilian Greeks are to be accused of indifference and lack of taste' (Dunbabin 1948: 245).

To a significant degree here Dunbabin was aided by the archaeological material now available to him and abetted by the manner in which it could be selected and interpreted. Much of this material was indeed Greek and the undeniable prominence of Greek artefacts in the material record went a long way towards supporting a study already predisposed to find the Greeks in a predominant position and defining through Orsi's finds what Dunbabin describes as the 'colonial spirit' (Dunbabin 1948: vi). Other features of Greek Sicilian culture such as linguistics showed greater influence from Sikel quarters and indeed were acknowledged by Dunbabin as the 'chief proved contribution ... to colonial culture' (Dunbabin 1948: 189). Such features today might be regarded as even more important than the material evidence, but they were not viewed as such around the middle of the twentieth century. In a Freeman-esque recourse to British colonization Dunbabin argues:

> The example of the British in North America and Australia shows that words and names and legends can be taken over from the native populations without miscegenation or profound cultural influence.
>
> Dunbabin 1948: 189

To some extent also, Dunbabin's interpretation of the archaeological material was limited simply by what happened to have been excavated in both the West and Greece. If, for example, the Archaic graves of the North Cemetery at Corinth had been available for him to study, he might have had to adjust his opinions regarding Sicilian taste and the early red-figure period burials of Sicily: the Corinthian graves contain relatively few goods and the distinctive Protocorinthian and Corinthian aryballoi so common in the richer graves of the West (in particular Syracuse) are conspicuous by their absence at Corinth (Blegen, Palmer and Young 1964: 52, 113-14).

Equally, that material which was less obviously Greek could be open to interpretation as such. One of Dunbabin's main arguments for the 'purity' of Greek colonies was that their cemeteries were of an overwhelmingly Greek character:

> The citizen bodies of the colonies were as pure Greek as those of Old Greece. In the thousands of graves excavated at Syracuse, Megara, Gela, and other sites of Sicily and southern Italy, there is only a handful of objects which can be ascribed to native industry or art, and very few indeed which would be out of place in a city of Greece proper.
>
> Dunbabin 1948: 192

Amongst the thousands of objects in the graves is a considerable amount of metalwork – a branch of technology and artistry for which Dunbabin did in fact give the Sikels credit for achievement (Dunbabin 1948: 173). Some of this metalwork, for example the dress pins, is probably Greek, but much of it finds parallels at indigenous sites in Sicily and Italy, and in particular the fibulae, which occur in a wide range of types, are now with only one or two exceptions thought to derive from Italy or Sicily. At the time Dunbabin was writing, however, the most common types – the *navicella*, leech and bone-and-amber fibulae (see Fig. 2.1) – were considered by himself (Dunbabin 1948: 265-6) and a number of others to be Greek. Their argument was based on the appearance of the fibulae at various sites across Greece, and Corinthian manufacture was suggested, due to the number found in that area. This Greek origin was strenuously argued in the face of considerable evidence to the contrary, particularly in the case of the bone-and-amber types, which were even admitted to be clearly derived from Italian versions and which occurred in greater numbers and arguably more pertinent contexts (graves rather than sanctuaries) in the West.[8]

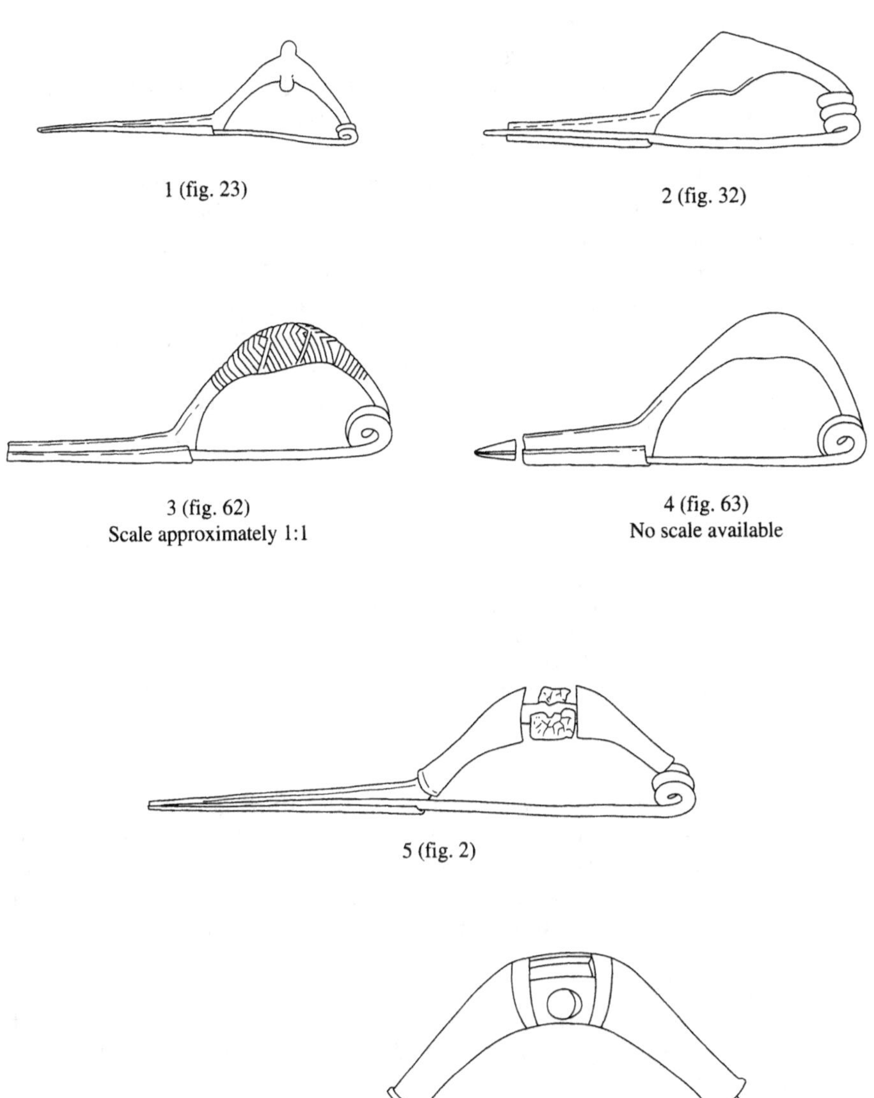

2.1. Fibulae from Syracuse. 1-3: navicella fibulae; 4: leech fibula; 5-6: bone and amber fibulae. After Orsi 1895, figs 2, 23, 32, 55, 62, 63.

Two points may be derived from this. The first is that there seems to be yet again a desire to prioritize the Greeks over indigenous populations (and Dunbabin is not alone in this) and credit the Greeks with the production of technologically sophisticated luxury goods, despite the admitted prowess of the Italians and Sicilians in this area: another example, perhaps, of the tendency to rank the various groups and reinforce a hierarchical arrangement in which the Greeks sat at the top. The other is that it was of course the mainland Greeks who were credited as the ultimate source of these items, not the Western Greeks. The latter were prime candidates as the producers on grounds noted above and indeed the site of Pithekoussai in the Bay of Naples has since revealed evidence for the manufacture of the bone-and-amber type (Ridgway 1992: 93-5), yet the possibility that they could be the producers of the fibulae was never entertained by the various scholars who debated their origins. Again, the modern colonial analogy is likely to be in operation here, as Dunbabin states in his preface:

> [The ancient colonies] were, like Australia until a few years ago, producers of raw materials, with a few staples on which they grew rich, and importers of manufactured goods. They bought most of their luxuries and objects of art from the mother country. In the period under study here, Corinth occupied the place as supplier of the rich western market and, we may believe, as chief port of consignment for corn and other exports, which Great Britain has held with the Dominions.
>
> Dunbabin 1948: vii

So once again the Western Greeks seem to be suffering from greatness of a colonial kind and come second to the mainland Greeks: they cannot themselves produce elite goods – despite the fact that it is difficult to see what technological or practical barrier could possibly have prevented them – but must derive such luxuries from the more sophisticated mother country.

Later, Dunbabin goes one step further to account for what he sees as the lack of colonial art in the seventh century as in part due to the colonists 'preferring things brought from the mother country' (Dunbabin 1948: 267) and here a glimmer of the concept of 'fidelity' may be detected: not only do the colonists refuse to adopt anything from an indigenous culture which was in any case inferior, not only are they incapable of producing their own elite goods, but they also regard objects from the mother country as inherently more desirable. This is not exactly the 'fidelity' which Ruskin recommended, which certainly included a degree of political dependence and associated loyalty which could never be applied to the politically independent ancient colonies, despite occasional slips in that direction such as Dunbabin's reference to Corinthian 'possession' of Syracuse (Dunbabin 1948: 17). Rather, it was a type of fidelity which may also have been encapsulated in Ruskin's use of the term: that of cultural fidelity, in which the colony bound itself to the mother country and maintained a relationship not only through the acquisition of objects derived from the homeland but also through the voluntary (and usually inferior) imitation of her material culture.

This in fact is one of Dunbabin's central theses. While Freeman emphasized race and hierarchy and to a lesser extent fidelity, the wealth of archaeological material which had appeared and been studied between the end of the nineteenth century and World War Two enabled the elaboration of a scenario of cultural fidelity for which British imperialism again provided the model. In the absence of complete political dependence, cultural dependence provided the necessary grounds for maintaining both Greece and Britain at the top of the hierarchy. In his preface Dunbabin is explicit in his use of a modern late imperial analogy, selecting this time not America, but Australia and New Zealand. These countries were of course politically independent by 1948, but they were part of the British Commonwealth and their citizens still carried British passports. Their situation was well understood by Dunbabin, who was himself Australian, and they provided him with a model for constructing the fidelity of the ancients; a more amenable model, perhaps, than the recalcitrant America which had won her independence by arms and cut all formal ties with Britain. He states:

> I have drawn much on the parallel to the relations between colonies and mother country provided in Australia and New Zealand. Here political independence is combined with almost complete cultural dependence, on which the colonials pride themselves. Difference in manner of life is due to difference of material circumstances, and is not enough to destroy the essential unity. This unity is the pride of most colonials; so probably in antiquity.
>
> Dunbabin 1948: vii

This unity, or to put it more crudely, duplication in the colony of cultural features derived from the mother-city, is perhaps the feature of the late imperial model which appears most conspicuously not only in Dunbabin's work but also in other studies of ancient Sicily and Southern Italy where the analogy is implicit rather than explicit.

One of the main features of the way the British thought about their empire in the nineteenth and earlier twentieth centuries has been described as a 'grammar of difference' in which the identification of and stress placed upon differences between various social groups were paramount in articulating and reinforcing British claims to superiority (Hall 2000: 20). Thus, for example, the contrasts between black and white, men and women, Christian and infidel (the last especially in the context of the Victorian missionary movement) were prominent features of social discussion and debate. A similar stress on 'difference' was employed in nineteenth- and earlier twentieth-century discussion of the ancient

Greeks and their contacts with other groups abroad. Predictably it emerges most clearly in Freeman's work through the process of defining his 'different classes of barbarians' discussed above, but appears from time to time elsewhere as well: in Dunbabin's reference to the 'distinction between Greek and Sikel' (Dunbabin 1948: 193) before the fifth century, for example, or Stubbings' argument that the bone-and-amber fibulae were Greek because they appeared in quantities at Syracuse and Megara Hyblaia where 'the colonists seem to have made a point of differentiating themselves from the natives' (Dunbabin 1962: 439).

If the 'grammar of difference' structured much contemporary discourse regarding the ancient world, then it follows that the corollary of a 'grammar of similarity' operated also. While the former was an effective tool for categorizing non-Greek groups, the latter was essential in establishing cultural dependence and 'fidelity': points of comparison rather than contrast needed to be pinpointed between groups which should in some way be similarly identified, and the imperial model demanded that the Greeks in the West did not deviate too much from the example set by Old Greece. The result was a tendency to ignore or gloss over real differences in the material culture of the Western Greeks and highlight the similarities: thus, for example, Dunbabin states in his preface that 'in spite of differences of circumstances, the colonials *were not in important ways* (my italics) unlike the Greeks of Old Greece, and held strongly to the traditions of the mother country' (Dunbabin 1948: vi), and later asserts that 'most colonial customs are seen to be directly derived from Greece' (Dunbabin 1948: 188). Differences could be dismissed as provincial aberrations, thus also reinforcing the superior position of the motherland: as for Freeman, in the eyes of later scholars the Western Greeks could never quite live up to their mainland counterparts.

The search for similarity combined with inferiority between Western and mainland Greece can be detected in various fields. Dunbabin found evidence for 'cultural dependence' in the fields of cult and art in particular. In the latter case he argued that styles were dependent on Corinth ('a province of Corinthian art', Dunbabin 1948: 268), even where differences existed: although Archaic terracotta revetments, for example, are admitted to be 'sufficiently distinct to be called Sicilian' (Dunbabin 1948: 269), the occurrence of similar elements in revetments in areas possibly influenced by Corinth leads him to the conclusion that 'though this style has not been found at Corinth, there is no doubt that it is Corinthian' (Dunbabin 1948: 269). Others have found points of comparison and links in commerce and epigraphy as well as various other cultural institutions (Graham 1982: 153-5; Boardman 1994: 137-8). In the case of burial customs I have argued elsewhere that distinctions in methods and accessories are more conspicuous and significant than the similarities with putative mother-cities and may be linked to a conscious attempt on the part of new states to forge their own cultural identities; the same could also be said for cult and religion, where evidence for interaction with mother-city sanctuaries is limited but interest in the panhellenic sanctuaries (and the opportunities there provided for display and posturing) abounds (Shepherd 1995). However, in one area in particular the desire to cast the Western Greeks as both culturally dependent and inferior even in imitation is particularly evident since it pervades the work not only of those scholars directly concerned with the Greeks in the West but also of those dealing with other aspects of ancient Greece. It is also the field in which the Western Greeks produced some of their most spectacular monuments: their temple architecture.

The morphology of Western Greek Archaic temple architecture vis-à-vis that of the mainland is well known, but it may be worth rehearsing some of the more obvious features here nevertheless.[9] The basic concept of a monumental peripteral temple following the canons of the Doric order (Ionic rarely appears in the West) is the same in both countries and could not be mistaken for anything other than a Greek temple; equally, however, it would be difficult to mistake a Western Greek temple for a mainland one or vice versa in the Archaic period. In plan as well as elevation perhaps the most obvious variation to the ancient eye as well as the modern is the frontal emphasis displayed by many temples in the West: whereas mainland temples tend to have the pronaos balanced by a matching opisthodomos at the rear and the whole cella complex centred within the peristyle, Western Greek temples display deep porches, often with double colonnades or other elaboration (see Fig. 2.2), and at the rear a blank adyton wall backed by a narrower pteroma. In addition the cella is relatively long and narrow and the flank pteromata correspondingly wider. Occasionally they display extremely unusual features which must surely be related to cult practice, such as the screen walls of the colonnades on Temples FS at Selinus and Zeus Olympios at Akragas; the latter seems also to have been decorated with Telamon figures on the exterior. Their size is impressive: Temples GT (Selinus) and Zeus Olympios (Akragas) rank amongst the biggest anywhere in the Greek world and for their time were matched only by the colossal Ionic temples of Asia Minor and not by anything yet constructed in Greece (Fig. 2.3).

To these may be added features of the elevation less apparent today: these include the ability of Sicilian architects to span wider distances, thus reducing the need for internal supports and potentially creating a very different interior space; the tendency to stretch frieze elements rather than employ angle contraction (as on the mainland) in order to meet the difficulties imposed by the demands of the Doric order; and distinctive architectural decoration, most notably the terracottas which included the lateral waterspouts and geison revetments, the latter occurring only on the mainland on buildings of Western Greek origin, namely on the treasuries at Olympia. Finally, their appearance within the landscape should

2.2. Temple of Apollo, Syracuse, *c.* 560 BC. View of the east end with double colonnade.

also be considered: like their mainland counterparts, Western Greek temples occupy high ground where they are most conspicuous. However, whereas the former tend to be isolated buildings on an acropolis, Western Greek buildings are not only incorporated into a city plan (as for example at Poseidonia, Selinus and Syracuse) but also appear in multiples: the wealth of the Western states allowed them to build temple after temple in close proximity to each other, with in some cases building apparently commencing on a new temple even before another had been completed. To a visitor from Greece, the urban landscape must have looked both recognizably Greek and at the same time unlike anything back home.

It is fair, then, to say that Western Greek architecture did not develop along entirely the same lines as in Greece itself. Communication between the two areas in this respect was clearly ongoing and intensive, since on current evidence there was no tradition of monumental Doric architecture at the time the Western states were founded, apart from the possibility of wooden prototypes. Increasingly, however, there is evidence to suggest that innovation did not always begin in Greece and spread west, but may have moved in the opposite direction also: the earliest evidence for sculptured metopes, for example, comes from the West and Ridgway has suggested their invention there (Ridgway 1977: 225-52 esp. 248); Klein (1998) has recently argued for the influence of Sicilian Greek roofing systems on those employed in the mainland; and the problems posed by

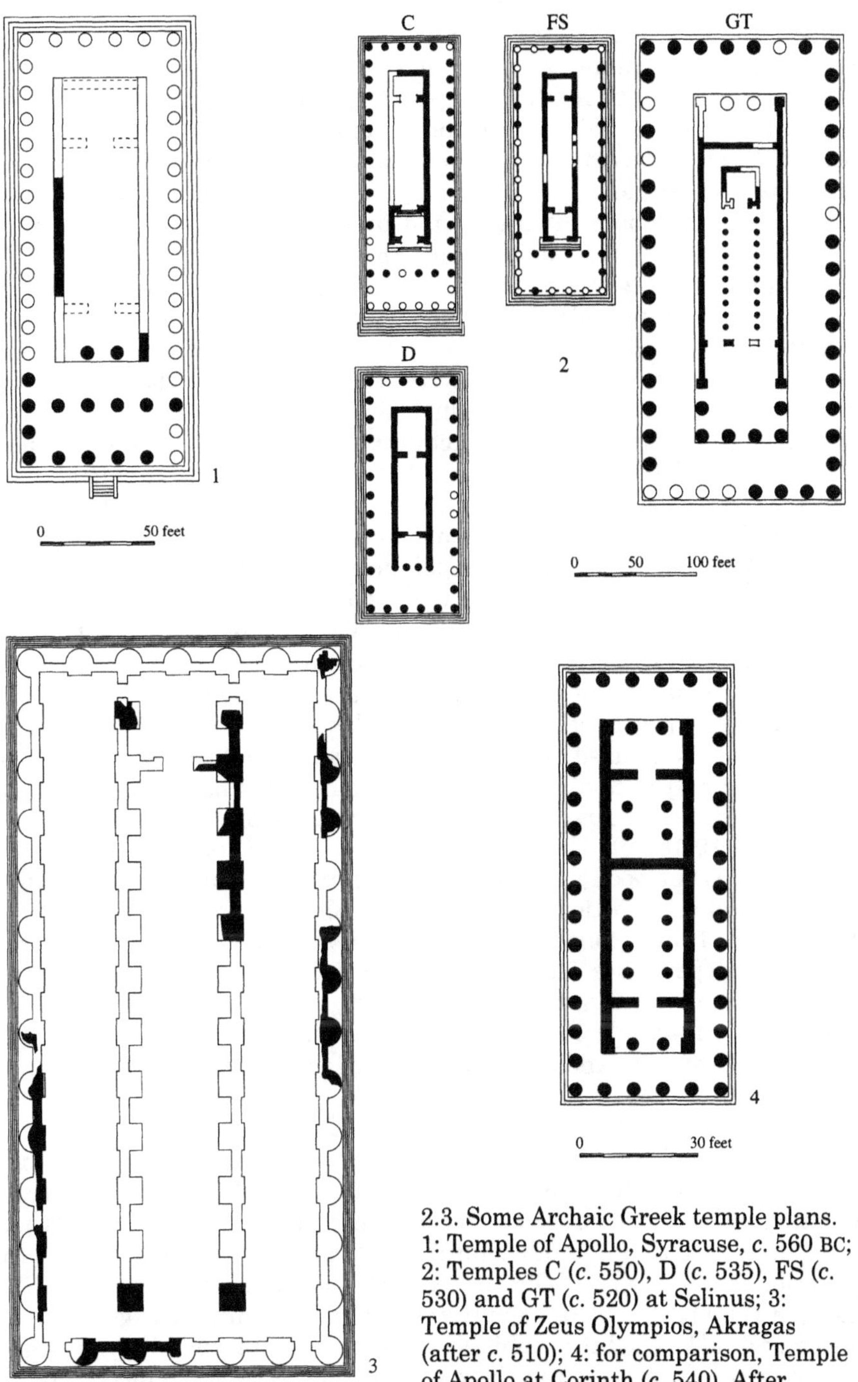

2.3. Some Archaic Greek temple plans. 1: Temple of Apollo, Syracuse, *c.* 560 BC; 2: Temples C (*c.* 550), D (*c.* 535), FS (*c.* 530) and GT (*c.* 520) at Selinus; 3: Temple of Zeus Olympios, Akragas (after *c.* 510); 4: for comparison, Temple of Apollo at Corinth (*c.* 540). After Dinsmoor 1950, figs 26, 28, 35, 40.

founding a new settlement from scratch in the West have long been recognized as instrumental in the development of town planning.

Earlier commentators, however, preferred to suggest that all innovation originated in Old Greece and divergences from the model there provided were to be explained as cultural lagging or provincial ineptitude on the part of the colonies. Their conclusions are less than complimentary and tend to cast both architects and patrons in entirely passive roles. Thus, for example, Dunbabin admits that some minor elements may be colonial innovations and admires both technical solutions and the ability to build on a large scale, but nevertheless concludes that Western and mainland (especially Peloponnesian) temples are similar in plan and elevation and the main characteristics of the former are to be explained as conservative preservations of features abandoned in Greece, thus indicating a significant time-lag in the architecture of the West (Dunbabin 1948: 281-4). Around twenty years earlier, Dinsmoor in *The Architecture of Ancient Greece* had compared the Greek colonies generally with America in their ability to outstrip the mother country but also betrayed surprise: the 'comparative insignificance' of motherland architecture is in his view 'astounding' (Dinsmoor 1927: 69); in the edition of 1950 his views regarding the divergences between Greek and Western Greek architecture are more explicitly expressed: he excuses the mother country by noting in the colonies a 'tendency towards ostentation, accompanied however by a certain amount of provincialism or "cultural lag" ' (Dinsmoor 1950: 75); Italy in particular is accused of 'barbaric distortions resulting from the intermixture not only of colonists of various origins but of native taste' and the reader is directed first to Syracuse for 'examples of provincialism' (Dinsmoor 1950: 75). The adyton was viewed by Dinsmoor as simply a peculiarity (Dinsmoor 1927: 80). These opinions remained unchanged in the 1950 and later editions of the book published over subsequent decades. By contrast, Italian commentators were pointing to Western Greek architectural independence and innovation: Gabrici stressed 'una fisionomia sua propria e un indirizzio alquanto divergente e indipendente' (Gabrici 1933: 229, 248) while Pace stressed the grandiosity of Sicilian temples versus those of mainland Greece and argued that Western Greek architecture played an important role in the development of Doric architecture generally (Pace 1938 (vol. ii): 211ff.; *contra* Dunbabin 1948: 283).

Later anglophone writers expressed views similar to those of their predecessors. The first edition of Lawrence's *Greek Architecture* (1957) credited the Western Greeks with originality in design, but damned them with the accusation of crudity until the Western Greeks woke up to the superior achievements of Old Greece in the fifth century (Lawrence 1957: 129); in 1960 Hodge, writing on Greek roofing systems, did argue that the Western Greeks used the sophisticated system of the truss for wide spans, but otherwise characterized their architecture as quite simply 'imitative and backward' (Hodge 1960: 41). In 1976 Winter, in one of a series of articles on Doric architecture, was more appreciative of Western Greek achievements, but nevertheless gives the impression that their architecture was provincial. He puts forward three possibilities to explain the divergent path of Western Greek Doric: these were the 'lack of hard and fast traditions' in Doric architecture at the time of the foundation of the colonies; softer stone, which aided experimentation; and a more adventurous spirit which allowed borrowing from other Greeks and was due to isolation amongst non-Greeks.

The common thread in all these interpretations is that the Western Greeks did not really know what they were doing and floundered about producing structures based on mainland models which were at best behind the times and at worst the bungled attempts of parvenus to ape their betters. This is surely both patronizing and implausible since the salient features of Archaic Western Greek architecture noted above are unlikely to be the result of unskilled counterfeit or provincialism. Such factors might account for clumsy copies, but these buildings are not copies: inept imitation does not explain such major divergences from the mainland format such as the addition of a second colonnade to emphasize the east end or the recurrence of the adyton; nor would it result in such substantial changes in basic proportions such as the narrow cella and wide pteromata; and nor would it allow for the development of such sophisticated building techniques such engineering for large scale construction, wide span roofing or alternative solutions to angle contraction. These characteristics all imply the deliberate and independent development of specific features from an early period which served to create a general architectural style in the West which was not to be mistaken for a product of mainland Greece or elsewhere and which could compete in size and splendour with anything else in the Greek world. Channels of architectural communication were clearly open and it is difficult to see what could have prevented the Western Greeks from copying mainland buildings exactly had they so desired; certainly the lack of 'hard and fast traditions' need have presented no obstacle.

As noted above, more recently there has been a move to credit the Greeks in the West with rather more active input into their culture. Yet the concept of colonial inferiority derived from the model of the British Empire encouraged a longstanding view that even the most impressive creations of the Western Greeks had to be overshadowed by those of Greece proper and relegated to the ranks of imitation and provincialism. The 'essential unity' which Dunbabin describes as the 'pride of most colonials', whereby colonies referred constantly to their mother-cities as both innovators and arbiters, was a motif of the British Empire which also became a major theme of the study of Greek settlement in the West. It was combined with a hierarchical structure which prioritized the Greeks at the expense of other populations, a structure equally derived from the period of high empire. The works of Freeman and Dunbabin provide the most obvious examples of this approach, not least because they took colonization as their main subject, but they were by no means alone. The imperial approach elsewhere tends to be implicit rather than explicit, but it occasionally appears in no uncertain terms. As late as 1962, for example, A.G. Woodhead could open his study *The Greeks in the West* by quoting Stanley Baldwin's evocation of the British colonial spirit:

> Wherever [the colonists] went, they carried with them the traditions, the habits, the ideals of their Mother Country. Wherever they settled, they planted a new homeland. And, though mountains and the waste of seas divided them, they never lost that golden thread of the spirit which drew their thoughts back to the land of their birth.
>
> Woodhead 1962: 17

It is Ruskin all over again, still going strong nearly one hundred years later as far as the Western Greeks were concerned. Woodhead applied it directly to the ancients, commenting:

> Stanley Baldwin spoke of British colonisation, but his words could as readily refer to the Greeks who left their Aegean cities to found new homes and farm new lands in Sicily and along the coasts of southern Italy ... surrounded by barbarian strangers ...
>
> Woodhead 1962: 17

Around the same time, Boardman noted in his fundamental work *The Greeks Overseas* that the West was a place where the Greeks had 'nothing to learn, much to teach' (Boardman 1964: 203). Neither of these assessments sounds unfamiliar: the model established in the late nineteenth century was still active in the second half of the twentieth, notwithstanding the fact that the basis for it – the British Empire – had all but disappeared. But in the earlier period the analogies with modern colonization – whether appropriate or not – had perhaps worked both ways and had become a circular analogy: while the British Empire structured the study of Greek settlement in the West, the alignment of the Greeks and British as both perched at the tops of their respective trees in turn reinforced British ideas of cultural superiority. The glory that was Greece was reborn in Britain.

The British were by no means alone in their appropriation of antiquity. As has often been observed, many European states somehow managed to line themselves up with ancient Greece, notably Germany; Rome also appears, with the French regarding themselves as direct successors of the Romans in North Africa (Van Dommelen 1997: 306-7; Morris 1994a: 11; see also Trigger 1984: 363-5). But the reverse impact of this link on the study of antiquity as opposed to ways of viewing the modern world and justifying modern politics seems to be a particular feature of anglophone scholarship, at least as far as the Western Greeks are concerned. If

Edward Freeman, one of its earliest exponents, at times comes close to being a caricature of his age – this was after all the man who could publish lectures on the Empire and America entitled 'Greater Greece and Greater Britain' and 'George Washington, The Expander of England' (Freeman 1886) – he nevertheless helped to establish a longstanding scholarly environment in which the presence of empire and its associated modes of thought informed the way in which scholars thought about ancient civilization as well as modern. For Sicily and Italy, this meant the superiority of the Greeks over all other groups and of mainland Greeks over Western Greeks, with the latter constantly looking to the former. These ways of thinking were very much part of the late Imperial age and, as Anthony Snodgrass points out in this volume, in some respects the reverse of what they had been earlier (see also Dalrymple 2002: xl-xliii with references). The high empire of the late nineteenth and earlier twentieth centuries would probably still have had its impact on the study of the Greeks in Italy and Sicily regardless: but if a study had been written in English one hundred years or more earlier in the eighteenth century it might have looked very different and maybe even have had something in common with twenty-first-century ideas.

Notes

1. Thanks are due to David Ridgway, from whose comments this paper has benefited, and Harry Buglass for illustrative work.

2. For discussions of modern appropriations of the past, see for example Trigger 1984; Jenkyns 1980, especially ch. XIII; Morris 1994a; Bernal 1987, whose first volume of Black Athena is entitled *The Fabrication of Ancient Greece 1785-1985.*

3. See, for example, Allcroft (BA Oxon) and Mason's *History of Sicily 491-289 BC* (1890) *passim*, but in particular p. 31 'Though so far removed from their original homes, the colonists of Grecian towns never forgot their relationship to their metropolis, which they regarded as a child regards its parents'; also on the Phoenicians (p. 18): 'Like most of the old Oriental nations, the Phoenicians tended towards a gloomy and morbid cruelty … '.

4. See Symonds 1991: 49, with references; also Freeman's *Some Impressions of the United States* (1883), with a review in *The Oxford Magazine* vol. 1 (18 April 1883), pp. 161-2.

5. For discussions of British and other European attitudes towards nineteenth-century America and American responses and 'cultural cringe', see for example French 1975; Morris 1994a, esp. p. 19. An illustration is the famous taunt of Sidney Smith in the *Edinburgh Review* (1820: 79-80): 'who … looks at an American picture or statue? …Who drinks out of American glasses? Or eats from American plates?'. See also Freeman's low opinion of the USA (Freeman 1883; reviewed in *The Oxford Magazine* 1883: 162).

6. One briefer study which also appeared was Walter Copeland Perry's *Sicily in Fable, History, Art and Song* (1908) written at the impressive age of ninety-four. While regarding Freeman's study as 'excellent' Copeland Perry asserts that it will only appeal to a 'few serious students' and excuses his own work on the grounds that nothing was available to the general reader 'who wishes to learn the *facts* of

Sicilian history' (pp. vi-vii). His opinions are very similar to Freeman's. For example, on the subject of the Sikans and Sikels he notes 'Happily, both these nations were Aryan ... and they had many points of agreement [with the Greeks] in religion' (p. 30); the Greeks he characterizes as 'the most intellectual and highly gifted people of the human race' and 'superior to the comparatively simple and guileless Sicels and Sicans' (p. 30); and on mother-city/colony relationships he claims 'the tie between the colonists and the mother-city was that which binds children to their parents – reverence and love ... It is to be remarked, and perhaps wondered at, that this filial piety did not involve political dependence' (p. 45).

7. Although published in 1948, Dunbabin's *The Western Greeks* was in fact substantially researched and written more than a decade earlier when he submitted an earlier version for a fellowship examination at All Souls College, Oxford under the title *Contributions to the History of Sicily and South Italy in the Seventh and Sixth Centuries BC* (1937). The scope of the two works differs somewhat – in the published book, for example, Dunbabin deals with the foundation period which he excluded from the thesis on the grounds that it had been adequately dealt with already by Alan Blakeway (Dunbabin 1937: iv) – but the theoretical approach is the same, with if anything the imperial flavour appearing yet more strongly (perhaps unsurprisingly) in the earlier version (*passim*, but see for example pp. 23, 92, 95, 115, 214, 227-8).

8. For full discussion of the fibula debate and references see Shepherd 1999, esp. pp. 278-83. The arguments that the fibulae were Greek came mainly from British scholars; others, notably Patroni (1896: 39ff.), Blinkenberg (1926: 26 with n. 1) and Sundwall (1943: Type GI βb) argued that they were of Italian manufacture. Interestingly, Dunbabin seems to have changed his mind on this subject between his 1937 study and the published version of 1948: in the former, Dunbabin suggests that simple objects such as fibulae were made in the colonies, where industry was nevertheless only very minor, while more complex metal objects were imported from Greece (Dunbabin 1937: 285-6).

9. For general discussion of the salient features of Western Greek architecture see for example Winter 1976; Mertens 1996.

3

'Lesser Breeds': The History of a False Analogy

Anthony Snodgrass

It has become common ground today in the study of early Greek overseas settlement that the whole subject was, for roughly the first three-quarters of the twentieth century, consciously or unconsciously dominated by the analogy with modern European imperialism. For work produced in Britain and the Commonwealth, that of course meant primarily the analogy with *British* imperialism; for work produced in other countries, including America which had once seen British imperialism from the other side, the same influence was less obvious. Scholars, as we shall see, made some effort to turn to the earlier stages of colonialism for enlightenment, and so as far as possible to compare like with like. But when it comes to drawing lessons from real life scholars, like everyone else, are apt to turn to the era lived through by themselves, their parents and their grandparents. Thus, inevitably, it was *recent* British imperial experience that shaped their subconscious thought.

It is equally common today to acknowledge the unfortunate aspects of the modern imperial analogy. It was bad enough in itself: among other things, it supplied most European languages – English, French and Italian and even German – with that profoundly misleading terminology for the process of early Greek overseas settlement, which many scholars now deplore. But the link with British imperialism took things another step further astray, because of the particular phase which was allowed to dominate the imagination. Britain's most expansive era of colonial growth – the first period when the phrase 'the British Empire' actually came into general use – was broadly speaking between 1875 and 1914. This intensification of activity was set in motion for a specific reason: Britain was losing her early lead in industrial development to other European nations and to America. To reverse this trend, she brought into play the main existing advantage that she had over her competitors: her huge share of the world's shipping tonnage, and the access to the pool of cheap raw materials and cheap labour in the Empire which this gave. This popular policy was strongly espoused by Conservative governments under Disraeli (between 1874 and 1880), Salisbury (between 1885 and 1902) and above all by Salisbury's Colonial Minister Joseph Chamberlain, who lasted on into the next Conservative administration under Balfour. To make it work, it was not enough to intensify the exploitation of existing territories:

new ones had to be added. On the whole, the policy did work; and it was Africa's fate to provide the main arena for its implementation.

*

To understand this period, when British imperialism was a mellow fruit in which few could yet detect any mildew, it is natural, indeed universal, practice to turn to the 'laureate of Empire', Rudyard Kipling. In 1897, as a tribute to Queen Victoria's sixty-year Jubilee, he composed his *Recessional*, once his most celebrated poem (until the later growth in popularity of the much inferior *If*), and soon to be set to music by Sullivan and to become a popular hymn. The whole of the first three stanzas – indeed, almost the whole poem – was to find its way into *The Oxford Dictionary of Quotations*:

God of our fathers, known of old –
  Lord of our far-flung battle-line –
Beneath whose awful hand we hold
  Dominion over palm and line –
Lord God of Hosts, be with us yet,
Lest we forget – lest we forget!

The tumult and the shouting dies –
  The captains and the kings depart –
Still stands thine ancient sacrifice,
  An humble and a contrite heart.
Lord God of Hosts, be with us yet,
Lest we forget – lest we forget!

Far-called, our navies melt away –
  On dune and headland sinks the fire –
Lo, all our pomp of yesterday
  Is one with Nineveh and Tyre!
Judge of the Nations, spare us yet,
Lest we forget – lest we forget!

It is an extraordinary exercise in dissimulation, ostensibly asking for God's leniency toward the British for their imperial presumptions, but taking the opportunity to revel, indeed wallow, in them. The lines which everybody in England remembered fell, without exception, under the latter description. No one quoted '*An humble and a contrite heart*'. Instead, it was '*Lord of our far-flung battle-line*'; '*Dominion over palm and pine*'; '*The captains and the kings depart*'. The fourth line of the next stanza is the one which provides my title:

If, drunk with sight of power, we loose
  Wild tongues that have not Thee in awe –
Such boasting as the Gentiles use,

3. *'Lesser Breeds': The History of a False Analogy*

Or lesser breeds without the law –
Lord God of Hosts, be with us yet,
Lest we forget – lest we forget!

What makes this line perhaps the most interesting in the whole poem is the general misunderstanding which it generated. The 'lesser breeds' were widely identified with the subjects, or victims, of imperialism. By 1942, nearly fifty years later, this misapprehension had reached such a pitch that, in an essay on Kipling, George Orwell felt it necessary to point out that the poet had meant nothing of the kind.[1] The briefest study of the context, provided by the preceding three lines, would have made this clear. Colonial subjects were neither 'drunk with sight of power', nor likely to indulge in 'boasting'. Kipling was in fact referring to the *rival imperialists.*

Orwell, himself writing in the middle of another Anglo-German conflict, took this to have meant primarily the Germans; and there is in fact documentary evidence that, since the previous year, Kipling had been much preoccupied with the German threat to British imperialism. He had been provoked by one incident in particular, the Kaiser's telegram to President Kruger of the independent Boer Republics (Transvaal, Orange Free State, Griqualand), expressing solidarity with him in the face of an unprovoked British venture, the Jameson Raid (of New Year, 1896) instigated by the arch-imperialist Cecil Rhodes, in which an armed force from Rhodesia had invaded the Transvaal to stir up an insurrection against Kruger, but with such spectacular lack of success that it was forced to surrender four days later. (Three years on, Germany was also to give aid and comfort to Britain's enemies when the Boer War broke out, but that lay still in the future).

But Kipling's animosity was not directed at the Germans alone. In a letter of 29 March 1897 he referred to '... the three despotic powers, Germany, Austria and Russia'; and on 21 July, immediately after finishing *Recessional*, he told one correspondent that 'we could kick many more races than the Teuton' and warned another of '... what manner of armed barbarians we are surrounded with'.[2] Closer to Britain and most blatantly 'without the law' were the Belgians: in 1885, an international conference in Berlin had awarded their King Leopold II the Congo as his private fiefdom, a single block of territory more than seventy-five times the size of his own country. The strong British opposition to this move met with some vindication when reports of the exceptional atrocities which followed in the Congo began to reach the British Foreign Office in the early 1890s (the final *dénouement* in the Congo will make a re-appearance shortly, in the unlikely connection of the British in Ireland). The acquisition of foreign territories by other European powers – including the Germans, but only since 1884 – was indeed a source of British irritation. But much more fundamentally, it had been the *economic* drive for cheap labour and resources which initially fuelled the last wave of British imperialism, and what was now developing was a show-down with the European economic rivals. Kipling was as aware of this as anyone else.

Some of the weaknesses of the analogy between ancient Greek and modern British 'colonial' activity will already have become clearer in the course of this digression. But it is worth while briefly to rehearse the objections to that analogy. First, there is no ancient counterpart, in Greece or anywhere else, for the nation-state, the medium through which modern imperialism was largely exercised. Thus it is strictly speaking anachronistic even to use the language derived from nation-states: in the phrase 'Greek colonization' it is not only the noun but the adjective which is inappropriate – as Nicholas Purcell perhaps implied in the opening words of his review of *The Archaeology of Greek Colonisation*: 'The archaeology of *what*?' (1997: 500). A series of further differences arises from this absence of nation-states in ancient overseas activity. One result of the prevalence of the city-state system in Greek culture was that the primary settlements overseas, by and large, were meant to be, and to a great extent were, permanently Greek towns – linguistically, institutionally, architecturally, and in their economies. To what extent was this ever true of the British Empire: which of its towns can be called 'permanently British' in the same sense? Some, encouraged by their naming after English country towns, may have temporarily tried to be – one thinks of Boston or Salisbury or Christchurch – before the forces of geographical and cultural context made them no longer recognizable as such, in a way that was hardly true of, say, Naxos in Sicily or Epizephyrian Lokri.

Next, only rarely could a mother-city lay permanent claim to *possession* of new territory overseas, however close its ties to its colony, as Britain and other modern states used to do (though T.J. Dunbabin, in his seminal book *The Western Greeks* of 1948, once let slip the phrase 'Corinthian possession of Syracuse' (1948: 17)). Nor should we assume that participation in a settlement was limited to citizens of the community from which the oikist himself came;[3] while oikists themselves show a certain tendency, at least according to Carol Dougherty, to be not respected pillars of that community, but rather misfits or outcasts of one kind or another (1993a: esp. 31-44). This contrasts with the modern phenomenon of expansion as a positive policy of the state, undertaken in the supposed interests of its home-based subjects who later became its electorate, even when operated by semi-independent entities like the East India Company (which, once they prospered, increasingly became a mere arm of the state). Again, the concept of rule over foreign subjects plays as small a part in ancient discussions of the *apoikia* as it does a large one in modern ones of colonialism. All these differences can be crudely summed up by saying that there was no notion of 'the flag', there was no thought of 'painting the map red' or any colour; indeed for a time there was probably not even a map. Overseas settlement could result in economic benefit, not only for the mother-city but for other homeland cities and for non-Greek peoples too;

but, from the point of view of state policy, its initial motivation seems to have been as much a negative as a positive one, to ease pressure on the land of the founding city and to rid it of restless elements. Equally absent, so far as we know, was any religious motivation, not only in the narrower sense of missionary efforts to convert indigenous populations to the colonists' religion, but more broadly in the sense of the desire to inculcate the values of that religion. Finally, it will be agreed that, however controversial the issue of the motivation of settlement overseas by the Greek cities, an immediate result was something I mentioned just now, the resettling of part of the home population on new land. In modern times, by the time of late nineteenth-century colonialism at any rate, this element had become a sharply diminishing one: the primary aim of all the territorial acquisition, except in a very few cases, notably Southern Rhodesia and Kenya, was not to resettle a part of the home population on new land.

Faced with such incompatibilities, it may seem remarkable to us now that the 'imperial analogy' found such acceptance. So let me next mention a few extenuating factors. First, as I conceded at the outset, Anglophone scholars of the twentieth century do seem to have made an effort to get back to an earlier phase of British expansion in their search for telling parallels and memorable phrases. Unlike Edward Freeman in the 1890s, who wrote openly of the possibility of the indigenous Sikels being converted into 'artificial Greeks' (1891-4, vol. I: 08), a vision borrowed from his own times if ever there was one, Thomas Dunbabin in 1948 turned to the early days of his native Australia for evidence on population-growth and the chronology of settlement;[4] Alan Blakeway's discourse about 'the flag' and 'trade' better evokes the seventeenth and eighteenth centuries than the mature British Empire (1932-3: 171; 202); while the same is largely true of John Boardman's often-cited phrase about 'the bright beads with which merchants are usually supposed to dazzle the natives' (1999: 200).

Secondly, the analogy does indeed become less preposterous when applied to those times. Episodes like the seventeenth-century Spice Wars in what is now Indonesia,[5] or William Hawkins' unsuccessful venture of 1609 to the coast of the Mogul Empire (Woodruff 1953: 21-9), or the way in which the early settlements in North America were reinforced by state encouragement, do evoke faint echoes of Greek settlement. Isolated, sometimes openly piratical ventures (in the Greek case mostly undocumented) led to permanent footholds on foreign shores, sometimes followed by agricultural resettlement. An important background feature, too, is that even in 1600 only some thirty-two per cent of the earth's land-surface, though more than half of its oceans, was known to Europeans.[6] There is the same feeling of pushing back the frontiers of the unknown.

There is another important background parallel too: the fact that, in these early years, there could be no necessary presumption of the cultural superiority of the new arrivals over the indigenous peoples. There is a good case for saying that, apart from its more backward political institutions, the Mogul Empire was a more civilized society than the British in 1600 – notably in regard to religious tolerance and to restraint in the exploitation of the peasantry. Much later, in 1785, Warren Hastings still felt it fair to remind his successor as Governor-General that 'Among the natives of India, there are men of as strong intellect, as sound integrity, and as honourable feelings as any of this Kingdom' (Woodruff 1953: 124).

But at this point I want to return to the era of Kipling, and to my earlier claim that its influence lay heavy on contemporary and later scholarship. This influence is not so easy to demonstrate, because of the essentially implicit way in which it was exercised: scholars were seldom so naive as to use it for a direct analogy. But little tell-tale signs of it are everywhere in the literature. The British high imperial age is distinguished from the earlier period between 1600 and the earlier nineteenth century by, among other things, a new or at least heightened sensitivity to race, and above all to colour. Illustrations of this are too numerous to count, but Gillian Shepherd touched on a delicate facet of it in her study of *intermarriage* in the early Greek settlements (Shepherd 1999).

This is, I think, not only a most delicate but also an absolutely central issue in the whole discussion of overseas settlement. It is therefore interesting to look at a more recent parallel. Mixed marriages had once been a recurrent, if subdued, feature of the British presence in India, and unofficial liaisons an absolutely ubiquitous one. It had started at the very beginning, when in 1609 Jahangir Khan had offered William Hawkins 'a white maiden out of his palace' as his wife; and Hawkins accepted on the one condition that she must be a Christian (the daughter of a Christian Armenian officer in the Mogul's army was duly found). The example of the Portuguese, who had been there first and who regularly took Indian wives, was presently followed by a number of highly-placed British civilians and soldiers. Mrs, or 'Begum', Johnson, the salon queen of British Calcutta in the 1780s, was the daughter or grand-daughter of a mixed marriage; Kirkpatrick, the Resident of Hyderabad in 1800, had a Muslim wife from a noble Hyderabadi family; William Fraser, commissioner for part of the territory of Delhi in the 1830s, had 'six or seven legitimate wives' who all lived together some distance away from his headquarters; even Charles Metcalfe, who rose to be Governor-General a few years later, had during his early service in the Punjab had for seven or eight years an Indian wife or mistress who bore him three sons.[7]

The second of these later stories, that of Major James Achilles Kirkpatrick, forms the central theme of William Dalrymple's splendid recent book, *White Mughals* (2002). Dalrymple (2002: 53) identifies a crucial period, from the 1790s to the 1830s, when society in the central seat of the British presence in India, Calcutta, first began to frown on a range of activities then still prevalent among the British officials in the outlying Indian courts, embracing religion, language, etiquette, medicine, appearance, dress and, above all, relations with Indian women. His discussion abounds in telling quotations that reveal the earlier extent of this 'integrating' movement, and the increasing condemnation which it now incurred.

By 1850, the battle in India itself was over: the new rule of strict separation of British and indigenous societies had been successfully imposed. This was to have an interesting sequel in the case of Burma. Substantial parts of that country were annexed by the British in 1826 and 1852, and placed under the Government of India. Here, where caste and purdah alike were unknown, intimacy and marriage with Burmese women soon became commonplace; and by the 1870s a shocked, India-trained Chief Commissioner was suggesting that promotion should be denied to those officers who indulged in such practices.[8]

So which of these successive 'imperial' attitudes can be detected among twentieth-century Classical historians considering the same phenomenon of intermarriage in the Greek West: that of the pioneer settlers and administrators, or that of their nineteenth-century successors? The answer seems to be, without exception, the latter. Gillian Shepherd's (1999) verdict is that scholars tended not only to argue against intermarriage having occurred at all widely, but to feel an instinctive disapproval of the possibility. This conclusion is extended in time to cover at least Dunbabin; not until around the 1980s can a real reversal of Anglophone scholarly opinion be detected. This then would be a distinctively 'late imperial' attitude, alive and well through the first half of the twentieth century. If so, it was a small part of a much larger concern with race and colour which crept over British imperial attitudes in the late imperial age.

This is where the point of Kipling's misunderstood phrase comes in. The late nineteenth- / early twentieth-century obsession with the subjugation of peoples with different-coloured skins, and the belief that it was justified by cultural superiority over these peoples, led to readers instinctively taking '*lesser breeds without the law*' to refer to them. In fact, as we have seen and as Kipling actually implied, a more significant factor in late imperialism was the rivalry with other colonizing powers. Kipling, like most of his British contemporaries, was as convinced of the superiority of the British over their imperial rivals as of their right to rule over their imperial subjects. His readers and contemporaries clung even more strongly to the latter tenet than the former: Kipling had after all been going on about the 'white man's burden' for so long that, apparently, they imagined him again to be talking about it.

*

We may now return briefly to the case of the Belgian Congo after 1885. The decision to award this huge territory to King Leopold as a private African domain had been opposed not by Britain only, but also by the

United States (which was hostile to empires generally) and by Portugal (which had a grand scheme of its own in mind, to unite its territories of Angola in south-west and Mozambique in south-east Africa into one huge colony). When the grim rumours of torture, massacre, even genocide in Leopold's Congo began to circulate, however, it was a British or more precisely an Irish agent who eventually brought them to the world's notice in 1904 – Roger Casement, who had served as consul in Mozambique and Angola, and then in the Congo. The uproar was such that the King was forced to set up a Belgian commission to investigate the facts: it confirmed the substance of Casement's reports and, in 1908, the Belgian government was obliged to take over the government of the colony itself. Casement was rewarded for his services with a knighthood in 1911, but this was not the last episode of his story, for history was to make one of its more playful links between two very different arenas of British overseas activity: Casement described Leopold's Congo as 'A tyranny beyond conception – save only perhaps to an Irishman alive to the horrors once daily enacted in his land' (Noyes 1957: 41); and it was as an Irishman that he was to meet his own end.

For the Achilles heel of Kipling and other imperialist writers was in fact the same as that of British imperialism itself: Ireland. Here of course there were no serious rivals to worry about; yet whichever period one is addressing, from the mid-twelfth century to the early twenty-first, there is always this grand, long-drawn-out failure of British imperialism to take into account. When it came to the Irish question, Kipling suffered even more acutely from pure prejudice than did most other Englishmen of his day (or ours). In April 1916 the myth-enshrouded Easter Rising took place, as a direct result of which Roger Casement, at that point a committed Irish nationalist based in Germany, was arrested and hanged as a traitor later that year. In April 1918, when World War One still had seven months to run, and partly in retaliation for the Easter Rising, the British Government introduced its Military Service Bill, whereby conscription (imposed two years earlier in Great Britain) was to be extended to Ireland. The government dithered so long about implementing this ill-judged measure – which disregarded the fact that tens of thousands of young Irishmen had long since enlisted as volunteers and fought with noted bravery in the British armed forces – that it was mercifully pre-empted by the end of the War. Its one decisive effect was to stiffen the resolve (and the popularity) of the Irish Republican movement, for the convulsion which was to bring partial independence in 1921.

Kipling was, predictably, a fervent supporter of Ulster Unionism. Two years earlier, in 1914, this had led him to indulge in perhaps the most indiscreet of all his public stances, in openly exhorting the Ulster Protestants to take up arms against the Westminster government's proposal to introduce Home Rule to the whole island. This itself would have been treason, had it happened a few months later when World War One had begun.[9] But, much less predictably, by 1918 Kipling was against Irish conscription too – but for different reasons. On 21 May, he wrote to an acquaintance: 'Personally, I wish to goodness we could do without Irish conscripts of any sort – carry on with common white men' (Pinney (ed.) 1999: 496). Among other things, this shows that, in the late age of imperialism, the appeal even of the race card could be trumped, however inappropriately, by that of the colour card. (Many years later still, at the dawn of the twenty-first century, this response was to have a farcical echo when the Metropolitan Police in London revealed that, out of a much-trumpeted increase of 218 new officers recruited from ethnic minorities, some 214 were 'white Irish' or 'other whites').

A cooler assessment of the Irish question might suggest that, here again, if one were to go some distance back into history, forgetting about the issues of colour, race and economic rivalry, one could find episodes that have some relevance to the study of Greek overseas settlement. The geographical distance – it is about sixty-five miles from Holyhead to Dun Laoghaire, as it is from Corfu to Otranto – and the slightly more distant cultural and linguistic affinities were not altogether different from those which applied to, for instance, the pre-colonial Greek relations with Apulia, where the Iapyges maintained early links with Illyria on the Greek side of the Adriatic. The difficulty is that, over the centuries, the English colonial experiments with Ireland took so many different forms. Here is what the writer and journalist Paul Johnson wrote in 1972, before his conversion from fiery socialism to equally fiery Thatcherism:

> The English had, at various times, tried every solution (save one): outright conquest, partial conquest, the *cordon sanitaire*, genocide, assimilation through settlement, settlement without assimilation, apartheid, military rule, civil rule, plantations, puppet parliaments ... The one thing they never tried ... was outright and total evacuation
>
> Johnson 1972: 483

At first sight, no item in this repertoire would seem applicable to the early settlement of Greeks overseas: the concept of the nation-state insistently intervenes to disrupt the parallels. Neither 'assimilation through settlement' nor 'settlement without assimilation' will quite do, in the absence of any real evidence for a conscious policy on the part of the Greek settlers overseas. But 'plantations' are a shade more promising. The reference here is, yet again, to the sixteenth and seventeenth centuries. A number of attempts were made in later Tudor times to settle groups of Protestant colonists in eastern, southern and western Ireland (Fig. 3.1). In a sense they were all too successful: the settlers took to the land and to the people, frequently married them and, horror of horrors, often embraced their Catholic religion; they became, as the saying went, more Irish than the Irish themselves. This meant that, from the point of view of the original

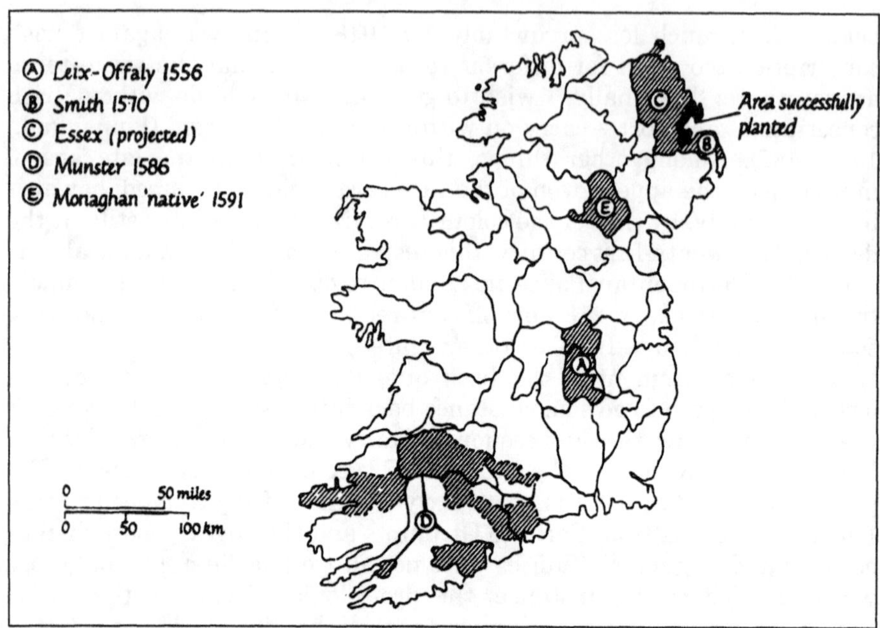

3.1. Tudor plantations in Ireland. After R. Dudley Edwards, *An Atlas of Irish History*, 2nd ed. (Routledge, 1981), fig. 50, p. 171.

objective, they were complete failures. But the most concerted of the plantation projects had a very different outcome, as we all have reason to know. After three Royal Commissions in 1608, 1609 and 1610, the biggest planned migration so far was sent on its way: Ulster, ironically because it had long been the most stubborn and ferocious centre of resistance to the English, was singled out as its destination (Foster 1988: 59-78). Care was taken to bring a large proportion of the colonists, this time, not from England but from Presbyterian Scotland. Celt met Celt, and there ensued nearly four centuries (and counting) of mutual animosity. Yet the sober fact is that, for much of these four centuries, the bulk of the population of Ulster have co-existed fairly peacefully, if (until recently) on terms set exclusively by the immigrant majority.

What, if any, are the lessons here for the study of the early Greek settlements? Several major factors have at once to be set aside: the fact that the Ulster settlement was brought about by the policy of a centralized government; the fact that (as in nearly all modern colonialism) the aim was to maintain, at least for the time being, close political subordination of the settlers to that government; and the fact that religion was the rock on which real assimilation foundered. It is difficult to establish the original number of settlers, but by 1622 it had risen to about thirteen thousand adults (Foster 1988: 72) – of the same order of magnitude as a large *polis*. And from here on, it is the similarities that catch the eye: regular and carefully worked-out land-apportionment schemes were applied when the settlers arrived; ascendancy was maintained above all by the privileged access which the immigrants had to the land, and later to the apparatus of industrialization; linguistic assimilation did take place; there is even a parallel to the founder-cult, in the annual celebrations of William of Orange as a spuriously late 'oikist'. Intermarriage might be disapproved of, but it regularly happened nonetheless: all manner of lesser expedients were therefore deployed to maintain separatism. At the same time, in accordance with biological principles, the cultural mix increasingly became a distinctive one: certain indigenous features crept in which helped to set Protestant Ulster as far apart from lowland Scotland as from the rest of the island. The link with the mother country, more fervently maintained on the settlers' side than it ever was in the early Greek world, was, on the other side, eventually more and more disowned – in approximate reversal of the ancient pattern. The extent of the Six Counties of Ulster, at about four thousand square miles, is today far greater than that of the largest Classical Greek *polis*. But the extent of Protestant settlement had expanded from a much smaller core: previously, in Tudor times, the area of successful Plantation had been confined to a tiny strip in south-eastern Antrim. Even today, beyond the thinly-populated *eschata* of Tyrone, Fermanagh and the Mourne Mountains there lies a line – a line which at times has become a fortified frontier; and beyond *that* lives an indigenous people, more numerous if till recently less advanced economically, which feels defrauded of a just claim on the same territory – for all the world like the Lucanians around Paestum or the Sikels behind Syracuse. This, I know, is a very facile analogy; but I find it more compelling than the half-conscious assimilation to late British colonialism which scholars seem to have adopted during, and well after the end of, that phase – above all, in their concern with racial differences between immigrant and indigenous peoples.

*

To make this argument fully convincing, it is necessary to find much more palpable and concrete illustrations of dependence on the late imperial analogy. A good place to start is with Sir Leonard Woolley, who after his great discoveries in the interior of Western Asia moved down to the Levantine coast in 1935 and found the Greeks at Al Mina. Anyone familiar with the scanty published accounts of that excavation will know his plans and reconstruction, in their later, rebuilt form, of the 'warehouses' in the town (Woolley 1938: 14-15; figs 3-4). His account implies not only that some of their predecessors took a similar form, but that the layout of *all* the excavated structures, from his 'Level VI' on, was similar. Woolley was keen to maintain his 'warehouse' interpretation for these buildings, and their use by 'merchants' who 'must have been Greeks'. His view had to overcome the awkward fact that a few (Woolley stresses 'a *very* few') burials were found under the floors of the rooms in these structures: others have accordingly wondered whether the buildings were not, at least in part, domestic in use. Woolley's view could (and no doubt did) derive direct encouragement from British colonial history as a whole. Warehouses (or 'factories' as they were initially called) were what early British overseas activity was all about. It was a 'factory' that William Hawkins wanted to build at Surat, while the Spice Wars largely arose from the desire of the British (and others) to build a factory on islands where the Dutch already had one: spices could then be bought while they were plentiful and cheap, and stored until the next ship from the Thames arrived. But Woolley perhaps slightly overdid things when later, in his *A Forgotten Kingdom*, he referred to the buildings as 'go-downs' (1953: 177). This term, a corruption of the Malay word *godong*, first entered the English vocabulary much earlier; but by the time that Woolley was writing it was redolent of the short stories of Somerset Maugham, or of events in then recent history such as the fall of Singapore in 1942, and there is little doubt as to the source and point of his allusion.

The text of Dunbabin's *The Western Greeks* has already been sifted through by Gillian Shepherd, in her study of the intermarriage question, for signs of the imperial imprint. Notwithstanding the extenuating factor that I alluded to earlier, namely his conscious recourse for analogy to the early phases in the growth of Sydney (from 1788) and of Melbourne (from 1837), she makes the telling point that he always looked for examples to existing Commonwealth territories, rather than to areas like New England (or Ireland) which had since won their independence (Shepherd 1999: 272). Apart from the fact that he was himself Australian, he undoubtedly realized that this would better support one of his central theses, that of the 'political independence, but almost complete cultural dependence' of the overseas settlements on the Greek homeland. That analogy itself, however, has a useful historical lesson to teach us, once we stop to consider how rapidly and completely such a view of the relationship between Australia and the mother country, common currency in the years around 1948, has become out-dated.

The corresponding analogy of mainland Greece with Great Britain ran into the serious difficulties that we have discussed, arising from the absence of the nation-state, but Dunbabin seems to have maintained it nonetheless. The Greco-barbarian divide was carried back to the beginnings of overseas settlement. Occasional sentences read as if they had dropped off a page written by Cecil Rhodes: 'In the colonies, however, the natives had no place' (1948: 47); 'for the native people had little to contribute to Greek civilisation' (1948: 186); 'the Greek regarded [the Sikel] as an inferior being and was proud of his own descent' (1948: 193). For this last statement in particular, it is very hard to find any explicit evidence, from the Archaic period at any rate, which would support such a confident assertion. The more plausible explanation is surely that it was triggered by the implicit and unexpressed analogy with late British imperialism.

Interestingly, where the Italian mainland was concerned, Dunbabin had to maintain his position, that intermarriage with indigenous women was exceptional, against arguments to the contrary from Italian scholars (1948: 46; 185): here we perhaps see nationalistic factors overriding those of recent colonial practice. At such points, we seem almost to be back in the world of Kipling-esque late imperialism; as also when Dunbabin writes that 'For the greater part of the sixth century [Sardinia] was anyone's who could take it' (1948: 341) – as though it were not an established island power in its own right, which at the time in question had just repelled a Carthaginian attempt at conquest. It is worth remembering at this point that the first version of Dunbabin's book had been finished more than a decade earlier, in 1937: the evening, but not yet the twilight, of Empire.

But Dunbabin's imperial paradigm is only in a few places a crude or aggressive one. With his teacher Alan Blakeway, it is again inconspicuous: there is an overwhelming sense of anachronism, but little of imperialism. Behind all this lies a wider and deeper truth about the Classical scholarship of their generation, and indeed of much of the past century: that this was a time when the prevailing current of international thought ran strongly in favour of assimilating the distant past to the present. To argue that the Greeks or Romans had acted 'like us' was attractive in its own right. The movement towards stressing the 'otherness', of the Greeks particularly, did not really begin to take over until about the 1970s, and this has helped to make a perhaps largely unconscious tendency so much more glaringly detectable to us today. The lay public, at least in Britain, still appears to find the older trend more satisfying than the new one.

What, though, is the academic corollary of my earlier point about the misapplication of Kipling's phrase 'lesser breeds'? Logically, it should be directed at the long-standing concentration on this same topic, of relations between Greek settlers and indigenous peoples, to the relative neglect of those between Greek and other navigators, migrants and settlers. Just as Kipling's phrase was misapplied, so the focus of scholarly interest made the same shift, to concentrate on the 'natives' and on the methods used to conciliate, assimilate and govern them. Now I freely concede that it would be churlish to complain of this tendency: it has produced some admirable results, particularly in the last two decades. It becomes a disadvantage only if it leads to the neglect of the strategies, methods and actual settlements of the other, non-Greek migrant peoples, as I think it has. Thus, it would be nice if future books on Greek colonization found room for a treatment of such topics as the partly-excavated layout of Phoenician Motya in Sicily, or of Carthage; or of the activities of the Etruscans in Southern France which preceded Greek settlement there; or for anything much about Sardinia.

But that is not the central issue. My main argument is that, in the particular field of early Greek overseas settlement, the older current – the Greeks as 'ourselves' – was allowed to run too far. Scholarship allowed itself to be diverted from pursuing legitimate analogies in the appropriate early modern era of colonialism, to applying the unexamined assumptions of the much more recent, and wholly *in*appropriate, age of the British Empire. The practice of 'thrusting the desired modern standards on to antiquity' was justifiably criticized by John Boardman, in the 1999 edition of *The Greeks Overseas* (1999: 268). But, as I hope this paper has shown, exactly the same process has been going on, if in a very different form from that of recent usage and to the opposite effect, for more than a century past.

Notes

1. 'Rudyard Kipling', in A. Rutherford (ed.) 1964: 70-84, at 71 [the paper had been first published in *Horizon*, February 1942].

2. See T. Pinney (ed.) 1990: 291-4, 305 and 306-7 respectively.

3. A point that seems to be freely conceded by Dunbabin (1948: 186), only to be contested much later by John Boardman (1994: 138).

4. See Dunbabin 1948: 450 on the population of early Sydney; 453 on the foundation-date of Melbourne.

5. For a popular account, see Milton 1999.

6. *dtv Atlas zur Weltgeschichte* 10. Auflage, München 1974, Band 1: 279.

7. These cases are cited in Woodruff 1953: 27-8; 160; 176 (the Portuguese precedent); 213; 237; and 269-70 respectively.

8. On the contrast with Burma, see Woodruff 1954: 128-30, 187.

9. See, e.g., Lord Birkenhead 1978: 257-8; even this laudatory biography refers to it as a 'crazy outburst'.

4

The Deceptive Archetype: Roman Colonialism in Italy and Postcolonial Thought[1]

Nicola Terrenato

Introduction

The idea that in the postcolonial world of today one needs to take a different look at the Roman Empire is at least fifteen years old (Millett 1990). In this time, postcolonial thought has been invoked and introduced in archaeological and historical discourse in a variety of ways. While many in our discipline are excited about the possibilities offered by the new dialectic and reflexive approaches, it is less clear how best to use them. At one end of the spectrum are those who see ancient colonial encounters in the Mediterranean as just another instance of the same processes that characterized modern ones (e.g. Van Dommelen 1998). Others make a more cautious use of postcolonial tools, preferring to focus upon specific concepts, such as creolization, that seem to be particularly relevant for the ancient world. Or there is a use of postcolonial thought mostly for epistemological, historiographical and reflexive purposes. This approach is more directly derived from literary theorists such as Bhabha or Said. It mainly deals with modern perceptions and constructions of the classical past, framed in the Foucaultian terms of the 'politics of knowledge'. Although occasionally discounted as 'ahistorical', it is precisely this approach that has sparked a number of important contributions (Hingley 2000; Marchand 1996) in recent years. In a way, there seems to be yet another split between substantivists and formalists, as it were, looming at the horizon. The former dismiss the latter, if only implicitly or between the lines, as having little practical impact on the reconstruction of the past (Van Dommelen 2002). In return, the 'formalists' defend their reflexive approach by emphasizing the gross assumptions that are necessary if one wants to apply postcolonial thought to the pre-modern world in a literal way, often with contrived and simplistic results.

The present chapter positions itself primarily in the reflexive field, but without giving up on the possibility of making substantive statements about the actual Romans. Indeed, as I have argued elsewhere, a full deconstruction of modern nationalist ideas about Roman imperialism, to name just one topic, is naturally conducive to the opening up of new historiographic perspectives, which can result in a reassessment of established concepts (Terrenato 1998a). In any case, if one really wants to take a fresh look at one of the most intensively studied segments of the human past, the only hope is to remove first some of the encrustations that an intensive scholarly activity has deposited over the years. This paper will therefore start with a critique of the analogy between Roman and modern imperialism drawn in Western nationalist historiography. Then it will briefly emphasize the structural differences that make a direct parallel between ancient and modern empires deeply misleading for the study of both entities. Particular attention will be paid to recent applications of postcolonial concepts, and the possible related pitfalls. Some avenues for a new interpretation of Roman colonialism will then be explored, and in particular of its possible comparative value within the broader debate on the archaeology of empires. It will be argued that pre-modern empires have very little in common with industrial ones, and that this structural difference, on issues such as ethnicity and social dynamics, can in fact provide us with a basis to generalize about ancient empires. However, a single thread possibly linking Rome and Western modernity may perhaps be found, not so much in the most obvious substantive aspects of the Roman Empire, such as economy or politics, but rather as the conquest unfolds in the growing number of individuals whose lives cease to fit traditional mentalities. These conclusions are based on a much larger work in progress on the archaeology of early Roman expansion and can only be briefly summarized here, but they will hopefully offer fresh alternatives to received models.

There are a few observations about the role of the Classical world in modern Western culture that are appropriate, even necessary, to introduce my deconstruction. It can be said that, despite their many strengths, the Classical disciplines do not have a strong record of contributing generalizations, comparative approaches and models to the wider field of the social sciences. At the same time, Romans and Greeks seem to have enjoyed a unique position in the imagery of Western culture, at the core of the very idea of historical development and with connections with issues that are still debated today, such as democracy, colonialism or ethnicity (Canfora 1980). There is hardly a major historiographical school that has not produced, explicitly or implicitly, strong views about the Classical world. Greece and Rome are maintained as the traditional starting point even in untraditional postmodern works (Said 1978). It is the only culture whose very name is a pre-emptive value judgment, defining the range of acceptable readings. It will be argued here, provocatively, that this range has been much narrower than one would think, in spite of the many trends and waves that have swept across the discipline, especially in the last fifty years.

In other words, while the world of Greece and Rome has always been assigned a major role within general cultural discourse, its specialists are averse to looking outside the traditional boundaries of the discipline.

Everybody should be grounded in the Classics, but it is fine for Classicists to be ignorant of everything else. It is not surprising, therefore, that the interpretative tools most commonly used in this subject area may appear very unsatisfactory to practitioners confronted with wider debates and new discoveries. A full analysis of this complex issue would go far beyond the scope of this paper, even if some observations can be made.

Inasmuch as a generalization is possible, there seems to be a marked tendency towards making modernist assumptions in many established approaches – what has been recently defined as a 'high modernist' bias (Scott 1998). In the most disparate schools and approaches, from idealism and historicism to positivism and Marxism, Classical antiquity has always been seen as containing prominent modern traits. There is a complementary reluctance to attribute any 'primitive' trait to the Classical world, as if this would in some way defile our ancestry. This is also probably the main reason why Greece and Rome are seldom included in any broad comparative framework, side by side with non-Western, 'savage' cultures. Greece and Rome simply could not be treated with the same tools used for the colonized 'natives'. For this reason, they are the only cultures that have remained outside the purview of anthropology, with only a few exceptions (e.g. Bettini 1991; Vernant 1983).

A mention should be made at this point of the so-called 'primitivist' school in the study of ancient economies, most prominently championed by Moses Finley (1973). While it raised interesting points in response to contemporary materialist formulations, its impact is effectively confined to the demonstration that the classic capitalist mentality did not exist in the Greco-Roman world. There is no real, sustained attempt at reconstructing a whole culture that functions along lines that are different from modern ones. Indeed one can perceive between the lines the idealist, anti-materialist notion that capitalism is not an essential, defining part of modernity. Its absence makes the ancient world not more remote from us, but simply a purer version of Western civilization, unsullied by the greed and the scepticism of the industrial age. The works of R.G. Collingwood (e.g. Collingwood 1956) are perhaps the clearest expression of this view.

The Classics play such an integral role in the construction of modern Western identity that virtually no one can push them away from us, in the primordial stew of 'primitives', without deeply shaking the received world-view (Terrenato 2002b). It is all the more surprising then that even approaches that supposedly transcend the constraints of nineteenth-century historiography, such as postcolonial and gender studies, have struggled to place themselves at an appropriate distance from the Classical world. As mentioned, ancient imperialism and gender relations are almost always still seen to contain distinctive elements of the contemporary world, and thus to be susceptible to analysis with the same tools we use for their modern counterparts.

There is an apparent paradox here, which needs to be addressed openly.

On the one hand there have been schools of thought that seem to agree on very little, such as nationalist, positivist, Marxist or postcolonial. On the other, all take for granted that a straightforward and unquestioned similarity between Classical antiquity and Western modernity exists and is a key element in the definition of both terms of the equation. The Westerners are those whose culture is rooted in the Classics and the Classical world is the one whose values live on in Western culture. What they have in common can be presented in a positive or negative light, but it cannot be doubted, it would seem. Indeed it is enough to consider the scholarship on Roman expansion to realize that whatever happens to be the interpretation of modern imperialism at any time becomes the explanatory framework for its Mediterranean predecessor. The modern term in the equation, whether nation-state or empire, determines how the ancient one is constructed. This, more than anything else, shows that the centrality of Rome in Western culture is a passive one. While apparently a revered piece of the past, it is in reality a highly flexible element which is freely shaped to fit current ideological needs (Terrenato 2002a). The only element that remains unchanged is the belief in the epoch-making significance of the Roman conquest and in its relevance as a model for modern events.

These reflections are not meant to be critical of the theories mentioned, but rather of the way in which they have been applied. Universal frameworks, such as Marxism or structuralism, often end up being distorted in order to interpret antiquity. One cannot escape the disturbing feeling that the choice of one or another of these theoretical options is made *a priori* with little consideration of its actual and specific heuristic value. Understandably, the vast majority of practitioners hardly ever ventures outside the boundaries of Classics, happy with empirical and substantive conclusions, or at best with ad hoc theories to explain a single event or trend. An alternative to avoid the stale dichotomy between comparativism and contextualism could be found in a 'middle range discourse' combining a global framework with sensitivity for the context. Borrowing from historical anthropology, it may be possible to come up with reconstructions that explain individual phenomena with reference to a general historical interpretation. The goal is the creation of a bottom-up historiographical theory, an *a posteriori* worldview. In this perspective, a re-analysis of Classicity can have crucial implications for our overall perception of Western history, if we only cast aside the blinkers that focus our field of vision on limited issues of local significance. We no longer need it as an idealized past, but we can study it as a crucial passage in the formation of the contemporary world.

Retrospective

Roman expansionism and colonialism perhaps best exemplify the issue being addressed here. It is precisely their role as archetypes for modern nationalism and imperialism that has long prevented scholarship from moving beyond some basic assumptions. It is enough to remark how the intense debate on Roman imperialism has always been focussed only on what happened in Rome, ignoring the role of the communities being incorporated (Keay and Terrenato 2001). Such basic choices actually make the historical inquiry in many ways a foregone conclusion, for Marxists and idealists alike. It is remarkable how much unexplored ground there still is in what could seem to be an overstudied subject; and looking at pre-nationalist historiography offers important evidence. That alternative approaches are possible is shown by the radical transformations that took place in the perception of the Roman Empire, in parallel with the emergence of nationalism at the beginning of the nineteenth century. Rome had of course been a key cultural and political icon ever since the Middle Ages (Folz 1953; Pagden 1995), but the political uses to which it had been put were very different. While the Roman Empire remained a paragon of clear laws and high moral virtues, a much greater space was left for pre-Roman and non-Roman components of the picture. Especially in the eighteenth century, the Enlightenment thinkers were very critical of the autocratic political system and, in Italy for instance, emphasized instead the importance of local cultures and autonomies, a trend known as '*municipalismo*' (Venturi 1984). Underlining the long tradition of small independent Italian states (or even city-states), Roman Italy was described as a federation of autonomous communities and the continuity between its *municipia* and the medieval communes was stressed and seen as a long-term trait characterizing the whole history of the peninsula.

It was only with the Romantic period that the idea that Rome had a mission to bring together and civilize disparate and ignorant peoples became dominant (Christ and Momigliano 1988). A crucial role in the creation of this new image was played by German scholars: Niebuhr's *Roman History* (1812) was the one of the earliest and most influential works in this sense, followed shortly afterwards by Mommsen's work. In this new wave of historical reconstruction, Rome's trajectory was believed to be pointing the way ahead for the fragmented geographical spaces represented by contemporary Germany and Italy. Tellingly, as observed by Jerzy Linderski (1984), Mommsen regarded Roman territorial expansion beyond the natural boundaries of the peninsula as a crucial mistake, ultimately responsible for the fall of the Empire. In his view Rome should have unified a nation-state, just like the ones that were being put together in Germany and Italy in his time, instead of a heterogeneous and far-flung empire. A role-model was created in this way for nationalists everywhere across Europe, who were often facing the precise problem of combining very heterogeneous communities.

In order to support such an ideological subtext, the making of the Roman Empire had to be described as the irresistible and pervasive triumph of a higher culture (Desideri 1991). Consequently, in archaeological terms, great attention was paid to those data sets (such as urban layout, public monuments and elite manifestations in general) which conformed to the expected pattern of cultural diffusion (Terrenato 2001). For most of these works what Philip Freeman (1996) has observed for British scholarship is generally true, that explicit comparisons between ancient and modern times were very rare, while they are much more common in popular literature or contemporary political writings. If clear evidence for the connection between ancient and modern empires is not easy to pin down, this may also be due to the reluctance that Classical scholars have always had for any kind of comparative argument (Vasunia 2003). It does not follow, however, that the contemporary situation was not playing a large role, implicitly shaping the belief that Roman culture had been pervasive, for the simple reason that it had been more rational, more politically and technologically advanced, more tasteful and more economically productive than any other pre-modern culture.

With the intensification of European colonial exploitation in the second half of the nineteenth century, the emphasis progressively shifted from Rome as a nation-state to Rome as a colonial empire. This image was becoming more and more appropriate for France and Britain as well as Germany and Italy, effectively universalizing the dominant view about the value of the ancient world. As observed by Frézouls (1983) and Hingley (2000) among others, Roman terminology and symbols were adopted to create a fictitious precedent to legitimize the unprecedented cultural treatment of colonized lands. The recourse to Roman terminology, imagery and symbols is a common thread linking the most varied forms of modern imperialism (see also the papers collected in Hingley 2001). Its use was almost always meant to convey the basic message that colonization is morally and materially a good thing for all those involved in it. By construing Rome as an idealized benevolent power, nobly taking on the burden of bringing light to the savages, scholarship performed an important reinforcing function for the dominant views in Europe of that time. Such a central role in colonialist ideology naturally placed strong constraints on how the history of Rome could be narrated. In Italy, this movement climaxed with Fascism, which made extensive use of Roman imagery, starting with the *fasces* themselves (e.g. Manacorda and Tamassia 1985; Munzi 2001). In short, the nationalist-colonialist view of the Roman Empire had a good hundred and fifty years, up until the mid-twentieth-century decolonization, to become crystallized and engrained in both scholarly and popular culture.

After World War Two, however, there was in theory no longer any need for frameworks of this kind, and materialist and Marxist approaches became more common, especially on the continent. Without entering here into the intellectual details, it is enough for the purposes of this paper to point out that Romanization was again perceived as a progressive and uniform phenomenon, which resulted almost mechanically from the integration of the peninsula in large-scale production (Carandini 1985a).

Indeed, the fundamental event, in these analyses, was suggested to be the introduction of a new mode of production, which was closer to modern capitalism. Archaeological support for this new model was sought and found in the mass production of artefacts such as amphorae or fine ceramic wares (Giardina and Schiavone 1981). The ubiquitous distribution of these indicators of intensive agriculture, specialized crafts and long-distance trade seemed to support the concept of Italy as a uniform economic system. Such modernist views on ancient economics show, even more clearly than in the previous idealist period, the influence that the industrial European world has had on our perceptions of Rome. Explicit comparisons were now drawn, for instance, between Roman and American slavery (Carandini 1985b). What concerns us here, is that again this perspective needed to assume that the Roman conquest had produced a homogeneous, more advanced entity, which came so close to early modern economic standards as to be called proto-capitalist.

All this thinking entrenched more deeply the image of the great empire as an archetype, having its own absolute and paradigmatic value. While the use to which this image was put changed according to the prevalent ideology, what is more important is that some basic elements became crystallized as inherent in this segment of the Western past (Woolf 1993). To give just one example, the idea that expansion was a process driven by Rome which revolutionized the Mediterranean has grown into an axiom that has held true for Romantic, idealist, positivist, nationalist, liberal and even Marxist reconstructions (Terrenato 1998a).

With the development of postcolonial approaches in the last two decades, research on Roman colonialism explored a number of new avenues, making use of innovative concepts such as creolization, hidden resistance or colonial anxiety (Mattingly 1997; Webster and Cooper 1996). However, the fundamental assumptions underpinning all modern views ever since the Renaissance still went substantially unchallenged, i.e. that Rome had been the closest pre-modern approximation of modernity. When, in post-colonial times, such a similarity became less palatable, it was simply recast in a negative light. Thus, even at a time of critical reconsideration of the colonial phenomenon, it still proved impossible to view Roman expansion independently of its alleged modern equivalent. It is only in some very recent comparative work on colonialism that a structural difference between ancient and modern situations has been explicitly theorized. In Chris Gosden's new book (2004), Roman colonialism is categorized among those that happen, at least to an extent, 'within a shared cultural milieu', in sharp contrast to more polarized modern encounters.

Thus we come again to the conclusion that Rome has had a surprisingly passive role in our historiography, and because of that, some major mismatches between antiquity and modernity have largely been ignored. A full comparison between ancient and modern imperialism would of course be a colossal enterprise, but basic differences are revealed as soon as the surface is scratched. Evidence that the very nature of the two phenomena is starkly different is provided by the situation of elites. Especially in the Mediterranean basin, which had largely been urbanized long before the conquest, non-Roman aristocracies played an important role in negotiating the terms of the incorporation of their communities within the Roman Empire and in participating in the benefits of the Empire. The wide-ranging horizontal social mobility that had characterized the Iron Age meant that ethnic boundaries were easily crossed, in a way that later would be made impossible by the emergence of nationalism. In many cases, incorporation can be described in terms of Roman and non-Roman aristocratic families building upon a tradition of intense political interaction to develop a new and stronger political network. They created (or joined) an overarching political structure that protected their common social interests vis-à-vis commoners. Evidence for this can be found in the brilliant careers that local leaders could make, all the way to the Senate and even to the imperial throne. To appreciate the deep structural differences with modern empires, it is enough to try to imagine an Indian Rajah becoming a member of the House of Lords in the aftermath of the British conquest.

That ethnicity was not a major determinant among the cultures of the Roman Empire is clear when one looks at citizenship, which had little to do with ethnic origin. Being Roman was mainly a political, legal and social status, and was perfectly compatible with citizenship of local towns. It was not an indication of cultural provenance in any way. Indeed it was routinely granted to descendants of former slaves, who could sometimes rise quickly within society, especially as protégés of the family of the ancient owners. Again, the modern equivalent would be represented by freed black slaves sharing the same grave and tombstone with their former masters, or by their descendants holding government offices in the United States before emancipation. These points may seem obvious and simple, and indeed the evidence supporting them has been well known for some time (Fabre 1981; Panciera 1982), but it was hardly ever brought to bear in discussions about Roman imperialism, which in itself is revealing. It should be added that the purpose here is not to disparage comparative approaches in general by highlighting superficial variability, but to emphasize the structural differences between Western modernity and Classical antiquity. Once this equation is removed, it becomes apparent that pre-modern complex cultures indeed display remarkable similarities and that there is much to be learned from comparisons that go beyond the Mediterranean (see Gosden 2004). The Greek and Roman world fits much more naturally in the context of other cultures centred upon aristocratic land-holding clans. This approach could only have been overlooked in the past hundred and fifty years because of the need to find precedent and justification (or damnation) for modern colonialism in the ancient world. In this perspective, it can be argued that the contribution that postcolonial thought could make to our discipline is to facilitate a consideration of ancient empires in their own terms, free from the heavy ideological baggage introduced by considerations of modern colonialism.

Prospective

For those who abandon the modern world as a yardstick for the ancient, exciting perspectives and spacious new vistas may suddenly open up. The Roman world can appear as a particularly well-documented case of interaction among a great number of heterogeneous small-scale communities, resulting in the creation of a much larger political entity. A major redefinition of the nature of the Roman Empire (and of other ancient empires as well) could be around the corner. Once again, only some quick observations can be made here. Conforming to the bottom-up approach advocated before, rather than attempting an *a priori* definition of Roman colonialism, it may be more productive to look at what actually happens in cultural terms to some social groups once they become involved in new forms of interaction within the empire. In the process, some key concepts may end up being reformulated in unusual ways. Postcolonial thought can indeed provide some of them, but they have to be discussed in terms that are appropriate for pre-modern societies.

A good starting point is offered by ethnicity, which figures prominently in Romantic and nationalist frameworks, but is now approached in a less straightforward way. As Woolf (1997) has proposed several times, it is time to go beyond the stale dichotomy opposing Romans and natives, and he has consequently emphasized the cultural novelty of what the colonial encounter produces. This can be taken a radical step further, assessing whether ethnic boundaries are really of any use in understanding the cultural implications of the Roman conquest. An interesting exercise is to see whether it is possible to describe the trajectories of broad sociological groups across the empire without any ethnic qualification; in other words, to see whether distinguishing, for instance, between Roman and non-Roman peasants is necessary to understand the cultural and social processes that are taking place. If we look at Mediterranean agricultural non-elite communities as they become part of the Roman Empire, we may see surprising similarities in different contexts. Almost everywhere rural peasants were bound by customary obligations to their lords and formed cohesive small-scale social entities that were resistant to change. The same can be said for all those other social actors – servants, small-scale craftsmen, clients and so on – who could only function with the protection and brokerage of their patrons. Individuals fitting within these networks clearly represented the vast majority of Mediterranean society, both before and after the conquest. Their cultural make-ups displayed a great variety, but they generally shared a stable, coherent and self-replicating worldview, which helped them to make sense of their experience. These common structures were only moderately affected by Roman expansion. While tastes and fashions among the elites quickly came and went, development in these conservative groups only happened slowly and within a limited range, allowing cultural continuity and self-consistency to be maintained.

Indeed, rural cultural structures, accounting for the bulk of the population, went practically unaffected in many regions, as is attested by the stability of settlement patterns, productive behaviours and vernacular architecture. When new events threatened this consistency, active resistance could be deployed to defend the customary arrangements, as some North Etruscan examples show (Terrenato 1998b). This was argued first for Britain by Reece (1988), but is now apparent in other, more central areas. It can be seen largely to hold true in the case of the original Latin groups, with the exception of Rome itself. Even the colonies founded by Rome are now viewed in a very different light. Rather than massive settlements of 'Romans' in 'native' lands, what went on in most cases was mainly a political and territorial reorganization, largely involving non-Roman people already residing in the area, and carried out by the central power with the co-operation of native elites (Bradley 2001). The world of interactions opened up by the emerging empire was experienced only very indirectly by these peoples. Their fine wares might now have come from two thousand rather than two hundred miles away, but this did not disrupt their perception of the world or challenge their identity in any major way. This, it is worth stressing once more, is in sharp contrast with modern empires, where there is an active attempt at imposing a dominant culture in a capillary way, by means of dominant discourses enforced in schools, churches, government offices and courtrooms, leaving no other option but silent resistance and counterculture for those wishing to retain their traditional order (Scott 1985).

The situation was completely different for elites, both Roman and non-Roman. Not only was it they who put the empire together, but their lives were radically changed in the process. Elite groups had been in contact across the Mediterranean ever since the Archaic period (if not the Bronze Age), but, as overarching structures came into being, the scope for such interactions was dramatically expanded. Although different in nature, a number of things that elites did to and with each other can be seen to fall within the same sphere of social behaviour. Exchanging gifts, establishing networks and factions, vying for power at the city and empire level, intermarrying and plotting, murdering and adopting, to name only a few, were activities that aristocrats engaged in to further themselves and the clans they ruled (Terrenato forthcoming). Roman expansion and colonialism delimited a new and fairly level playing field where such games could be played with a degree of order and for higher stakes. Here ethnic origins counted for very little (again in sharp contrast with modern situations). Factions and networks easily crossed cultural and political boundaries, but rarely social ones. There seemed to be a basic understanding that elites would always stick together in the face of commoners, above anything else. Elite competition and conflict was virtually never allowed to disrupt the social hierarchy. Thus, families of all sorts and backgrounds, as long as they were of the right social extraction, had access to an unprecedently vast arena of enormous potential and relative fairness. Clan leaders from the four corners of the known world had a reasonable chance, unknown in modern empires, of influencing the decision-making process, through the Senate or the magistracies, or simply by lobbying their friends, pulling strings and throwing their weight about.

Of course, all good things come at a price. This was not so much in the giving up of a theoretical freedom (as Romantic historians maintained), but rather in a strain on the relationships with their communities of origin. The majority of aristocrats under the Empire came from a line of quasi-feudal chiefs who owed their status and protection to their subordinates. Throughout the conquest, such ties were generally honoured as much as possible. Ideally, the best strategy for those elites was to act as brokers for their communities' relationships with the larger state, without relinquishing the culture they shared at the local level with commoners (Slofstra 1983). To accomplish this, they often developed a Janus-like quality, with different identities for different contexts. Combining the role of feudal lords at home and cosmopolitan jet-setters in the capital was no easy juggling act, as the Russian nobles in Chekhov's plays painfully come to realize. In the long run, such fragmentation of social roles, such multiplication of identities and personas began to tell on the cultural stability of many elite groups.

While the internal homogeneity of most small-scale communities was never under a severe threat and they were able to go on as self-contained organisms able to deal with empire-wide political and economic convulsions, things were less easy in other contexts. The elites that had resettled to the big cities tended to lose contact with their backgrounds, especially as they became embroiled with new social actors, who represent a third broad sociological group. The very organizational structure of the empire, linking together slow-moving communities, necessarily produced fast change in some specific contexts. The enhanced long-distance networks, represented by trade, warfare or administration, required some individuals to become part of new cultural and social groups. This was a by-product of expansion which in all likelihood was not expected by the empire-builders themselves. The alliance of aristocracies that underpinned the Roman state always had as one of its major aims that of preserving traditional loyalties and existing social orders. But the human machinery required to make the empire work ironically ended up producing an increasing number of individuals who fell outside the sphere of traditional values and thus were potentially a threat to the traditional order.

Uprooted from their contexts of origin, thrown together in a few huge commercial and administrative centres, enriched or impoverished beyond expectation, a growing number of members of the Roman Empire were faced with a reality for which their upbringing was of limited help. New identities became necessary. Thus, some people came to think of themselves as belonging to a certain legion, or trade guild, or even as supporters of a certain chariot racing team. This only very partially compensated for the lack of a traditional world view or a shared cultural grammar. What set them apart from the majority was not any specific ingredient, but rather the inherent heterogeneity of their mentalities. This phenomenon might occasionally be associated with colonial situations, with new settlements, but it was certainly not confined to them and was not determined by any conscious colonizing attempt. It was the price to be paid for having brought such a big empire into existence.

Conclusions

Roman expansion and colonialism have been brutally simplified here, characterizing them by looking at the actual actors involved rather than at the process as an abstraction, for two main reasons. The first is to try to provide a model, which can be of use to archaeologists dealing with other colonial cases. It has been argued here that the main cultural tensions in the Roman Empire were between small-scale conservatism and global trends – between customary power and Mediterranean-wide political games, between traditional forms of surplus circulation and elements of market economy – more than between Romans and natives or colonizers and colonized. Indeed – and here lies the other reason – such generalizations can apparently stand for entire social layers, irrespective of ethnic or political boundaries. This means that we are moving on a completely different plane from that of most postcolonial discourse, at least in its most frequently used forms. Some of its key concepts, such as resistance or creolization, assume colonial encounters in which ethnic factors have an overriding importance. While this might be appropriate for the modern world, its retrojection onto antiquity seems largely a hangover of that passivity discussed above. We have to come round finally to the notion that pre-modern empires were structurally different from later ones, not more primitive (in fact one can argue that an obsession with ethnicity is not a good thing in itself) but simply different, organized along different fault lines from modern ones.

In this perspective, the one element that can be construed as working in a similar way in both worlds is cultural identity and the factors impinging on its integrity. For the Roman Empire, it has been suggested that, as cities, empires and other sophisticated networks emerged, a growing number of individuals were faced with new challenges requiring adaptation and questioning of the established cultural order. The responses to these stimuli varied according to the contexts. Traditional communities actively resisted elements that threatened their internal consistency. This, incidentally, was the only form of resistance that we see happening regularly in pre-industrial times. It is important to stress that resistance of this kind, in contrast with what befalls modern popular movements such as the Vandée in France or the Sanfedisti in Southern Italy, was largely successful in allowing communities to retain their distinctive traits and to slow down change to an acceptable tempo.

In some other cases, arguably the minority, such strategies do not or cannot work. Traumatic events may unsettle existing communities or clashes may emerge in newly formed ones. Such fragmented communities naturally strive to regain a degree of cultural balance, of homogeneity. Refunctionalizing existing elements and adding new ones may reduce internal contradictions. New local power structures regrow and rearrange themselves along more traditional patterns. Such reorganization cannot be effected all at once, however. Each generation can only adjust to a point, without upsetting further the delicate balance. Given enough time, they may succeed in coping with the stress of change, in digesting it, as it were. Many traditional communities indeed probably have one or more such episodes in their past. This may have been as true of Roman colonies as it was of early Spanish colonialism in central America.

In some areas and in some contexts, however, change keeps following change, and newcomers newcomers. The imperial administration, for instance, grew and evolved rapidly throughout the Empire. Long-distance trade ebbed and flowed across the Mediterranean. Armies were mobilized and restationed all the time. All this, let me repeat once more, happened on a level that affected only a minority of the people living in the Roman Empire. But those who were involved in it might find themselves continuously trying to keep abreast of their ever-changing life conditions, thus accumulating further contradictions as older surviving traits kept clashing with new ones. This is where a sort of colonial anxiety could really become an issue for specific individuals in different ethnic contexts. In a way, this anticipates what would happen on a much larger scale in modern colonial encounters. Only, because in the latter case cultural disruption happened on a major scale, anxiety and contradiction become a global problem that defines the process itself, rather than just a minor side-effect.

Loss of identity apparently increased as the parable of the Roman Empire unfolded. For example, a growing number of people placed their hopes for harmony on cults promising deferred salvation. They characteristically spread where traditional culture had lost its grip, in large cities, among the soldiers, the traders, the elites. While the bulk of the Romans stayed safely within the bounds of cultural self-replication, the fate of some of them may indeed remind us of some of the challenges of modernity. Not forgetting that a general problem of today was limited to a minority then, some useful comparisons can perhaps be drawn. Roman colonialism, far from being a cute scale model of our own, can at best show us a germ of what went hugely wrong in modern Western culture.

Note

1. This chapter was originally conceived as a submission to a session on the archaeology of colonialism at the Third World Archaeological Conference (later published in Lyons and Papadopoulos (eds) 2002), but did not become part of it. It was given in Cambridge in 2001 at the invitation of the editors and later developed and presented at a session of the 2002 meeting of the Society for American Archaeology in New Orleans, organized by Sara E. Bon. Thanks are due to the many who provided interesting feedback during the long gestation process of this work, and especially to Peter Van Dommelen, Sara Bon, Greg Woolf and Phiroze Vasunia.

5

A View from the Americas: 'Internal Colonization', Material Culture and Power in the Inka Empire

Elizabeth DeMarrais

> ... Tawantinsuyu [the Inka Empire] ... [was] more a complicated and extensive network of relationships than it [was] the apparently monolithic and showy apparatus of power that the chroniclers described in the sixteenth century.
>
> Pease 1982: 190

Introduction

In recent years, postcolonial theory has influenced Classical scholarship, leading to the reworking of concepts such as 'Romanization'. Views of Romanization as a progressive, steady spread of a monolithic culture are being supplanted, replaced by more nuanced understandings of the interactions between Romans and native groups. An increase in the evidence available to scholars through the accumulation of reports from systematic excavations has drawn attention to variability in material culture throughout the Roman provinces. Seeking to explain this patterning, researchers have tried out a range of approaches to social processes, including acculturation (Slofstra 1983), emulation (Millett 1990), or innovation, co-optation and hybridity (Alcock 2000). Taken together, these new approaches reflect an increasing interest in considering ancient empires and their territorial expansion in terms of ongoing struggles for power, negotiation, and compromise among diverse sets of protagonists, Roman and native, elite and non-elite.

Romanization, seen from this perspective, requires that the archaeological evidence be understood in terms of the intentions and goals of social actors who, by virtue of their social positions, have widely varying access to power and resources. Recent theoretical currents reflect archaeologists' efforts to move beyond simple contrasts (for example, domination versus resistance, or elite versus non-elite) to develop a more nuanced picture of the complex social and political realities of the past. Mattingly (1997: 135), following Said (1993), has set out one conception of this 'discrepant experience', writing that:

> Imperial discourse involved a complex interplay between the different aims and aspirations of the principal actors against a background of drastically unequal power relations ... [Researchers] would do well to explore the interplay of resistance and accommodation and the gradations of behaviour lying in between, rather than to highlight only the significance of evidence for the former. That is what I would characterize as the discrepant experience of empire ...

Theoretically satisfying, Mattingly's agenda nevertheless poses distinct challenges for archaeologists. One aim of this paper is to consider, in practical terms, how the material records of ancient empires can be approached with these questions in mind.

Another dimension of the debate about Romanization involves the extent to which Rome's policies should be seen as interventionist – as a set of deliberate, top-down strategies. While Rome's policies involved less direct intervention than, for example, those of more recent colonial empires, the degree to which Romanization should be attributed to deliberate action or to a coherent set of policies remains unclear (Blagg and Millett 1990: 3). Millett's (1990) study of Roman Britain, for example, attributes the spread of Roman culture not principally to imperial strategies, but instead to the agency of local elites, who sought out Roman customs and culture in an effort to secure prestige or power. Members of subordinate classes, in turn, emulated indigenous elites, setting up a 'trickle-down' process of which the end result was a wider distribution of Roman styles and material culture.

That historians and archaeologists of the Roman Empire have long thought in terms of Romanization is understandable, given the abundance of material remains – buildings, roads, cities, statues and inscriptions – found across a vast territory. Processes of acculturation, emulation and hybridization had sufficient time, sometimes centuries, to take shape, changing through time in response to new political developments that altered local circumstances. In contrast, the Inka expansion unfolded over little more than a single century, cut short dramatically by the arrival of the Spanish conquistadors in AD 1532. One consequence of the limited duration of Inka expansion is a more variable, patchy distribution of Inka material culture across the Andes. Even taking into account this restricted time frame, there exists little archaeological or documentary evidence for a coherent policy of 'Inkaization'. Inka officials, like their Roman counterparts, faced problems of communication, maintaining security, and administering disparate groups of colonists, but Inka solutions differed, in some cases significantly, from those implemented by the Romans. This contrast is a starting point for considering the discrepant experience of Inka colonists, undertaken here with comparative reference to the Roman record.

Perspectives on power

In American archaeological theory, 'practice' perspectives (Ortner 1984), together with models of agency (Dobres and Robb 2000), have drawn attention to struggles for power, the negotiation of conflicts of interest, and factional competition as central dynamics underlying sociopolitical change (Earle 1997; Feinman and Marcus 1998; Alcock et al. 2001). Yet the emphasis on conflict has also (as Ortner (1984: 157) feared two decades ago) led scholars to '... lose sight of cooperation and reciprocity'. Because models of early empires have disproportionately viewed power in negative terms, a clearer view of the discrepant experience requires, first, a redress of this imbalance.

Foucault's (1980, 1984) notions of power and governance provide us with a broader perspective. Foucault recognized that societies could not function if power were solely punitive or repressive; for him, analysis must also consider power as a '... productive network' of social relations (1980: 119), so that power is seen as '... a set of actions upon other actions' (1984: 427). Governance, in turn, involves structuring the '... possible field of action of others' (1984: 429), so that the exercise of power involves guiding 'conduct' or, alternatively, putting in order an intended outcome.

This conception of power arguably facilitates a wider view of the social and political interactions that characterized relations between early states and their subjects. If, as Mauss (1990) argued long ago, material objects mediate social relationships, then a close examination of imperial styles will shed light on the state's varied attempts to communicate, dominate, persuade, manipulate or reward subjects. Analyses of variability in Roman symbols and styles in colonial settings (as mentioned earlier) have emphasized the two-way, interactive nature of these processes. To consider the intentions that lay behind these activities, it is helpful further to ask how they articulate with different 'forms' of power relations. Here the typology of Wrong (1997) can be used. In Wrong's framework, forms of power are distinguished according to the interests and motivations of social actors on both sides of the power relationship. Power relations are seen fundamentally as *social* relations (except in extreme cases of coercion); hence coercion, symbolism, propaganda and ideology, and legitimate authority represent distinct strategies (with variable costs and effects). These 'forms' of power will, importantly, evoke different responses from subordinates, including many responses that lie (as Mattingly suggests) somewhere between the extremes of accommodation and resistance.

Hence, a closer look at the 'forms' of imperial power and their implementation in colonial settings can reveal how power was imposed and elaborated, on one hand, but also how subjects responded to the demands – and opportunities – that followed conquest. My approach is a balanced one, in line with Alcock's (2000: 224) view that:

> If comparative studies help to combat old unhelpful myths, there remains the danger of new ones cropping up, not least as the result of an over-exuberant paradigm swing. For example, reacting to previous overly-uniformitarian views of the empire, one recent trend has been to seek out, and indeed to expect, great regional variations and tenacious local tendencies. This can slide toward an unwillingness to contemplate or even out-of-hand rejection of, any form of top-down models ...

It is of course exceedingly difficult to reconstruct attitudes and beliefs of people in the past, but it is nonetheless important that archaeologists assess – using as much evidence as possible – how imperial activities affected local groups. We should expect to encounter evidence for a range of reactions, as subjects may – at a given time – act out of a sense of loyalty (to indigenous elites or imperial personnel) or respond on the basis of a religious commitment or a sense of moral obligation or duty. Further influences include fear of sanctions or a desire for rewards (material or symbolic) (Bell 1992: 39). Subject groups may resist directly and forcefully, or, more often, they may simply 'put up' with the demands of a powerful state (Cowgill 1988) and they may benefit from it. A realistic approach to the discrepant experience must also anticipate that imperial projects or activities will from time to time fail to achieve intended outcomes.

The Inka Empire

In the Andes, in the decades just after AD 1400, the Inka Empire expanded through military conquest and diplomacy to become, in about a century, the largest polity in the pre-Hispanic Americas. The Inkas gained sovereignty over more than twelve million people, controlling an area that extended from southern Colombia to central Chile and Argentina, across the rugged mountain setting of the Andes (Fig. 5.1). At its greatest extent, the empire incorporated over eighty ethnic groups, creating a complicated mosaic of ethnic and linguistic diversity (Lorandi 1992). Corvée[1] crews built a vast infrastructure of roads and settlements to link disparate areas of the empire. The expansion of the Inka Empire is often compared to that of Rome, despite important differences. The Inka expansion took place without the aid of a written language, draft animals[2] or wheeled transport, and in the absence of a well-developed market system. Among early empires, the Inka state was unusual for its reliance on corvée, as well as for the lavish, large-scale feasting events that served as payment for labour service (Morris 1985, 1998).

During the early stages of imperial expansion, Inka emperors focussed efforts upon the conquest of new territories using force. Later emperors turned their attention to the consolidation of territories and the strengthening of frontiers. Inka efforts to manage internal security and, in particular, the administration of labour service, led to extensive resettlements within the borders of the empire, amounting to a policy of 'internal

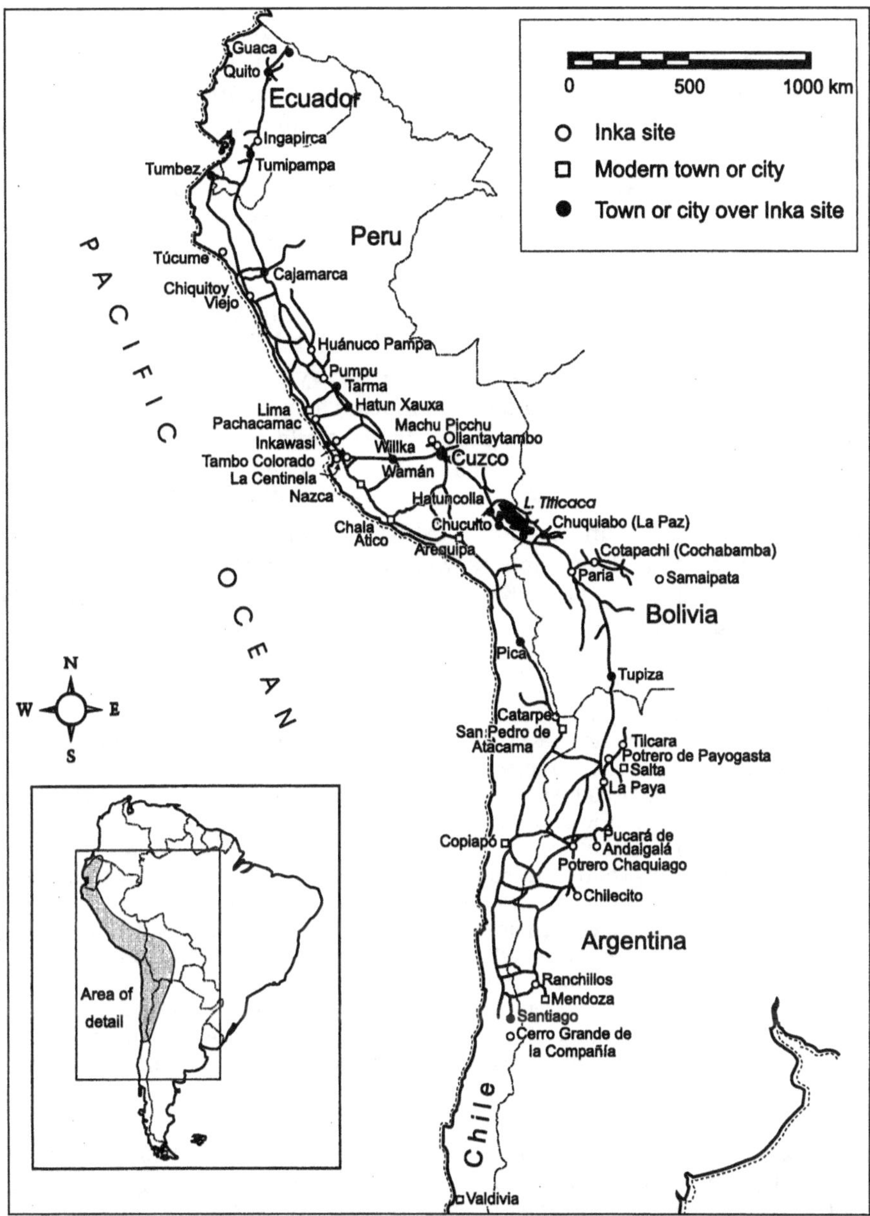

5.1. Map of the Inka Empire, showing important sites and the road network. Courtesy of T. D'Altroy.

colonization' (D'Altroy 1992: 74). Vast numbers of households – in some cases entire ethnic groups – were moved to new locations. The rationales for resettlement included security, as rebellious groups were frequently resettled, often under the eye of more loyal groups, to reduce the likelihood of rebellion. In addition, because corvée crews formed the military, constructed settlements, storehouses and roads, and tilled state lands, the Inkas often moved labourers, either temporarily or in more permanent arrangements, to ensure that labour was available where it was needed (Rowe 1946: 269-70, 1982).

Although the Inkas intensified agricultural production to provision provincial administrative centres, the state did not supplant local subsistence; local communities retained responsibility for the welfare of their own members (D'Altroy 2002: 264). These *ayllu* (kin-ordered corporate groups) had a long history of colonization before the Inkas (Murra 1972). Usually based in home settlements in the highland river valleys, members of each *ayllu* established colonies or temporary settlements high in the mountains (for pasturing llamas and alpacas) as well as in lower elevation zones, where maize, cotton, coca and fruits could be grown. Because all members of the *ayllu* maintained rights to goods from distant zones, reciprocity (rather than exchange) was a key mechanism for the integration of highland Andean economies (Murra 1972).

The scope of Inka resettlements was vast. D'Altroy (2001: 460), drawing upon information from the sixteenth-century Spanish chroniclers, reveals some of the specific intentions behind the state's activities:

> No state policy affected the Andean social landscape more than resettlement. Perhaps three to five million people out of a total population about twelve million moved to new locales. Cobo (1979 [1653], book 2, ch. 23: 189) wrote that, in principle, the Inkas selected six or seven thousand families from each province (of 20,000-30,000) to be resettled as part of their standard approach in new territories. Rowe (1982: 107) has estimated that 10-80% of the population of individual provinces was resettled. The most renowned program moved entire communities hundreds of kilometers to create enclaves of internal colonists called *mitmaqkuna*. ... [early sources] detail how particular groups of people were used to meet military, political, and economic ends ... Another motive for resettling colonies arose from the Inkas' interests in claiming a divine mandate over the peoples of the Andes. That vision was given its most conspicuous form in the ethnic microcosm created around Cuzco, but the sanctuary that housed members of 42 ethnic groups at Copacabana, on Lake Titicaca, may have been designed for the same purpose ...

Relations between the state and colonists were managed through diverse means, including ceremonial hospitality, acts of gift exchange, diplomacy, and coercion. The scope of Inka feasts and other acts of gifting were impressive enough to have led one sixteenth-century chronicler, Garcilaso de la Vega, to view the state as an early manifestation of a socialist state. He perceived the state as '... benevolent and paternal, simultaneously capable of guaranteeing a social peace that some called socialism [through redistributive activities] and of brutally repressing the opposition' (Pease 1982: 183).

Inka diplomacy involved '... a persuasive combination of threats of destruction for those who resisted and incentives for those who acquiesced' (D'Altroy 1992: 75; Bauer 1992). Punishment for resettled colonists who returned to their home territory involved torture for the first transgression and death for the second (Cobo 1979 [1653], book 2, ch 26: 206). As D'Altroy (2002: 236) points out, the existence of the second sanction provides clear evidence of repeated acts of resistance.

Making an impression: coercion and threat

For the Inkas and the Romans alike, military conquests provided an initial, unambiguous expression of the state's capacity to impose its demands upon a subject population. The chronicler Cieza de León (1984 [1553]: ch. 53) records that reports of the emperor Pachakuti's impressive victories in the Lake Titicaca region led members of other ethnic groups to travel to Cuzco, the Inka capital, to surrender to the Inkas without a struggle.

At the same time, the costs of provisioning an army are high, and military intervention is more effective as a deterrent than as a means to encourage desired actions (Wrong 1997). For these reasons, threats are as important as the implementation of military force. Luttwak (1976: 3) recognized this point clearly in his analysis of Roman militarism, writing that:

> ... the Romans clearly realized that the dominant dimension of power was not physical but psychological – the product of others' perceptions of Roman strength rather than the use of this strength ...

In the long run, threats may be farther-reaching and, ultimately, more influential in dealings with subject groups than the use of coercive force. Moreover, threats are enhanced *not* through proportionately greater investment in the physical means for violence (Luttwak 1976: 192), but through actions and images. In short, threats depend upon effective *communication* as much as they do upon the use of force to back up the threat.

The Inkas relied heavily on the communication of threats through a range of channels, including ceremonies, severe punishments meted out to rebellious groups or individuals and impressive displays materializing power asymmetries (DeMarrais et al. 1996). The royal court in Cuzco staged dramatic festivals to celebrate Inka military victories. Successful generals were rewarded with lavish food and drink, as well as gifts of finely woven textiles and objects made of gold, silver or precious stones. Threats were integral to these celebrations; in one instance, two Qolla leaders who had led an uprising against the Inkas were flayed, their skins made into drums played at the celebrations following their defeat (Cobo 1892 [1653], vol. 3, book 12, ch. 14: 169).

Corn-planting and harvest rituals undertaken by Inka nobility in Cuzco also made manifest a close association between warfare and the power of the emperor. Inka rituals commonly made reference to mythic origins; through re-enactments, myths were literally brought out of the past to reassert their continuing validity in the present. Bauer (1996: 331) writes that:

> Within the corn rituals of Cusco the ruling Inca stood as a majestic figure. He alone had the power to defeat and capture the reproductive powers of nature for society. Thus he was the first to ritually break the earth ...

Following the initial conquest of an ethnic group, one of its lords was sent to Cuzco to be held as a hostage to prevent rebellion. In addition, the most sacred local cult object was removed to Cuzco, where it, too, was kept as a hostage (Cobo 1892 [1653], vol. 3, book 12, ch. 22: 221). The presence of subject lords and their sacred icons in Cuzco ensured the good conduct of subject groups (MacCormack 2001: 428-9).

Further from Cuzco, landscape elements, especially roads, symbolized the connections between territories, materializing a threat of rapid retaliation by the army in case of rebellion. Although archaeologists frequently emphasize the symbolism of 'landscapes of power', less attention has been paid to understanding the ways that built environments conveyed threats, as well as facilitating surveillance and monitoring of subjects. Hingley's (1997: 90) study of *civitas* capitals in Roman Britain examines their role as instruments of social control. Borrowing from Foucault, he argues that these settlements facilitated elite oversight of ritual, control of resources, and even the monitoring of the daily lives of inhabitants. For the Inkas, Foucauldian perspectives remain largely unexplored, although my colleagues and I (DeMarrais et al. 1996) have argued that Inka roads reinforced the threat of a rapid response to rebellion.

Although some threats involved generalized messages directed at the populace as a whole, others messages targeted individuals. Local lords, appointed to administrative positions within the Inka hierarchy, were threatened with summary removal if their loyalty or abilities came into question (Rostworowski 1999: 148). Frequently, too, the privileges and honours offered to individuals carried strong coercive undertones. *Aqllakuna* (chosen females) were selected by the state from among the daughters of provincial elites. In the Andes, elite women were traditionally weavers of the finest cloth, the most highly valued of crafted goods. Taken from their households at a young age, girls chosen to serve the emperor were sequestered by the state, awarded high status, and taught to weave and brew maize beer. Some *aqllakuna* continued to serve the state in these capacities, while others became sacrificial victims. Still others were given as wives to men as rewards for exemplary service. Costin (1998: 135) observes that:

> ... we cannot underestimate the political significance of the act of the state appropriating the productive and reproductive potential of the daughters of former rulers, taking from conquered elite households the creators of wealth (as weavers) and producers of heirs and attaching them symbolically to the household of the emperor.

The high status granted to *aqllakuna* came, quite literally, at the price of their physical freedom. As no comparable price was exacted from male craft specialists, it is clear that, at least for some individuals, gender differences affected the discrepant experience of empire.

Importantly, although threats were an effective basis for Inka control of indigenous elites, as well as for managing colonists, they were less useful to the ruler in Cuzco. There, ceremonies – intended to persuade rather than to threaten – were the basic idiom for negotiation with members of the royal lineages, as MacCormack (2001: 432) has argued:

> Outside Cuzco, the Inca's will was law, enforceable by warfare. Within Cuzco, on the other hand, the Inca's will was law only to the extent that he could persuade the royal lineages to accept it as such, and the same was true of his view of past and future. Within Cuzco, acceptable means of enforcement, as far as the available information goes, seem not to have gone much beyond ceremonial ones ...

Yet in distant colonies, the significance of threat and coercion cannot be underestimated. Repeated convincing victories over rebellious groups, dramatic ceremonies, and swift and summary punishment for those who resisted were cornerstones of Inka policy.

As argued in the following sections, however, threat and coercion *alone* were insufficient means by which to govern. Threats are unlikely to secure more than 'pragmatic acceptance', the situation in which an '... individual complies because he [or she] perceives no realistic alternative' (Mann 1970: 425). Moreover, because – as mentioned previously – threat and military force are more effective for preventing actions than for facilitating them, states must develop and implement other means of communication and negotiation to inculcate loyalty and to create incentives for compliance.

Power made visible

The logistics and infrastructure that supported the Inka army and its movements provided tangible evidence of the state's readiness to quell rebellion. Similarly, the ruler surrounded himself with extraordinary splendour and wealth, as part of claiming a divine mandate to rule.

5.2. Illustration by the chronicler Guaman Poma de Ayala, showing the body of emperor Wayna Qhapaq being carried from Quito to Cuzco.

Whenever the emperor went forth, he rode on a golden litter surrounded by emblems of sun and moon and other sacred symbols of the royal lineage. Such displays guaranteed that '... the Inca ruler ... was so far exalted over the rest of humankind that no one dared so much as to look at his face or to appear before him without carrying a gift' (MacCormack 2001: 424). In death, as in life, this divine status was maintained, as seen in Guaman Poma's (1936 [1615]: 377; see also http://www.kb.dk/elib/mss/poma/, p. 379) drawing of Wayna Qhapaq being carried back to Cuzco after his death (Fig. 5.2).

Other categories of material culture – especially monumental architecture – fulfilled goals of communication. Architecture signalled the Inka presence in distant territories, advertised the organizational capacities of the state, and imposed order on the landscape. The Inkas called their empire Tawantinsuyu, 'land of the four quarters', a name that reflected their view of its organization. Cuzco was the centre of the empire (Garcilaso de la Vega 1989 [1609], part 1, book 2, ch. 11: 93-4), and a complicated system of radiating lines (sight lines: the *zeque* system) expressed and ordered relationships between corporate groups, their lands and the cosmos (Hyslop 1990; Zuidema 1964, 1983). When groups were resettled in the area surrounding Cuzco, they were arranged to create, in the capital, a microcosm of the territorial organization of the empire as a whole (Espinoza Soriano 1987: 320). Physical and sacred geography were interlocking elements shaping a carefully constructed cultural landscape in and around the capital.

Inka architecture and monumentality

The symbolic messages expressed by Inka buildings and landscape features were multiple and overlapping; many of these, executed on a grand scale, were designed to be awe-inspiring. Scholars have increasingly recognized that the analysis of power cannot rely *solely* on a reckoning of the rational aspects of human thought and action. Instead, we must instead acknowledge that the rituals and art (and architecture) of early states were deliberately designed to be:

> ... *compelling*. They use various means to arouse, capture, and hold attention. Both are fashioned with the intent to affect individuals emotionally – to bring their feeling into awareness, to display them. A large part of the compelling nature of rituals and art is that they are deliberately *nonordinary* ...
>
> Dissinayake 1995: 46, emphasis in the original

Trigger (1993) observes that lavish expenditures on symbolic displays, splendid buildings and religious iconography are common to civilizations across the ancient world. The ubiquitous presence of these activities suggests that they had a considerable *affective* impact. Cowgill (1993: 57) emphasizes that – beyond rational thought – human actions are shaped by 'nonrational propensities'; that is, human beings '... experience emotions and hold moral sentiments that often influence ... actions, and [individuals] often ... act without thinking, either from habit or impulsively'. To call these propensities 'nonrational', however, is not to suggest that they are irrational. Cowgill refers carefully to experiences that make sense in a given context, but that may not easily be subject to analysis. As Geertz (1957) argued long ago, vivid performances and events induce not only intellectual, but also emotional, assent to the interests of the group over those of the individual.

Taking the debate a step further, Wilson (1988: 132) argues that a monument displays not illusory power, but real power – in his words – *power made visible*. A monument conveys the concrete, physical existence of collective capacities and organization, as well as aesthetic properties reflecting skills in design and artistic execution. It is the outcome of planning, co-ordination of labour, and the marshalling of resources, sometimes on a grand scale. In short, a monument signals capacities that are anything but illusory.

The Inkas were noteworthy among early Andean states for their planning, for their monumental constructions, and for creating – at both a conceptual and physical level – an ordered universe.[3] As with warfare, Inka myths attributed substantial creative powers to the ruler. The rebuilding of Cuzco, for example, was said to have been a creative act undertaken by Pachakuti to provide a proper home for the Inka nobility (MacCormack 2001). The scale and scope of Inka building activities, together with large-scale feasting events and festivals, were impressive. Kus (1989) has interpreted such acts – 'bread and circuses' – as repeated evidence of administrative competence that provides unambiguous proof to subordinates that tangible benefits (such as resources, security and protection) flow directly from the state. A particularly good example of this last point involves vast Inka storage complexes:

> ... it was the storehouses, prominently on view on the hills above the Inka installations, that assured that the workers would be fed wherever they were needed ...
>
> Morris 1993: 44

The Inkas built monumental structures of fine cut-stone masonry around Cuzco itself, but further afield, monumentality was most often expressed in the provision of enormous central plazas in administrative centres, used for feasts. At Huánuco Pampa in the central highlands of Peru, a massive plaza measuring 547 x 370 metres dominates the site (Morris and Thompson 1985). This standard layout, including the plaza with a central platform and large rectangular structures along the edges, was repeated in Inka sites from central Argentina to Ecuador. The site of Potrero de Payogasta in the Calchaquí Valley, Argentina, shows the careful export of Inka architectural canons to a distant, marginal province over 1500 km south of Cuzco (Fig. 5.3).

The messages expressed in architecture and roads were blunt and direct, yet their distribution throughout the empire was uneven. Fine pottery and architecture, the most abundant, well-preserved Inka artefacts, co-occur in notable concentrations in only three regions outside Cuzco. These include the south coast of Peru, where the state established a collaborative trade relationship with the Chincha; Lake Titicaca, an area rich in economic resources and site of an important religious sanctuary;

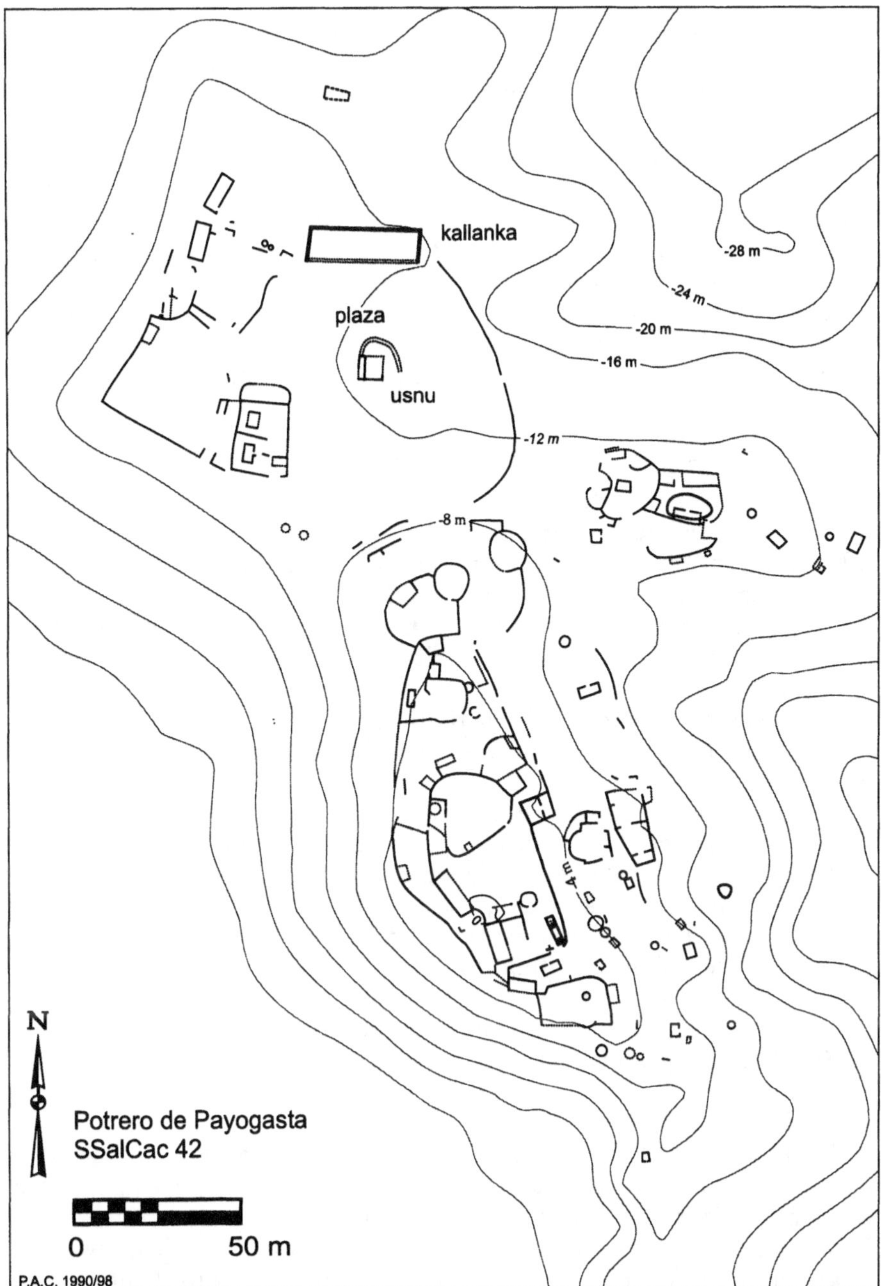

5.3. The Inka administrative centre of Potrero de Payogasta in the Calchaquí Valley of north-west Argentina. The layout of the plaza, *usnu* platform, and rectangular *kallanka* building (in the north sector of the site) is typical of Inka sites throughout the empire.

and finally the Quito/Cuenca regions of Ecuador, where a secondary capital was emerging. Chroniclers' accounts reinforce archaeological evidence that reflects the economic and strategic value of these regions (Hyslop 1993: 344).

Yet in most other areas Inka architecture was less prominent and Inka-style ceramics were scarce. D'Altroy (2002: 253) observes, for example, that '... [i]ntriguingly, there is little material evidence for Inca rule away from the grand center and roads [near Huánuco Pampa]'. Along the north coast of Peru, another economically significant region, relatively little architecture was built in the Inka style. These patterns suggest that although architecture had diverse symbolic and functional roles, decisions about construction involved tactical and strategic considerations.

Inka architectural canons in local communities

In some local communities, architecture reflects local elites' emulation of Inka canons. In the Yanamarca Valley of Peru's central highlands, the Inka conquest imposed a regional peace, allowing inhabitants to relocate closer to the best arable lands (Earle et al. 1987; D'Altroy and Hastorf 2001). My research (DeMarrais 2001) on local architecture and community layouts indicates that newly built sites such as Marca (as well as the pre-Inka period site of Hatunmarca, remodelled under the Inkas), had larger areas devoted to public activities. Public buildings at both sites incorporated Inka features including rectilinear floor plans and trapezoidal niches.

At both sites, residential compounds also incorporated Inka features (Fig. 5.4), most notably a shift from a circular or D-shaped floor plan to a rectangular design. Morris and Thompson (1985: 138-43) report a similar pattern for the local site of Ichu, not far from Huánuco Pampa, where an important local leader apparently built several structures following a rectilinear floor plan. In a final example of emulation, local lords in the Lake Titicaca region – who were traditionally buried in stone towers – began to incorporate fine Inka masonry into their burial towers (Hyslop 1990: 248). The presence of Inka features in domestic architecture and burial structures suggests attempts by local people (most probably elites) to emulate Inka designs.

The Inkas also imposed their own architectural imprint upon some local communities. Sectors of Inka architecture were built within existing local settlements in the far south of the empire, as a recent survey of the Calchaquí Valley (Argentina) reveals (DeMarrais 1997). At least two local communities have intrusive Inka sectors. One local site (Guitián) was modified to accommodate a plaza with a central platform and a kallanka along the side. The other site, El Director (Acuto 1994), has a central plaza with a rectangular structure at its centre.

Finally, some important sites on the south-central coast exhibit a

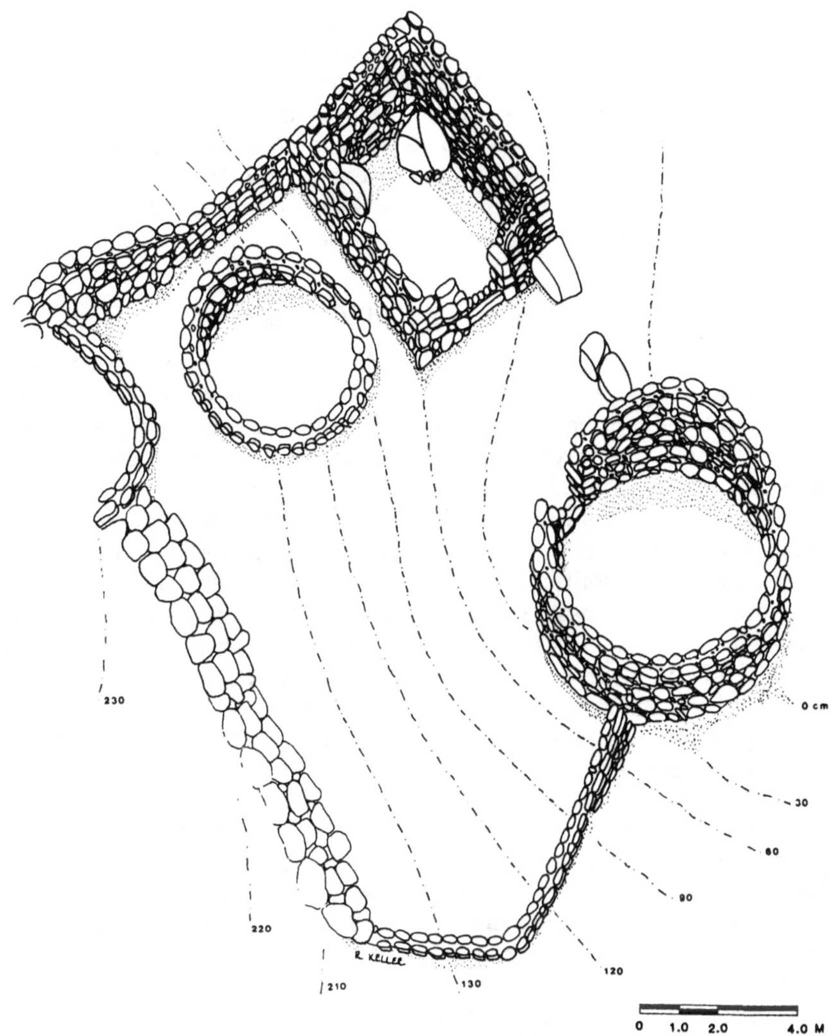

5.4. Drawing (by R. Keller) of a local residential 'patio group' from the site of Marca, showing the incorporation of a rectangular structure alongside two circular structures.

hybrid architecture that mixes Inka and local building styles. Analysis of La Centinela, a local site modified to incorporate Inka features, led Morris (1998: 296-7) to suggest that architecture served as a 'sensitive indicator' of the peaceful coexistence and collaboration of the Inkas with the Chincha ethnic group. Thus, architecture and site layouts were – for both the Inkas and for local elites – a flexible medium for signalling power relations, for asserting physical presence and for advertising political affiliation. For archaeologists, the same buildings provide a useful index of the varied nature of local responses to the imperial presence; the adoption of Inka styles in local settlements may be one of the best archaeological measures of emulation by local elites. Similarly, construction of intrusive Inka sectors in local settlements suggests the forging of a new type of political relationship, although this may have been imposed, rather than negotiated, by the state. The hybrid architectural styles that emerged in the Chincha region demonstrate that architecture was also an effective medium for materializing a collaborative, two-way political relationship.

Propaganda and ideology

A close examination of propaganda and ideology is essential to considering the discrepant experience of empire because these phenomena shaped the attitudes and perceptions of both powerful Inka officials and their subordinates. Propaganda involves speech, art or writing formulated with the aim of influencing attitudes (Marcus 1992: 10). Ideology, in turn, is '... a system, or at least an amalgam, of ideas, strategies, tactics, and practical symbols for promoting, perpetuating, or changing a social and cultural order; in brief it is political ideas in action' (Friedrich 1989: 301). Both propaganda and ideology represent the interests of the state disproportionately over those of subordinates; ideologies provide 'rationales for action' (Wolf 1999: 280) that reinforce hierarchies and legitimate the state's right to extract tribute or to enforce laws.

Ideologies and propaganda involve communication and messages designed to convince subjects that their subordinate positions are natural, inevitable and permanent. Importantly, however, unlike 'power made visible', which provides a more or less accurate picture of the state's capacities, ideology and propaganda often involve the misrepresentation of social or political reality. An ideology may mask contradictions (Leone 1984) or present arbitrary social conventions as if they were natural or timeless, even phrasing them in 'mythic terms' in order to 'place [them] beyond criticism' (Rappaport 1971: 35).

By obscuring reality, then, ideologies and propaganda mediate resistance (Miller and Tilley 1984: 7). Further, because their messages may be veiled, hidden, or indirect (Wrong 1997), these forms of power are less susceptible to overt resistance, since they rarely present subjects with a visible or clearly defined adversary. Ideology and propaganda operate through symbols, through the manipulation of the built environment, and through ritual. These symbols are sometimes overt and obvious, influencing conscious thought and activity, but frequently, too, they are more subtle in their effects. Subtle but pervasive cues in the built environment, for example, can influence unconscious behaviour and even the routines of daily life.[4]

The Inka use of propaganda was obvious to one Spanish chronicler, Bernabe Cobo (1892 [1653], vol. 3, book 13, ch. 1: 302, translated in Conrad and Demarest 1984: 109), who observed that:

> The truth is that Inca religion did not remain fixed and unchanging from the birth of the realm onward; they did not cling to the same few beliefs or worship the same few gods … They were induced to make changes in [religious] matters because they began to realize that in this way they could strengthen themselves and keep the kingdom under tight control …

Although the Inkas had no written history, the manipulation of royal genealogies and oral narratives, and even alterations to the image of a particular ruler were common practices, as noted by Cieza de León (1967 [1551]). The effectiveness of propaganda is further attested to by the careful attention given to these matters by Inka – as well as by Roman – imperial personnel. Whittaker (1997: 153) describes Roman regulations setting out the appropriate dimensions for statues of the emperor placed in colonial settings, as well as numerous other details of the cultural programme.

Certain portable goods, used to negotiate relationships with individuals, depended heavily upon ideological associations with the emperor that dramatically enhanced their value. Gifts were distributed in ceremonial settings as rewards for loyalty, payment for services and markers of identity or social position. These goods – especially metals and intricately woven textiles – were mobilized from artisans working under close state supervision. Access to Inka-style goods was highly regulated; sumptuary laws ensured that only those of appropriate social rank could wear fine cloth or other valuables (Costin 1998).

The Inkas also sought to create incentives – through gifts and honours – for selected individuals to develop new identities, loyalties, or linkages to the state. As Rowe (1982: 97) has argued:

> The source of honor and privilege was the Inca government; the more closely a person was identified with the government, the greater was his or her chance of attaining the rewards available in the system …

The state awarded titles to individuals; some were awarded the status of 'Inkas-by-privilege', while other named statuses included *yanakuna*, individuals selected from the 'best people' of a province to serve the Inka ruler (Santillán Par. 36; 1879: 39 cited in Rowe 1982: 99). Some *yanakuna* were rewarded with administrative positions. Artisans were also frequently resettled and awarded agricultural lands in return for their labour in the state's workshops.

There were, then, ideological and financial incentives extended to selected individuals, encouraging them to participate more fully in Inka culture and politics. Gifts also played a key role in diplomacy with less privileged subjects; the bestowing of gifts on newly conquered peoples was intended to foster a traditional Andean relationship of reciprocity. Murra (1980) described this practice as 'priming the pump', a gesture that would secure the state's ongoing rights to recruit labour. The chronicler Cieza de

León (1967 [1551]: 74) also describes gifts – including gold or silver bracelets, cloth, women, and special privileges – awarded to resettled colonists, possibly as compensation for the disruption caused by relocation (D'Altroy 2002).

All of these activities fostered wider dissemination of Inka material culture, but these symbolic expressions of generosity and reciprocity masked the reality of the state's exploitation of its subjects' labour. Neither should we view these activities as manifestations of a coherent policy of Inkaization. Rowe (1982: 94) summarizes this last point:

> We need not be very concerned over the degree to which the Incas tried deliberately to encourage cultural unification. Probably all imperial regimes consider some cultural unification administratively convenient, and a case can be made that the Incas shared this common view, particularly with regard to language. Some Inca policies, however, seem to have been designed to perpetuate local differences. My impression from much reading of sixteenth-century sources is that cultural unification was probably not a primary goal of the Inca government. I am inclined to agree with Bernabé Cobo, who said of the Incas in 1653, 'The whole foundation of their policy of government rested on means designed to keep their people subject and deprive them of the zeal to revolt against them' (Cobo Lib. 13, Cap I; 1890-5, vol. III: 302).

A further range of Inka policies maintained and even strengthened perceptions of ethnic and linguistic difference among subject groups. Chroniclers describe severe penalties imposed upon subjects who abandoned their traditional costumes or head ornaments. Rowe (1982) has interpreted these punitive measures as a means to discourage the emergence of a shared Inka culture among subordinates. The absence of shared culture, customs and language would have limited opportunities for the formation of alliances against the state. In general, Inka policies worked to discourage horizontal linkages amongst subject groups, while at the same time propaganda and ideology were designed to strengthen the vertical ties that bound subordinate groups to the state.

Legitimacy and authority

In recent years, scholars have been sceptical about the extent to which ideologies are believed by subordinates (Abercrombie et al. 1980; Scott 1985). Exploring alternatives, Brumfiel (2001) has suggested that ideologies bind specific interest groups *within* a society (such as artisans or warriors) but that they are less successful in inspiring strong loyalty amongst the general populace. Such an approach applied to the Inkas might imply that the blunt messages directed at the masses did little more than inspire 'pragmatic acceptance' or 'tactical obedience', while privileges, honours and incentives given to individuals were more effective in securing loyalty.

Evaluating these questions involves an assessment of how far the Inkas suceeded in exercising *legitimate authority*. In Wrong's framework, legitimate authority differs from each of the forms of power discussed previously. Coercive force, threat, power made visible, propaganda, and ideology all depend upon the *content* of the message for their effectiveness (it must be convincing). Legitimate authority depends instead upon the *source* of a command; it also presupposes *shared values*. Legitimate authority involves '... a relation between actors filling, or "playing", social roles rather than [a relation negotiated] between individuals' (Wrong 1997: 50). Since it implicates enduring social relationships and institutionalized forms of leadership (Mann 1983: 1031), legitimate authority is far more reliable than ad hoc solutions (Wrong 1997: 52).

The other advantage of legitimate authority is its efficiency. Exercising authority is less expensive than provisioning an army or distributing payments, incentives, or rewards (Wrong 1997: 52). Hence to the extent that a polity can monopolize meaning, worldview, or aesthetic and ritual practices, using these to underwrite the exercise of legitimate authority, it has access to substantial collective power. Perceptions of shared interests, a sense of moral obligation, or even collective forms of identity, shared between rulers and subject groups, can contribute to the exercise of legitimate authority. Although archaeologists following recent theoretical trends have strongly emphasized conflicts of interest and struggles for power as central dynamics in past societies, these perspectives have, in my view, obscured another reality of power relations (if we recall Foucault's insights). Some degree of consensus and acceptance of legitimate authority must have co-existed alongside elements of discord in early empires.

For example, the evidence from both the Roman and Inka empires for massive investments in symbols and iconography associated with religious ideas suggests that in both cases a close association with the supernatural was viewed as a key basis for authority (Trigger 1993: 75).[5] It seems likely, too, that sacred traditions, religious ideas, or cosmologies could – and did – hold sway over substantial numbers of adherents. As Mann (1986: 23) has argued:

> People are not manipulated fools. And though ideologies always do contain legitimations of private interests and material domination, they are unlikely to attain a hold over people if they are merely this. Powerful ideologies are at least highly plausible in the conditions of the time, and they are genuinely adhered to ...

In Mann's view (1970: 425) such adherence is important because it involves the 'normative acceptance' of ideas promulgated by priests or rulers. In this case, subordinates internalize '... the moral expectations of the ruling class' and view their own inferior positions as legitimate.

Assessing the effects of the state cult and ideology on Inka colonists is nevertheless difficult. In general, one would expect that highly visible, redundant or standardized symbols would be associated with the most important messages or religious ideas. While such symbols are costly, their messages are easier to decode and are less likely to be misinterpreted (Clark and Parry 1990: 295). As discussed earlier, Inka Cuzco was resplendent for its buildings, its ordered layout, and also for its festivals. Cuzco's main temple, the Qorikancha, was remarkable for its fine ashlar masonry walls, further decorated with gold plates. Inka religion granted the ruler a sacred charter for leadership, and myths and rituals recapitulated traditional Andean practices including ancestor worship. The ritual maintenance of these ancestors – including the mummies of deceased emperors – reinforced linkages among royal lineages and reasserted hereditary rights among members.

The symbolic importance of Cuzco's architecture and city plan, and particularly its role as a setting for ritual, finds strong parallels in descriptions of Rome and other provincial cities. Whittaker (1997: 148; see also Zanker 1988) stresses the ways that religion and politics were inextricably linked through ritual, an observation as relevant for Cuzco as it is for Rome:

> The Roman city was literally stuffed with political imagery which was, like advertising, ubiquitous, inescapable, and subliminally absorbed... But the buildings and organization of space in the city were not merely images. The medium in this case was also the real message ... The theatre, for instance, was not just a building for theatrical performances but a reproduction of the moral order of the city in symbolic form ... In Rome the theatre and amphitheatre were the setting for a public re-enactment of power relations between rich and poor.
>
> Whittaker 1997: 145-6

Under the Inkas, sons of provincial elites were regularly invited to the capital, ostensibly to learn the Inka language and customs (Levillier 1940: 132; Rowe 1982: 95), but the impact of their exposure to the splendour of the capital and its multi-layered symbols must have been substantial.

While it is possible to imagine that those who enjoyed the largesse of the royal court more willingly embraced its ideals, it is more challenging to explain why those in the hinterland, who never travelled to the capital, might also have seen Inka religion and rule as legitimate. To the extent that subjects accepted the state's demands as legitimate, that legitimacy is most likely to have come from two principal sources. The first was the state's institutionalization of ceremonial hospitality, and the second depended upon Inka officials' ability to phrase labour and tribute demands in a traditional ideology of reciprocity.

Feasting lay at the centre of Inka relations with subjugated peoples.[6] With their immense central plazas, Inka '... [a]dministrative cities were built to support a vision of rule based on gift giving and generosity by the ruler' (Morris 1993: 37). Morris (1985: 481) has argued further that '... the salient feature of Inka control ... was the amplification of many of the principles of Andean reciprocity from the village level'. The Inkas recruited labour according to long-standing Andean principles that governed rights and obligations between leaders and followers. Individuals who laboured on community-sponsored projects were traditionally repaid through hospitality. By sponsoring lavish feasts in state installations, the state was literally 'earning authority' (Morris 1985) directly from the populace, phrasing a new (exploitative) political relationship in a familiar (corporate) idiom. Tradition gave coherence and moral authority to Inka practices in a manner alluded to by Giddens (1984: 200), who observed that '... [t]radition ... represents the moral command of "what went before" over the continuity of day-to-day life'.

Once again, gender affected an individual's access to the largesse of the state. Evidence from skeletal remains from the central highlands suggests that males attended feasts more often than females, presumably because males were more likely to serve in the army or work on state projects (Hastorf and DeNiro 1985; Hastorf 2001). Studies of stable isotopes indicate that, after the conquest, some males consumed greater amounts of preferred foods, including maize (probably in the form of *chicha*, maize beer consumed at feasts). Values for females suggest lower levels of consumption of these prestige foods and, by inference, more limited access to state-sponsored hospitality.

Other archaeological measures of the intensity and importance of feasting include distributions of Inka pottery. Hyslop (1993: 347) stresses the central importance of distinctive pottery, arguing that:

> In some places the Inkas could, and did, run an empire without their fancy settlement layouts, but they could not do it without the state hospitality, which required pottery that symbolized the state ...

Pottery thus signalled the state's generosity. While some Inka pottery is found in most provinces, the finest Inka ceramics are more limited in their distribution. In a recent study of provincial pottery production in the Leche Valley, Peru, Hayashida (1999) found that Inka officials retrained local potters selectively, only enough to ensure reliable supplies of the distinctive vessels (*aríbalos*) used in feasting. The state's policy in this region does not, therefore, suggest a policy of Inkaization; instead, local elites continued commissioning fine pottery in the local style, suggesting that indigenous markers of status remained important despite the imposition of Inka rule.

Elsewhere, fine Inka ceramics are usually found in burials or households of local elites. Even those elites who maintained good relations with the state had relatively few vessels in their households. In the Yanamarca Valley sites of Marca and Hatunmarca (discussed earlier), where local

5.5. A hybrid-style *aríbalo* from the Calchaquí Valley, Argentina, showing a mix of Inka and local traits.

elites were closely affiliated with the Inkas, proportions of Inka pottery from excavated from households rarely exceeded twenty-five per cent (D'Altroy 2002). More generally, local potters throughout the empire imitated Inka pottery forms and styles, producing a widespread hybrid style combining Inka and local traits (Fig. 5.5). Only in frontier regions, where the Inka presence lasted just a few decades, are these hybrid styles absent (Hyslop 1993: 350).

How far did these efforts go toward securing 'normative acceptance'? Present evidence suggests that Inka efforts to compel loyalty and to legitimate the state's authority achieved only partial success. For example, when the Spaniards arrived in 1532, many Inka subjects, perhaps inspired by memories of their relatively recent conquest by the Inkas, allied themselves with the foreign invaders. After a decisive victory by the Spaniards, resettled colonists were offered the chance to return to their ancestral lands, and, again, a majority chose to do so (Pease 1982: 176-7). Finally, with the end of Inka domination, Inka provincial centres were rapidly abandoned. These administrative centres had been to a large extent 'artificial' cities. Useful as dramatic settings for feasting on a grand scale, but located long distances from local centres of population and occupied by temporary and transient administrative personnel, these settlements were readily abandoned as the state's authority waned (Morris 1972).

Conclusions

Although the Inka and Roman empires shared common elements, such as a strong emphasis on militarism, extensive roads, elaborate buildings and cities, and the proliferation of imperial styles in distant provinces, they also differed in important ways. The Inka expansion was meteoric, cut short by the arrival of the Spaniards, while Roman imperialism unfolded over a longer period (although it too underwent meteoric phases as in the second/first centuries BC). In the absence of a writing system, the Inkas relied heavily on distinctive material symbols – especially architecture, textiles, and pottery – for communication with subject groups. Yet, despite this emphasis on material culture, the Inkas failed to implement a policy of 'Inkaization'.

Analysis of Inka material culture and its distribution suggests that, while the Inkas invented new forms of hierarchy, imposed a state religion, and created overarching institutions of leadership, the state's relations with subject groups in the provinces relied heavily on traditional forms of authority, mediated largely through ceremonial hospitality. In its overall patterns of governance, the state was 'scaling-up' political relationships more commonly associated with smaller-scale polities (Morris 1993: 36-7).

The 'discrepant experience' of Inka rule varied across the empire. All subjects lived under the threat of coercive force and severe punishment for transgressions. The logistical and bureaucratic skills of the Inkas were made visible in the over-engineering of the roads, which materialized the capacities of the state to quell rebellion and to co-ordinate labour on a grand scale. Those awarded positions of authority in the Inka hierarchy were given financial and ideological incentives for loyalty, including privileges, access to agricultural lands, and finely crafted goods or political insignia. The state also promoted an ideology that credited the Inkas (and particularly their ruler) with the creation of a physically ordered universe and gave them a divine mandate to rule.

Each of these strategies – ritual and pageantry, personal relationships maintained through gifts and rewards, and feasting – placed heavy demands on the state (D'Altroy and Earle 1985). Through time, as the ranks of retainers grew larger, demand for both subsistence and wealth goods increased. The maintenance of the Inka system depended upon intensification of staple finance (to supply administrative centres with food for feasting and for support of the bureaucracy) as well as upon wealth finance (state control of artisans to ensure a continuing flow of valuables). Murra and Morris (1976: 276) have described the resettlement of artisans as follows:

> Potters, weavers or smiths ... [were reorganized to] provide the benefits of mass production, under workshop conditions, which could fairly be compared with the 'industrial' establishments of Europe at the same time.

These activities reflect the importance of rewards to local elites and other retainers. It seems clear, however, from the rapid deterioration of the empire after the arrival of the Spaniards that the Inka Empire was fragile. Strongly dependent upon threat and coercion, Inka ideology was reinforced by an impressive visual display of power and logistical competence. Yet these messages appear to have done little to win support amongst those in the hinterland. Finally, because of the Spanish conquest, we shall never know how long Inka strategies would have sustained the empire; nevertheless the study of the Inkas provides a wealth of insight into the nature of the discrepant experience of one empire in the pre-Hispanic Americas.

Notes

1. Corvée is forced, unpaid labour service. Under the Inka system (known as *mit'a*) each household was required to provide labour service for state projects, as assessed by the state each year.

2. The llama was an exception; along with the alpaca, it was a source of meat and wool. Although llamas could be used as pack animals, their capacity was limited to loads of about thirty kilograms.

3. MacCormack (2001: 434) observes that among contemporary Andean peoples, 'the definitive social and political order that people like to look back to is that of the Inca. That they were the creators of such an order is precisely what the Incas in their day endeavored to communicate to their subjects.'

4. Along these lines, Bourdieu has argued that 'Of all forms of "hidden persuasion" the most implacable is the one exerted, quite simply, by the *order of things*' (Bourdieu and Wacquant 1992: 168).

5. I am inclined to agree with Trigger's (1993) observation that – despite the lavishness of expenditures on religion by rulers of early empires and the importance of these institutions for legitimating authority – the power of these rulers nevertheless depended ultimately upon control both of a hierarchy of administrators and of an army.

6. In their concerted efforts to maintain face-to-face interactions with their subjects through feasting the Inkas differed from the Romans, who were more likely to overlook the rural poor, leaving their control in the hands of local elites (Whittaker 1997).

6

Excavating Colonization[1]

Carla M. Antonaccio

Introduction

The phenomena that made up Greek settlement 'abroad', usually characterized as colonization, are clearly an integral part of Greek history and the development of Greek culture(s). Yet, although the so-called Western Greeks fully participated in panhellenic cult, politics and economics, and culture[2] the colonies are often not integrated into the master-narratives of Iron Age and Archaic Greek history. This is starting to change with an expressly comparative archaeology of colonization or colonialism that is now coming to the fore and making its way into Classical Studies (e.g. Lyons and Papadopoulos (eds) 2002; cf. Dyson (ed.) 1985, Descoeudres (ed.) 1990, esp. Birmingham 1990), following hard on the heels of a recent profusion of scholarship on the archaeology of ethnicity (see below). Excavating colonization has also occasioned digging into the history of the study of Greek colonization and into the relevance of other colonialisms, and led to a long-overdue dialogue between Anglophone and European scholars with their respective perspectives and agendas (Morris et al. forthcoming). This paper offers a contribution to the broader framework within which archaeology is working to understand the intricate interplay between material culture and identity, specifically in the colonial context of Sicily.

The Sicilian context

Sicily's eastern coast was among the earliest regions where Greeks founded permanent, independent settlements near the end of their Iron Age, in the eighth century BC. The path to the foundation of these *apoikiai*, literally 'homes away from home', was not an entirely new one; Mycenaean contacts with Southern Italy and Sicily are attested by the archaeological record and contact between Western Greece and the Salentino may never have been completely disrupted (Malkin 1998 with references; see also Papadopoulos 2001). Greek voyages to the central and western Mediterranean had several effects: the diffusion of elite practices and commodities (possibly including epic poetry, mythological genealogy and elite burial practices) to the Etruscans and other groups in central Italy; the foundation of permanent settlements (Pithekoussai) that seem to have had trade as their primary purpose; and the creation, from scratch, of new and durable Greek *poleis*.

All of this activity has often been considered a kind of chapter, or subplot, in the main narrative of the development of Archaic and Classical Greek culture and society, like the 'Orientalizing' turn in Greek material and other culture of the seventh century. That narrative has emphasized the development of discrete centres or nodes (mainland *ethnê*, *poleis* and sanctuaries) and their interaction. Yet the 'Orientalizing' of Greece has been re-evaluated in recent scholarship, which suggests that the seventh century is not the only Orientalizing period, and indeed that Greek culture was always Orientalizing on some level (Morris 1992). So too should Greek voyaging, trading, and settlement 'abroad' be considered an integral part of Greek history. At the same time, just as a variety of conditions led to intensified orientalism in the culture of many Greek communities in the seventh century, so, too, was the eighth century a pivotal moment in the Greeks' long experience of journeying across and around the Aegean, Mediterranean and beyond.

The earliest colonies of coastal Sicily (Naxos, Syracuse, Lentinoi, Katane, Megara Hyblaia – as well as Gela and Selinous on the south coast) present complex problems to researchers because of the existence of historical and para-historical source materials as well as the fragmentary archaeological record (Leighton 1999: 222-5). Interior settlements of indigenous Sicilians were not affected in the same way as coastal communities by the arrival of Greeks and in many instances these places continued to be inhabited through the period of colonization, though not unaltered. Many interior sites have been fitfully excavated since the days of Paolo Orsi's wide-ranging explorations in the late nineteenth and early twentieth centuries, and study and much new fieldwork has occurred in the past few decades, especially in the centre of the island (Leighton 1989, 1999).[3]

Morgantina

Morgantina, in Enna Province, illustrates changing approaches to Greek colonization very well. Princeton University chose this site from among a number of possibilities in the Mediterranean during the early 1950s to offer training in excavation for graduate students in the programme in Classical Archaeology on a Greco-Roman site.[4] The first years of work at Morgantina located its agora and revealed many of the hallmarks of a Classical urban site, including city walls, a theatre, several stoas and other public or civic buildings, houses, and modest shrines, as well as the quantities of pottery and other small finds that excavation usually produces. In nearly fifty years of excavation undertaken by five different American universities as of this writing, Morgantina has produced some important artefacts and architecture of Greek origin or type. The preliminary reports graphically display the place's Greekness from early in the sixth century BC. Leafing through the annual preliminary reports published in the 1950s and 60s brings before the reader the highlights of each season: shops in the market, fortifications, mosaics, the classical visages of votive terracottas and coins. In addition to an impressive red-figure krater by Euthymides, the Athenian Pioneer vase painter (Neils 1995), the site boasts one of the earliest tessellated mosaics anywhere, the earliest preserved *macellum,* and a rare fountain-house at one corner of the agora. Fragments of a large Doric building (temple or altar) and fragments of a monumental Ionic altar of the early fifth century have been found (Bell 1988). Morgantina coined its own money, inscribed with the name of the city in Greek letters, using devices borrowed from Sicilian Greek city-states (Buttrey et al. 1989; see further below). Indeed, to all appearances, Morgantina was a Greek city, a *polis,* and attained its most extensive and elaborate urban expression during the Syracusan Hellenistic hegemony. The few ancient texts that speak of it offer no contradictions. No record exists of any Greek foundation of Morgantina, but the historian Diodorus Siculus said it was, in the first half of the fifth century, a 'city worth talking about' (*polis axiologos,* XI.78). Thucydides says that it was transferred from the control of Kamarina, a colony of Greek Syracuse on the south coast, to that of Syracuse itself in 421 BC (Thucydides 4.58.1; Bell 2000).

On the other hand, there are some uncomfortable anomalies. Almost no sculpture in stone has ever been found at Morgantina, even in fragments. Inscriptions, aside from short graffiti scratched onto pottery, are very few. The foundations (and functions) of the monumental Archaic structures mentioned, the sanctuaries in which they were located, as well as any later successors, have proven elusive. It is hard to conceive of a Greek city without a temple (though a temple does not prove a city Greek – witness Elymian Segesta). These facts might be explained by Morgantina's location in the interior and on the periphery of the territories of several major colonies, so that it was in essence a provincial place.[5] A different past comes into view, however, with the 'pre-Greek' sherds illustrated in the report for 1957, and in two 'Siculan' vessels shown from the excavations of 1959. These served to illustrate the evidence for a continued native presence on an outcrop below the site well into the sixth century BC (Sjöqvist 1958, 1960). They are also nearly the only non-Greek (or non-Roman) objects from the site to be pictured in the preliminary reports published during Princeton's tenure at the site (1955-67). In fact, Morgantina was an inland indigenous settlement whose earliest occupation may be Neolithic; it was certainly inhabited in the Early Bronze Age, and continuously inhabited from the tenth century BC (Leighton 1993). Like other inland sites, Morgantina came to be strongly affected by the Greek colonization of coastal Sicily in the eighth century and implicated in the political and military struggles of the fifth and fourth centuries; it was taken by the Romans at the end of the Second Punic War in 211 BC and finally abandoned late in the first century BC.

Despite its earliest history, though, the site has usually been regarded as culturally and politically Greek from at least the sixth century, mostly on the basis of its material culture. But in fact, and contrary to the impression given by the preliminary reports, a large percentage of the material recovered from the excavations of Morgantina's Archaic settlement is not Greek, but can be described as local, Siculan or Sikel, indigenous, native – as identifiably different from metropolitan Greek material culture, either from the old homelands or the colonies. Thus, taken as a whole, Morgantina's material culture, especially in the Archaic and early Classical periods, is actually neither wholly Greek nor indigenous, but hybrid (Antonaccio 2003, 2004). The very term hybrid, of course, is borrowed from the world of animal and plant domestication; a hybrid is a cross of two distinct species or varieties to produce something new that combines both.[6] Cultures are, metaphorically, like animals or plants: originally separate creatures with their own genealogies, to be bred, transplanted, crossed with others. Such concepts are deeply embedded in our thinking, since we also speak of the birth, florescence, maturity and decline of culture in a cycle borrowed from nature.

Hybridity

Hybridity, as a term of criticism, was developed in Postcolonial Studies, where it denotes a status or quality between colonizer and colonized, a 'third-space' of 'in-between-ness' where communication between the parties takes place and negotiation happens in whatever form, engendered by the need for communication among people who utilize different languages, cultures and ideologies (Bhabha 1994; Gandhi 1998). This 'third space' can be compared to Richard White's notion of a 'middle ground' of colonial negotiation as recently discussed by Irad Malkin (White 1991; Malkin 1998, 2002). Hybridity applies not only to colonial space but to culture and persons. The formation of a specifically Sicilian Greek, colonial identity, as *Sikeliotai*, a self-differentiation from other Greeks within a colonial context (Antonaccio 2001) is a consequence of this as well. Colonial hybridity thus must start from separate types, namely the Greek colonizer's culture and the native or indigenous – which invokes a version of what Annie Coombes terms 'strategic essentialism' (see below). The usefulness of the concept of hybridity is not limited to small and arguably peripheral, or 'native', places like Morgantina only. It offers a more productive approach than either the polarities of Greek and barbarian, or the unidirectional process implied with the term 'Hellenization' (and it should be noted that postcolonial theory was being applied to 'Romanization' somewhat earlier than to 'Hellenization') (Van Dommelen 2001 with references). Almost from their beginnings, Sicily and Southern Italy's colonies produced some of the most impressive Greek architecture anywhere. Yet approaches to the study of the material culture attendant on colonization have usually focussed on distinctively colonial forms, especially in architecture (e.g. Shoe 1952). At the same time, however, architecture produced in Sicily and Southern Italy is often considered non-canonical by mainland standards, and sometimes regarded as eccentric, even semi-barbarous (Ceserani 1999; Dietler 1999; Hall 2003).[7] This attitude stems from the notion of colonies as culturally dependent and their culture as derivative. The Euthymides krater mentioned above provides an object lesson, as it were; it was celebrated at the time of its discovery in 1958, and since, as a major, perhaps singular work of an important Attic red-figure pioneer, but its recontextualization at Morgantina, where it was long used and found in the debris of a destroyed fifth-century settlement, has lagged (Neils 1995, Antonaccio 2004).

Ceramics and ethnicity

As exemplified by the Euthymides krater, not only the colonies but many communities in Sicily were the destination of an impressive range of ceramics and other objects imported from Greece, and the colonies also developed their own ceramic industries that are discernibly Greek in the techniques they use, forms they produce and surface treatments they feature. Yet, because of the structure of the field of study ('vase painting'), decontextualization is a symptom of ceramic studies in particular. Ceramics are the archaeologist's and ancient art historian's staple, plentiful and nearly indestructible. Greek pottery has been studied for centuries and, especially for Attic and Corinthian pottery, basic chronological frameworks, and changes over time in shape and decoration, are well understood. There are many studies of ceramic imports and their implications for trade and economic activity. Ceramic studies have tended, however, to neglect cultural and archaeological contexts, since the material is so widely distributed, emphasizing instead the workshop, shape, dating and so on, even the modern collection within which a given object is currently situated, without considering the rest of the assemblages with which a given object is found. Even when the context is included, as when tomb groups are published, the standard catalogues are organized for specialists who wish to study the objects as part of the body of work produced by a given painter, workshop or city, or as representatives of a shape, ware and so on. The focus is on the object and its production, not as much on its context of use and its meaning within that context (see Antonaccio 2004).

Such approaches are, of course, meant to address particular problems and concerns. They are not themselves illegitimate or mistaken. But the standard catalogue is one of a number of factors that have tended to fragment and dis-integrate comprehension of antiquity in particular ways. The division of the ancient world into homeland and colonial, indigenous and Greek; of periodization inappropriate to colonial contexts; of excavation publication programmes into specialized studies of different ceramic styles (among other topics) in isolation from one another addresses some problems but creates others. Pottery has also borne a particularly heavy interpretive burden. Ceramic style has often been considered what Polly Wiessner calls 'emblemic', especially in a colonial context: it functions to communicate something expressly, i.e. ethnic identity in this case, by expressing a social boundary through a distinctive style (Wiessner 1983, 1990). Recent research indicates that style does not reliably express ethnicity per se (Antonaccio 2004 with references). But Wiessner herself also observes: 'Styles without distinct referents that work through association ... may be both active and effective means of communication giving powerful aesthetic impressions and stirring strong feelings through associations' (Wiessner 1990: 108).

The question of what style means, how it functions, is critical to understanding the material record (see Conkey 1999). Yet it is not at all easy to take Wiessner's analytical first step: 'Determining how actively or passively style is used in communication' (Wiessner 1990: 107). The general assumption is that indigenous style in particular is emblemic, but most archaeologists these days would not assume the same of Greek pottery: the presence of Corinthian pottery, for example, on a given site does not necessarily indicate Corinthian colonists (cf. Boardman 1994; Snodgrass 1994). Yet, conversely, Greek pottery in native places is often cited as evidence of intermarrying with Greeks, or Greek presence in the form of political and military control of a given site.

This is because until recently Classical archaeologists worked within a culture-history paradigm whereby the boundaries of a cultural and political territory were defined by material culture styles. These styles, in turn, signalled the presence of a particular people: Greeks or Sikels, for example. Thus, the archaeological record has been used to verify the truth of myths relating migrations of native populations before the arrival of colonists, and to fix the boundaries of their territories in default of written histories. Attempts to trace the movements of Greek settlers after colonization began, based on the assumption that artefact types and style are markers of Greek identity and presence, form a related endeavour (see Graves-Brown et al. (eds) 1995; Jones 1997). Whereas anthropologists and archaeologists privilege the role of culture in defining and expressing ethnic identity, Jonathan Hall, writing as an historian, has emphasized criteria of descent and ancestral territory to distinguish ethnic differentiation from cultural difference and avoid the difficulties that ensue when trying to find consistent expressions of ethnicity in material culture (Hall 1997, 2002, 2003). Hall distinguishes these criteria from cultural 'indicia' that may, but often do not, articulate ethnic identity.[8]

To take a specific example of a transculturated or hybrid object from the ancient colonial Greek world, consider a pair of ceramic vessels now in the

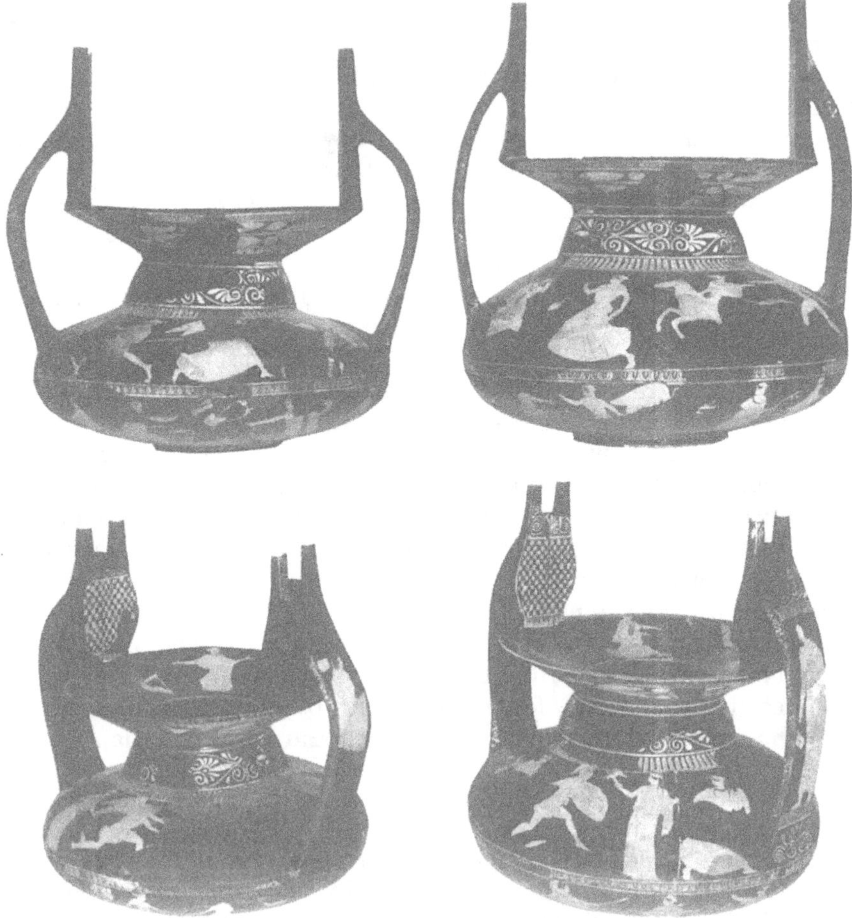

6.1. Attic red-figure nestorides attributed to Polygnotos, 450-440 BC.

J. Paul Getty Museum in Malibu (Fig. 6.1; Jentoft-Nilsen 1988, 1990). Dating to the mid-fifth century BC, these objects are hybrids in several senses. In shape, they most resemble a South Italian form with roots in pre-colonial culture, more the *olla* than the *trozzella*, the latter a kind of amphora with knobbed handles, or the related *nestoris*, which was its late Classical colonial descendant and named for the two-handled drinking cup of Nestor (Jentoft-Nilsen 1990: 243; Trendall 1989: 10, and 1990). The latter shapes are specific to the ancient territory of Daunia (modern Puglia) and not used in contemporary Greek communities of the 'old country', but they are produced for the South Italian Greek (and indigenous) market in the fifth century. All these shapes have a broad, everted rim, but the *trozzella* and *nestoris* are larger and more suitable for serving, featuring a low foot and more elongated shape. Moreover, the handles of the Getty vases lack the knobs of the latter two types, but instead sport the horned projections that appear on local *ollae* (Iannantuono 1986; cf. Mazzei 1986). Boardman claims that 'The market for the vases was principally local and Greek though they spread generally, as had the Greeks, through South Italy, seldom much beyond. Shapes are as expected but there are signs of observation of local, native shapes, either because they had some functional convenience or to encourage sale to non-Greeks' (1991, 217-18). Boardman specifically cites the *nestoris* as an example of the latter.

The decoration, however, firmly places the Getty vases in the metropolitan, rather than native, tradition: the painted scenes are executed in the Attic red-figure style, and not the South Italian variation that takes off in the later fifth century. The date is about 430 BC. The Attic artist associated with the style of the figures has been suggested as the Polygnotos Painter – i.e. the vases are 'Polygnotan' (see Matheson 1995: 249, 483). As Jentoft-Nilsen noted, the shape is practically unique in the Attic repertoire, recording a few other, similar, examples of the shape, all decorated in Attic style (1990: 243). The shape of the Getty examples might have been adopted by an Attic artist who had direct experience of South Italian examples, either as imports or while in Italy himself; other examples simply might no longer be extant; the pots could have been made for the colonial market (like the production of Attic black glaze stemless 'Castulo' cups, designed specifically for the challenges of export shipping); or they might have been the commission of an itinerant South Italian patron. Jentoft-Nilsen concluded that, whatever the case, these items were a warning against the assumption that the direction of all 'influences' was from east to west, instead of west to east.

These vases, whose provenance is unfortunately unknown, but is likely to be South Italy, are transculturated or hybrid objects, produced in a metropolitan centre in response to the colonial experience, possibly of Athens herself (Thurioi was founded on the site of Sybaris in 443 BC by Athenians). Thurioi, however, may not itself have been the home of early South Italian red-figure, a distinction that apparently belongs to Metapontion (Boardman 2001: 110; cf. Trendall 1989: 17, who notes that Furtwängler, the scholar who isolated South Italian pottery as a class, also connected the style with Thurioi).

Metropolitan products from other times and places may at times be produced by 'natives' under the direction of colonial patrons (Antonaccio 2003) and thus document a contrived and manipulative hybridity. There are any number of cases in antiquity and in more recent situations where exotic, foreign or luxurious objects are borrowed from other cultures and domesticated to the purposes (however trivial or decontextualized) of metropolitan consumers. But a similar kind of hybrid object can be found in other kinds of colonial contexts: for example, at Morgantina, in the form

6.2. Corinthianizing krater, Morgantina, Necropolis 2 Tomb 32, *c.* 625-600 BC.

of a Corinthianizing krater of the late seventh century (Fig. 6.2). This object's shape and the rays emanating from its foot are derived from the mixing bowls of Corinth in the late Protocorinthian period, perhaps by way of Syracuse, whose somewhat earlier Fusco kraters may have provided models. The handle plates and stirrup handles are particularly clear borrowings, and the light colour of the clay may also be imitating that of Corinthian exports (Lyons 1996: 77, 213-14). Yet, the wavy line motif and syntax of the ornament as a whole is not found in the Corinthian, or other Greek, tradition. The actual place of production is unknown, though it must be local to Morgantina if not Morgantina itself; it is certainly not a colonial (Sicilian Greek, or 'Sikeliote') product. Thus, a local potter produced a vessel that combines elements from the indigenous and colonial repertoires to create something that is not merely an imitation of a Greek original, but an object that partakes of two different cultures and their idioms.

As noted above, pottery has carried the flag for interpretation along the lines of the culture-history model. 'Personal' artefacts such as jewellery and tools, on the other hand, have been regarded as expressions of personal identity, which extends to gender and class. Yet, despite the clear influence of Greek pottery on indigenous potters in eastern Sicily, they produced neither close copies nor direct imitations of Greek wares, as discussed in connection with the Corinthianizing krater above. The entire 'Siculogeometric' class of pottery, therefore, should be considered a hybrid category. At the same time, indigenous carinated shapes continued to be very prominent, as well as one handlers, basket-shaped bowls with three vertical handles on the rim, *askoi*, *amphorai* and cups with high-swung handles. Yet it would be misleading to emphasize only the survival of elements from the indigenous tradition. Indigenous forms were used side by side with imported wares, from the end of the Iron Age right through the fifth century (Antonaccio 2001, 2004). Thus, not only particular objects, or single categories of objects, but the entire assemblage of ceramics found in inland sites during the seventh to fifth centuries is hybrid, composed of elements from several origins and dominated by a hybrid category, Siculogeometric. As alluded to above, local pottery may very well not have been emblemic of ethnic identities, nor expressive of the boundaries between ethnic groups at all. As this author has suggested elsewhere, relationships based on individual or community links may account for the similarities in indigenous culture in eastern Sicily (see Antonaccio 2003). The construction of hybrid assemblages associated especially with drinking, and the creation of hybrid objects, suggests that a very complex and continuous negotiation of status and identities was taking place in interior communities, and echoed in the colonies and even their *metropoleis*.

Irad Malkin has proposed a relationship of *xenia* between early Greek settlers and traders and indigenes, especially in the region around the Bay of Naples (Malkin 1998, 2002). Through this structure, according to Malkin, Greek and native elites exchanged customs, including mythic narratives of *nostos* and heroic genealogies, as well as practices of feasting and ritualized drinking. Yet, stories of descent and migration in Greek and Roman sources reflect Greek and Roman mental maps. In the case of the Elymians, for example, it is dubious that the indigenes of western Sicily would have believed they were descended from Trojan refugees before the arrival of Greek (and/or Punic) settlers.

In the case of Morgantina, the only such criterion known is Strabo's account of Morgantina's founding (6.1.7). Rather than record a Greek foundation, however, this narrative traces the city's name to the eponymous hero Morges, who led a band of Sikels from South Italy to Morgantina and lent his name to both the town and the ethnic group said to live there, the Morgeti. It is possible that Greek-Sikel exchanges of *xenia* in a colonial 'middle ground' may lie behind both the adoption of Greek drinking pottery in interior Sicilian settlements, like Morgantina, and the invention of a native founding *nostos*, i.e. Morges, in early phases of the colonial encounter, though no historical narrative so indicates. The earliest coinage, dating to the 460s BC and the late Archaic apex of the town, shows a bearded male head on the obverse that has often been identified, after Greek prototypes, with a local river god (Fig. 6.3; Antonaccio 1999). While there is good reason to maintain this identification, it could be proposed that this image is instead that of Morges, in which case the mythological founder might have been invented, or at least prominently expressed, at a time of political and cultural stress during the Douketios episode. Such an invention might coincide with finally 'becoming Sikel' as much as the Greeks of Sicily had to become Sikeliotai (Antonaccio 2001).

6.3. Morgantina silver coin, *c*. 465-459 BC. Obverse: bearded male head, ?Morges; reverse: ear of grain.

Discussion

Whether we emphasize cultural identity and material culture or ethnicity and an affinity based on kinship and territory, these are constructed statuses, often arising in oppositional situations, like colonial or other encounters with different groups. How identity plays out in material culture, or if it does, remains a question. As I have argued elsewhere, what people do is as important as what they say (on 'discourse and praxis' see Hall 2002: 19-29). Whether or not objects have anything to do with ethnicity, material culture should be considered to comprise an entire discourse of its own. If this discourse does not map onto criteria of descent and territory, then the discourse of things should be considered as challenging, contradicting, ignoring or coexisting with spoken or written discourses of identity (Antonaccio 2001). Moreover, we should be wary both of taking on faith the testimony of ancient authors that in the Greek period Sicily was shared by three distinctively different indigenous ethnic groups, and of assuming that anything in material culture that appears distinctive to us expresses ethnic difference *per se* (Antonaccio 2004). But colonial hybridity of necessity sees both 'Greek' and 'Native' as distinctly marked at the start, and the categories of native, Greek and then hybrid or transculturated, and/or in some taxonomies, 'colonial' – as in colonial architecture – also beg several questions: do they recognize any categories that were operative in antiquity? Do any differences in material culture enact meaningful differences in identity, and is this a cultural, or an ethnic, identity, rather than a question of class or gender or some other category?

At least as early as 1971, Filippo Coarelli argued against seeing in colonial encounters the interaction of a purely Greek culture with a purely Other.[9] In the same decade, too, Erik Sjöqvist's Jerome Lectures at the University of Michigan explicitly acknowledged the native presence in Sicily by including them in his narrative of Greek colonization and using the types and styles of artefacts and aspects of the built environment to identify them (Sjöqvist 1973). Sjöqvist taught at Princeton with Richard Stillwell and was his collaborator and co-director at Morgantina; it was Sjöqvist's field report in 1959 that published the two non-Greek pots. In that period, too, Serge Gruzinski and Agnes Rouveret collaborated to produce a comparative account of Greeks and 'barbarians', on the one hand, and Spaniards and indigenous Mexicans on the other, treating both pairs as case studies of acculturation. Since art historical and aesthetic methods and principles usually are brought to bear on figured objects, as Gruzinsky and Rouveret point out, colonial art, judged against the standards of the core region or colonial motherland, is found wanting – judged as barbaric, provincial, primitive or naïve. In their refiguring, contact between colonizer and colonized is a continuous and direct experience that produces changes in cultural patterns in one of the two parties, and assimilation is only a phase in this process (as is diffusion). While thus denying the false dichotomy between colonizer and colonized, Gruzinski and Rouveret nevertheless maintained the attitude of the colonizers in both case studies to be the quintessentially patronizing, if benign, one of adults towards children: 'Ellos son como niños' (Gruzinski and Rouveret 1976).

This early scepticism about the traditional polarity of colonizer and colonized foreshadows the adoption by art historians and archaeologists of concepts – including hybridity, creolization, *métissage* – developed in Postcolonial Studies. The general trend among archaeologists in the last two decades has been a much greater awareness of the native populations and towards a more contextual analysis, at least among field archaeologists. The study of colonial cemeteries provides an example. Recent analyses have considered how various identities – ethnic, social, and gender, for example – might have been articulated in burial, and to chart how interactions both between colonies, and between colonies and indigenous groups, shaped the burial records in colonies and in interior sites (Shepherd 1997, 1998; Lyons 1996). Meanwhile, Italian, French and Spanish scholars were much occupied with the effects of colonial encounters that took place within the borders of contemporary national, imperial or ethnic territories, particularly on the indigenes; reflections of recent colonial empires have been detected in early studies of Classical colonization (see for example the papers in *World Archaeology* vol. 28, 1997; de Angelis 1998; Ceserani 1999).

Such recent work has presented a more complex picture of acculturation and assimilation than the term 'Hellenization' traditionally implies, and as it was defined a generation ago by the relatively enlightened Sjöqvist: 'the assimilation process signified the absorbing of the indigenous element by the Greeks, rather than vice versa. When that process had come to an end, after three or four generations, the Hellenization of central Sicily was completed' (Sjöqvist 1973: 72). As Michael Dietler has recently observed, the very term 'Hellenization' expresses 'the idea that a desire for Greek objects, and Greek culture in general, was a natural and inevitable result of contact' (Dietler 1999: 476). Early attempts to reframe the Greek versus barbarian opposition as both Eurocentric (insofar as 'the Greeks' and their 'culture' are construed as the founders and foundation of European identity) and colonialist presage the emergence of postcolonial discourses about hybridity and creolization that have moved out of the sphere of literary criticism to the study of material culture. Important to this perspective, obviously, are comparative colonialisms – broadly defined as incidents of deliberate settlement (rather than migration or relocations of populations) that strive to reproduce an entire society and its material culture in a new place (see most recently Lyons and Papadopoulos (eds) 2002). Rather than a simple insertion of a new society, and the inevitable destruction of its host population, the process of colonization may be argued to be more reciprocal than is implied by terms like 'Hellenization', a notion that is, finally, a specific form of assimilation. Rather than assimilation (of the indigenes), acculturation takes place, which produces new identities and cultural variations. 'Hybridization' or 'creolization', and closely related ideas like White's 'Middle Ground' and Serge Gruzinsky's *pensée métisse* and *métissage* all imply the mixture that the process entails (Gruzinsky 1999). These frameworks stress accommodation as well as confrontation, and the creative productivity that may result from colonialism.

Yet these grounds for compromise are not uncontested. Coombes has criticized the category of hybridity with respect to museum exhibitions in the 1980s that attempted to challenge the usual contrasts of West and Other, centre and periphery, and so on. Coombes pointed to the careful selection of 'transculturated' objects for the shows, objects that signified not only cultural, ethnic and national identities but also mutual exchanges between cultures. Coombes argued that the display of hybrid objects by museums demonstrated how Western institutions' celebration of cultural diversity, propped up by a bland multiculturalism, 'ultimately invoke [a] misleading ... rhetoric of equality ... laying claim to an impossible relativism that declares objectivity at the expense of a recognition of the multiple political interests at stake in such an initiative' (Coombes 1994: 104). While noting that hybridity constituted 'an important cultural strategy for the political project of decolonisation', she stressed that 'the problem is not to question the validity of hybridity, either as a strategy of oppositional identity ("roots revivalism") or as an instance of creative transactional transculturation' both of which she accepts as 'contingent and conditional'.

Instead, Coombes propounds a 'strategic essentialism' – a return, in essence, to a modified notion of original purity – refusing hybridity because, she argues, that concept already carries too much baggage.

Obviously, Coombes is dealing with modern colonial and postcolonial societies that have a critical and vital stake in the construction of their identities and histories by powerful Western institutions. The adoption of hybridity for ancient colonial contexts, moreover, adopts a framework invented for other situations in which race is the dominant concern. She may well be right that 'transculturated' and hybrid objects should not be taken as typical, and emblemic, of a Middle Ground that reassures Western inheritors of colonialism that postcolonial outcomes are not all bad, or erases conflict and difference. We must bear in mind Coombes' concern not to overemphasize such objects, which are not especially common, or we would not remark upon them. In addition, Coombes, Rouveret and Gruzinski, and others are mostly concerned with hybrid objects and styles, while in many colonial contexts transculturated objects or styles are only part of the picture. In the case of Greek colonies, and post-colonization interior communities, we are sometimes confronted with styles, objects and practices that are hybrid, but also with entire categories of material culture that combine native, colonial and hybrids into an entire discourse of recombinant difference. A further observation should be made: while the vocabulary of the discourses is composed of the emblemic or marked elements from the originary groups, the combinations are telling. In Greek colonies the dominant notes are almost exclusively Greek, though the sources can be quite varied. In the interior, the discourse is more dominated by the local traditions.

*

The Getty vases must have a fascinating biography now lost to us because of the circumstances of their modern recovery and acquisition. What they are, however, is a part of the discourse noted earlier: one that is parsed not in single, hybrid or transculturated objects, but in whole assemblages of artefacts, and in built environments, in language, foodways and customs. Turning to architecture, a similar story can be told. Western Greek monumental architecture is notoriously non-canonical by mainland standards; however, viewed from within rather than from without, it is precocious, monumental from the start, and not playing by the same rules as mainland architecture, but is no less Greek for all that. Though not influenced by early Greek Iron Age forms and practices, like the chieftain houses and their communal use that are now well documented in many Iron Age Greek communities of the homeland, the early Greek temples in the West were numbered among the early innovators even by mainland standards (Mertens 1990; Barletta 2001: 75 with references). Architects were sometimes eclectic in the Archaic period, combining elements from different orders and ignoring principles shared by mainlanders. Thus West Greek architecture comes to express a local or regional variation on Greekness in a way comparable to how the variations on Siculogeometric in indigenous communities express local variation on native identity. On the domestic front, the indigenous house form was the so-called hut (*capanna*), really a kind of longhouse; a very large complete example at Morgantina measures eighteen metres in length (Trench 31, Leighton 1993: 37-48).[10] The Greek colonists built houses on other plans and used different materials, but the quick adoption of the *naiskos* form in some interior communities may owe something to its similarity to the scale and basic plan of the longhouse. Once interior communities adopted the Greek house type, with its tiled roofs and mudbrick walls, and its significantly different plan and, presumably, domestic routines, the communal functions of the longhouse may have been displaced onto the *naiskoi* and other monumental structures.[11] As with drinking customs that may have been engaged in these spaces, indigenous Sicilians adopted the Greek built environment in ways that made cultural, ritual and social sense to them (Antonaccio 2001; Hodos 2000).

I finish with an apparent exception to the general observation that Greek colonies constructed their hybridity through combinations of Greek material culture: Himera, a late and somewhat isolated foundation on the north coast of Sicily by Zankle in 648 BC. Hemmed in on the west by the Punic presence, embedded deep within indigenous territories, Himera nevertheless prospered from the first and peaked with the eponymous battle against the Carthaginians that famously took place on the same day as the similarly decisive naval battle of Salamis that defeated the Persians. The city, like several Greek colonies on the south coast, was destroyed in 409 BC, ending its brief existence. What is particularly interesting is the notable proportion of indigenous material found within the city itself. The foundation deposit of Temple A contained a matt-painted oinochoe, and the distribution of indigenous pottery in the settlement has been plotted by Stefano Vasallo, demonstrating that indigenous ceramics are not restricted to dedications (a context in which native pottery is found at Gela also, for example at the extramural sanctuary at Butera). Instead, native pottery has been recovered throughout the city in domestic contexts (Spatafora and Vassallo 2002). While this could be taken (and often is) to indicate an ethnically mixed population, what it seems to echo is the particular mix of material culture of the indigenous interior settlements like Morgantina, and not the wholly Greek, if hybrid Greek, assemblages of the older colonies on the east and southern coasts, which were founded by displacing the existing indigenous presence. Himera's colonial identity may thus be expressed with a different kind of hybridity from that of Syracuse, for example (Antonaccio 2004).

The hybridity of colonial Sicilian material culture thus seems to extend both to the colonies themselves and to the interior sites which experience a gradual acculturation over the course of the seventh to third centuries, but are not themselves colonial foundations (or re-foundations). Rather than the concept of ethnicity, which smacks of the strategic essentialism championed by Coombes, an emphasis on local and regional, hybrid identities may be a more appropriate and productive focus of future discussion.

Notes

1. This chapter is drawn from my book-in-progress of the same title, to be published by the University of Texas Press. Some of its ideas were first formulated in 'Ethnicity and Ceramics in Post-Colonial Sicily', a paper presented at the annual College Art Association meeting in February 1998. I thank Ann Gunter for inviting me to participate on that occasion and for her interest and encouragement then and since. Other aspects have been presented at the University of Newcastle-upon-Tyne in 1999 and Wellesley College in 2000 (Antonaccio 2003, 2004), as well as the State University of New York, Buffalo, the University of North Carolina, Greensboro, and Duke University; I wish to thank the audiences on those occasions, as well as the seminar at Cambridge, for their interest, comments and criticisms. Thanks in particular to Jonathan Hall for sharing his work with me in advance of publication, and to Keith Stanley for discussing Attic ceramic oddities with me.

2. E.g. as competitors in the crown games, and also as patrons of epinician poetry and the more durable victory monuments.

3. Unfortunately, much of the fieldwork and analysis is presented in local conferences and publications largely unavailable outside Sicily, with two exceptions: the journals *Kokalos* and *Sicilia Archeologica.*

4. As revealed in a letter to then-President Goheen from Professor Erik Sjöqvist in the expedition archives housed at the Department of Art and Archaeology at Princeton.

5. In contrast to this interpretation, Malcolm Bell has vigorously propounded the view that Morgantina was an integral part of the Hellenistic kingdom of Hieron II and as such benefited from royal patronage – which accounts for the theatre, stoas and so forth mentioned above.

6. The term appears in English in the early seventeenth century, according to the *OED*, when its usage followed the original (rare) Latin and applied to cross-bred animals. It was not much used until the nineteenth century, when natural historians use it of both plants and animals; it is often pejorative in tone though it also denotes vigour. The Latin word is probably related to the Greek *hubris:* dangerous, even violent, over-reaching.

7. Cf. A.J. Graham in *CAH*^{2} III.3, 193 speaking of architecture among other arts: 'work of respectable, and sometimes high, standard was achieved, but it is clear that the western Greeks followed the lead of artists in Greece.'

8. In his most recent book (2002), Hall reflects extensively upon the interplay of ethnicity and culture; further response is beyond the scope of this paper, but Hall continues to defend the primacy of the discourse of descent even when admitting cultural attributes to the construction of identity.

9. 'La cultura greca <ut sic> è un astrazione, non esiste; come non esiste d'altra parte un mondo indigeno, che a quella si oppongo in un complesso sisteme di influssi e relazioni in una facile e illusoria dialettica' (quoted by Gruzinski and Rouveret 1976: 162). The quotation is from comments made by Coarelli at the

Eleventh Congress on Magna Grecia at Taranto in 1971, *Le gente non greche della Magna Grecia* (Naples 1972): 331.

10. Continued excavation in 1999 and 2003 of the building in Trench 16 West at Morgantina, published in its incomplete state in Leighton 1993: 21-7, has demonstrated that its length was at least twenty metres, making it perhaps the largest such structure of its time known in Sicily.

11. For example, the monumental Four Room Building at Morgantina, with its elaborate architectural terracotta decoration, which is sited contiguous to the longhouse in Trench 16 West: see previous note and Antonaccio 1997.

7

Colonization and Mediterranean History

Nicholas Purcell

Empire is the art of putting men in their place.
Charles Maurice de Talleyrand-Périgord, 1797

Introduction

This chapter explores some merits and difficulties of using comparison with other periods of Mediterranean history to investigate episodes which ancient historians and archaeologists usually call 'colonization'.[1] These social and economic changes are unusual in Mediterranean history in being *traditionally* studied in a comparative spirit, which doesn't shrink from adducing even twentieth-century case-studies. As the late Ettore Lepore said of 'Greek colonization', 'des modèles de comparaison historique sont presque aussi nécessaires que les témoignages mêmes' (2000: 68). For all its popularity and importance, however, 'colonization' is a category in crisis in the study of the ancient Mediterranean.

Long-term comparison in Mediterranean history is the theme of the monograph *The Corrupting Sea,* which sought common denominators in social responses to the frantically diverse, unpredictable and fragmented productive environment of the Mediterranean coastlands, and the opportunities provided in such a world by the sea itself (Horden and Purcell 2000). A whole gamut of social behaviour, from simple productive logic to complex structures of organization and control, has drawn its character from these basic givens; it was this that made attractive a systematic comparison of many aspects of apparently very different Mediterranean communities.[2]

Among the most significant variables in such comparative history are access to diverse opportunities in the productive landscape, the deployment of human labour, and the mobility – often on a far from local scale – of what is produced and of those who are involved in production and its organization. These variables are also central to the ancient instances of 'colonization', including the activities of Greek-speakers on a Mediterranean-wide stage from the eighth to the fourth centuries BC. Accordingly, *Corrupting Sea* made a trial-attempt to compare episodes of the imposition of 'far-flung power', such as the Phoenician diaspora, or some of the initiatives of imperialistic states from the Hellenistic period to the Islamic and Christian Mediterranean (and especially in the Levant in the age of the Crusades), and the extensive economic networks of Genoa and Venice (Horden and Purcell 2000: 278-87). In this chapter I develop this approach in relation to the Greek diaspora in the Archaic and Classical Mediterranean, illustrating it with the example of Southern Italy.

Agrosystems and seaways

Over the last generation, interest in the ethnography of traditional Mediterranean communities has combined with new methods in archaeology to bring about an 'ethnoarchaeological revolution', offering a novel repertoire of points of comparison over the long term – against the earlier orthodoxies which promoted a radically differentiated periodization, between the prehistoric and early historic periods, for instance, or between antiquity and the Middle Ages. In explaining traditional Mediterranean primary production, this enquiry has especially emphasized the explanatory potential of risk and strategies for reducing it. The preponderant natural source of danger is the unpredictability of rainfall from year to year, and of its distribution within each season. This risk is intensified and modulated by the fragmented topography of the Mediterranean coastlands, which entails marked variation in precipitation from microregion to microregion. The three principal responses to this problem are to diversify production, to store the product, and to redistribute it. The cultural significance of this triad is, therefore, a given of the Mediterranean ecosystem. It is less pronounced in neighbouring areas where microregional fragmentation, and the variability of precipitation, generally fall off.

The avoidance of risk in the Mediterranean promotes net average surplus. To survive, you must produce every year as much as you can towards the store which you might need if next year is bad. If you do not do this, when the bad year comes, you die. So everybody attempts to diversify and overproduce. But bad years, though common, come less often than half the time (and in some places much less). Even when they do come, they affect some productions more than others. So, averaged across a landscape or a region, and over a decade or a half-century, there should be net overproduction. The obvious concomitants are to store – in the broad sense which includes 'social storage' – and to redistribute: that is, to exchange products of differing seasonal production between microregions.

The terminology is general and deliberately bland. It is not actually a cosy picture. The notional autonomous individual, *homo Hesiodicus* as we might call him, is a phantom. The reality is the *demoboroi basileis*, the leaders who consume their people. Productive choice, accumulation, disbursement, processing, exchange, and mobility all sustain elite power. The average benignity of Mediterranean conditions has therefore frequently not sufficed for the survival of the people who do the work. Storage means Mycenaean palaces and Medieval monastic granges; mobility means slavery, forced depopulation and exploitative resettlement; redistribution means piracy, tribute and war.

The uncertainties of ancient primary production and the strategies available for overcoming them created opportunities for certain recurring kinds of disposing power. Because of the extreme fragmentation of much of the Mediterranean landscape, the portfolios of even those with quite limited disposing power tend to be extended in space: such as the scattered parcels of land distributed within a village community by partible inheritance. For the wealthier and more powerful, the widely extended portfolios which we call *latifundia* are a common expedient. It is not uncommon for such holdings to be widely dispersed. The highest term in the sequence is the 'patrimonies scattered across the globe' of the pan-Mediterranean elites of the Roman hegemony. It is not surprising that Marx could regard ancient agriculture as essentially more colonial than capitalist (1887: 3, 6, 24). We can turn the aperçu around: ancient 'colonization' is more like agrarian power-structures than political hegemony. In this section I present examples of how Mediterranean conditions promote a single set of exploitative behaviours, deployable within communities or capable of being extended at the expense of outsiders.

Production for redistribution makes specialization and intensification significant indirect responses to risk. These vary according to whether they are planned by a more-or-less autonomous producer, or (as is commoner) by a figure who controls a larger segment of the landscape. Patterns and prototypes can be traced in such areas as property, crop- (or animal-) type, productive technique and equipment, labour-management, processing, and the arrangements for storage and redistribution.

The powerful 'allotted' opportunities for production, a process for which Greek used a characteristic verb, *nemein*, *nemesthai*, with a special cultural/economic reference.[3] This 'allotment' took many forms, but one of the most important historically is the division of space into actual lots and their assignation, creating 'allotted landscapes' of which Roman centuriation-schemes are the most dramatic. Such allotments have often been misinterpreted as essentially an organized form of subsistence production, but were in fact usually associated with production for redistribution. Take the extreme example of the management of Messenia by Classical Sparta. The due which the Spartans demanded from the helots was an *apophora* fixed at the outset, to be paid from profits. A curse was laid against anyone who charged more, on the grounds that the expectation of profit would reconcile the helots to their position, and that any departure from the fixed due would endanger this.[4] Allotted landscapes, then, are found among the communities of the Greek homeland (the cleruchies of fifth-century Athens are another celebrated instance), but the form is also characteristic of overseas settlements.[5] Here too the title to a lot (*kleros*) was a significant opportunity rather than a minimum for survival. The lot offered to the lyric poet Philoxenos in a *Sikelike apoikia* offered a livelihood (*bios*) and an abundance of what was needed for a household (*oikos pollen euporian echon*): he high-mindedly sailed away rather than abandoning himself to the *truphe, hedypatheia* and *amousia* (uncultured pleasures and luxuries) associated with the opportunity.[6] In the Black Sea, the archaeological record of the territory of Pontic Istria and its allotment infrastructures cannot be made to fit emergency settlement or apologetic 'land-hunger' explanations: these Milesians, like the lot-holders of Philoxenos' Sicily, are not the very poor.[7] The combination of successful agriculture, political might and elite success that was the dream of those who participated in new settlements was most potently evoked in the Greek tradition by the story of Sybaris: the *apoikia* whose elite succeeded so brilliantly that the city was ultimately doomed. For all the moral condemnation of Sybarite excess, *truphe* was the underlying aim of Greek overseas settlement.[8]

Away from Greek landscapes, the disposing power wielded on a small scale at home was extended across wider landscapes, in which more people could become grateful beneficiaries of their allotment. The purveyance of opportunity was made routine, as later in the territories of Roman chartered towns, and to some extent in Medieval overseas settlements. A classic case, indeed, is the Christian settlement of the most favoured landscapes of the Iberian peninsula, the *huertas* of the river-mouth plains of the south-east, an unusually promising ecological niche which compares well with others, such as the plains of Sybaris, Siris or Campania. A recent study describes the allocation by Christian rulers of six thousand hectares to favoured recipients, in large or small lots; and if some of the recipients were the Muslims who had already been living there, the *donadio* allotment system dispossessed many Muslims in areas which had been reserved to them by treaty (Menjot 1995, esp.162). Allotment is a complex political language in which statements are made about the relative rights of many different groups.

Allotted landscapes are only the most developed case of the general tendency for overseas settlement to be accompanied by dramatic interventions in the agrosystem (for the case of Medieval and early modern Crete, see Triantafyllidou-Baladié 1981). Some features are celebrated, especially the development, against the usual dictates of prudence, and often against environmental sustainability, of monocultures; powerful outsiders can compel producers to take risks, and are short-termist by nature; the profits of monocultures outweigh the dangers. The exportation of the fruits of such enterprises helps establish the importance and shape the economic behaviour of certain key commodities (such as wine, oil and bread-wheat, cf. Horden and Purcell 2000: 209-20).

Viticulture is the most famous of such strategies, as conspicuous in the ancient as in the Medieval Mediterranean, and spectacularly combined with the landscape of allotment in the territory of cities such as Chersonesos Taurike (Saprykin 1994). Also from the Crimea comes clear palaeobotanical evidence that the wheat-species which the settlers of the coastal cities and the neighbouring peoples developed so successfully as a commodity was not indigenous but brought from the Aegean by the first settlers, cultivated and commercialized anew in the new context.[9] Sophisticated systems used for the collection and storage of cereal crops are attested by the distinctive silos of the retroterra of overseas settlements in Spain (Adroher et al. 1993). The coastal lowlands came to form a cerealicultural *koine* which commanded surpluses in Sicily and South Italy at the level of what Gelon could offer to the Greeks in 480 or the Romans receive in years of shortage in the early fifth century. Already in the *Odyssey* (6, 8) an alien land such as Scherie is characterized as being 'away from the eaters of cereals'. But animal husbandry also formed part of the agrosystem, and here too scientific analysis of animal remains suggests that selective breeding in antiquity produced animals of greater size and yield than in neighbouring communities (or again in Medieval contexts before the eighteenth century: Kron 2002). Specialized technology was characteristic of the imposed agrosystem: it was costly, and justified only by the pursuit of high returns. The presses used for wine and oil, or the equipment deployed in the most famous colonial monoculture of all, the sugar-cane of the late Medieval Mediterranean, are obvious examples: but the sophisticated techniques required for formal land-division, and the notarial infrastructure required to maintain such a regime, should be mentioned alongside the hardware.

More important is a further variable: labour. Labour-regimes are a part of the system specially open to manipulation. Environments away from home offer some distinctive possibilities. Traditional labour-relations, tied to a landscape inhabited over some generations, can be altered in a new setting. The mobility entailed by the displacement opens the new society to further settlers who can contribute to labour needs. But, above all, the successful violence implied by the maintenance of an overseas settlement in a new location very often results in relations of dependence and compulsion with local sources of labour, on a scale leading up to chattel slavery. The process of acquisition may not stop with the provision of what the settlement itself needs, but can make possible mobilization of labour for disposal elsewhere, through slave-dealing.

In all these respects the landscape of opportunistic production needs outlets, gateways for interaction with the wider world, through which its surpluses can be distributed, and the people on whose mobility it variously depends come and go. This brings us to the other great common denominator: the Mediterranean itself. The long coastlines and archipelagos provide a perfect medium for redistribution between microregional environments. The range of modalities of redistribution, as well as the scale, becomes vastly greater because of seaborne transportation (not forgetting the role of rivers too). And since redistribution is part of the agrosystem, this too is subject to the interventions of disposing power, an instrument of domination.

Inter-regional contacts at many periods of Mediterranean history have been mapped by the archaeological documentation of widespread and sometimes massive movements of small artefacts, above all pottery, including material such as transport-amphorae which is diagnostic of the movement of other commodities. Such movements might in theory be outside the calculus of domination, all parties to the exchange being equipollent. More usually, these too reflect gradients of economic and political power. The archaeological record maps patterns in these movements, which relate to some extent to the literary and documentary record of centres of redistribution: the *emporia* of the Greek world, as they are beginning to appear as the result of outstanding recent work, are a classic case.[10] The institutions of the *emporion*, and especially the exactions that were made there on the movements of people and materials, help to identify a network of harbours, gateway-settlements, centres of exchange, subject to intensification, the coherence of which is discernible in the regularities of the practice of exaction (Purcell 2005).

Seaborne redistribution enables particularly fluid labour management/deployment – the slavery-piracy nexus. Its speed and the diversity of markets also make cash-crop specialization less risky. It is thus an agrarian strategy. There is no sensible way to separate primary production and the movement of goods and staples – whether domestically or abroad, the two are closely intertwined. The *emporion*, then, the commercial outlet, far from being a different form of settlement, is integral to landscapes of allotment and opportunistic production. The dichotomy between land and trade as factors promoting overseas settlement, dear as it has been, especially to British scholarship, must be abandoned.[11] The archaeology of 'colonization' *is* the archaeology of redistribution, and like other aspects of the subject, this allows no sensible distinction between the practice of homeland and elsewhere.

Greek 'colonization' is therefore the continuation of agrarian domination by elite groups in new environments whose accessibility is one of their enticements. That accessibility is due to the distance-shrinking effect, by which, for all the miseries and dangers of seafaring, the sea brings within reach places which would normally be far beyond the horizon. It is almost too obvious to point out how many instances of the power relations which we are studying have been seaborne.[12] The sea creates a hugely enlarged theatre of opportunism, an expansive stage for domination, by comparison with continental space. It is enough of an obstacle to help in the creation of legitimating myth: it is a painful experience to reach Outremer. But the geography of 'overseas' is part of the rewards of the effort, like environmental advantages, labour-supply, or raw-materials, and should not be turned into a major principle for classifying these aggressive opportunisms, which take place in many other contexts too, if with less spectacular returns.

Frontiers and mobilities

The Mediterranean of connectivity, fragmentation and risk has margins, albeit fluid and difficult to define. It exhibits all around transitions to zones of different ecological conditions. Many different parameters might, of course, be used in identifying the transition zone. Formerly climatic or botanical patterns were popular. But primary risk-buffering strategies may offer a more promising way of mapping the ecotone.

The more specialized the social and economic superstructure, the clearer the transition away from the Mediterranean towards other ecologies. Thus allotted landscapes – developed intensively and ambitiously by force – delineate the ecotone quite sharply: this is one of the reasons why Greek overseas settlements can present such interesting examples of boundary and frontier institutions. But ease of communications is perhaps the key element in this ecological differentiation (Purcell 2004). If we imagine a cartography based on the degree and nature of connectivity experienced by localities at a given time, tracing lines of equal connectivity in the manner of contours, and so delineating 'connectivity gradients', it would map a universe of waterborne communications comprising the Mediterranean and extending along rivers and through lagoons as a coherent territory. Around it, a 'great frontier' might be evoked, dividing the world of the sea and the coastlands with their engagement with water-borne *cabotage* from the regions whose interconnections depend on haulage on two legs or four – the long-sought-after ecological boundary of the Mediterranean world.

But that would be both to exaggerate the uniformity and comprehensiveness of the connectivity, and to give a too static and definite impression of a 'boundary' which is in fact innumerable ecological transitions, local and transient, sharp and gentle. Importantly, it is also to risk what has been called 'Mediterranean exceptionalism', in at least implying that more is better, and that the communicative world of the maritime somehow has an advantage over terrestrial spaces. These too can have high connectivity, and for that reason the notion of a connectivity gradient needs to have a qualitative element. The movements of migrating peoples along mountain chains or across semi-arid spaces, the exchanges of traders travelling across the North European plain, in caravans in West Asia or across the Sahara, may be parts of connective networks – but they are ultimately different in kind.

Since 1967, when Ettore Lepore proposed the idea, there has been considerable interest in applying the ideas of 'frontier history' to the relations between Greeks and non-Greeks in the Mediterranean world of the ninth to fifth centuries BC.[13] Frontier history has had to develop denominators of a high level of generality to accommodate comparisons between societies (Burns 1989: 310), so that it should help formulate generalizations about colonialisms too. It was first formulated to describe the westward ambitions of European settlers in North America in the eighteenth and nineteenth centuries. The frontier in that context was a zone perceived as open to extensive colonial settlement for the purposes of primary production. The 'perceived as' is vital, since, as in North America, the openness has often been in the mind of the beholder. The beholder's mind is also the location of the other, and perhaps more fruitfully enduring, element in the agenda of frontier history, the effect on the culture of a settling community of the effort to extend settlements into a hostile frontier zone. The *protos heuretes* of frontier history, F.J. Turner (1861-1932), applied the idea, notoriously, to the self-fashioning of the United States (see especially Turner 1921). Lepore, however, largely reversed the Turner model – the frontier of the Hellenic was of crucial significance to cultural formation, but it was not an inevitable triumph for settlers over indigenes. It was a dialectic, involving both parties.[14]

This sense of the double direction in which frontier exchanges work is essential for understanding the ecotone too. The Mediterranean coastlands are a debatable zone, now oriented to the sea, now engaged more with the life of the land. They may be a channel through which enterprises, opportunisms and aggressions are directed from the sea into a given interior; or they may be the springboard through which people whose base has been the interior 'become maritime' and embark on the pursuit, peaceful or not, of the possibilities offered by maritime communications. This reversibility is a key element in what is distinctive about the Mediterranean as an ecological space. In the context of the Maghreb, it has been usefully labelled *recursivity* by Brent Shaw (2004).[15] Like Mediterranean islands, the seaboard niches most open to recursive re-occupation become centres of adaptation, and the flexibility of their societies promotes innovation and makes them influential on others.

Ecological frontiers, then, are also defined by the gateways where they are breached as much as, if not more than, by any linear impediments. The nature of the gateways – more varied than, though not unlike, the ports-of-trade of Polanyian analysis – is therefore of crucial historical importance. It is vital to discover who controlled them and how, who moved through them and how.

The primary consequence of the distinctive Mediterranean opportunity of redistribution is human mobility, which has different patterns in the ecological zones of the sea, the frontier, and the interiors.[16] There are specialists in redistribution, such as the *caboteur*, or the travelling craftsman. More significant for this chapter is the adaptive movement of the primary producer and above all the relocation of groups of producers and consumers in different microregional niches. The 'adaptive movement of the producer', though, is another misleadingly bland phrase. Aggressive opportunism involving pre-emptive seizure of others' resources and the forcible occupation of their environments comes under this heading: and such relocations are more often executed by the powerful than spontaneous emigrations by families under environmental pressure. This movement, in other words, is the building block of colonization, decolonization and recolonization, the art of relocating the people which Talleyrand saw as quintessentially imperial (see the epigraph to this chapter). Nonetheless, domestic survival strategy is echoed in the language of Mediterranean colonization: risk-avoidance through extending the family underlies that rhetoric which first gave us the metaphor of mother- and daughter-cities (Wilson 1997: 199). In antiquity, the domain of the colonial is the backyard of the extended family. This background of response to normal risk explains why Mediterranean colonization is so often accompanied by an exculpatory rhetoric of need and *force majeure*, demographic necessity or 'land-hunger'.

Seeing this, Adam Smith described Greek colonies as emancipated children. And it has sometimes been maintained that their relative independence rules out considering ancient aggressive settlements as colonial.[17] The boundary between public and private initiative in ancient settlements is, however, usually too porous for this insistence to be reasonable. What is more, we are clearly in that thought-world in which the empire is the macrocosm of the small-holding, and the decisions of kings about estate-management are those of the householder writ large. Mobile labour and its management is something that the primary producer and the emperor alike understood. A single scale linked decisions about the tasks of the children of the house and the forced resettlement of whole populations.[18] There are three tiers of mobility: to move in order to diversify or to redistribute; to be moved for those purposes; to move in order to see to the moving of people for those purposes. A further bridge between the levels in Mediterranean colonization is the mobility of the last kind, in which members of the elites and their immediate dependents move. 'Aristocratic diasporas' are well-known in Medieval Mediterranean contexts, such as the Crusading states (Bartlett 1989), and may be more relevant to the Classical Mediterranean than is usually thought.

This mobility, then, in which communities resemble the opportunistic family, seeks the larger opportunities and wider landscape in which to extend the strategies which conduce to survival. Just as the enhancement of the family's portfolio may take advantage of weaker neighbours, so the larger mobility also has frequently taken the form of successful aggression. But there is a particular set of opportunities for open-ended extension of the landscapes under control, and that is generated by the ecological abutment, the Mediterranean frontier, that we have already defined – indeed, this is one of the ways in which the ecological transition-zone most resembles the subject-matter of 'frontier-history' as it is usually conceived (Bartlett 1989: 31-2, cf. 43). That 'open-endedness' ultimately derives from the advantage afforded by the differences in organization and behaviour which in turn result from the different regimes of connectivity. One mainly pastoral people contending with another, one coastal polity based on a carefully divided landscape competing with its similar neighbour, reach stalemate quite quickly. Across the divide, the opportunities are much greater, whence – recursively, as we must again insist – the extension of seaborne colonialism toward the interior or the takeover of the resources of the coast and the world of the sea by communities from inland, 'becoming maritime', in the Greek phrase (Bresson 1993; Prontera 1996).

Just as colonial landscapes may be 'non-contiguous conquest lordships' of aristocratic diasporas (for the term Bartlett 1989: 40, on Ireland), so the object of colonization can be the web of connectivity itself rather than the productive terrains. And a relatively few people on the move can give the impression of vast demographic possibilities. A ditty from late Medieval Genoa runs:

e tanti son le Zenoexi
e per lo mondo so distexi
che unde li van e stan
un'altra Zenoa ge fan.

Racine 1995: 149

(the Genoese so numerous are,
and scattered through the world so far,
that wheresoe'r they chance to go or
stay, they make a new Genoa.)

But for Genoa, as for Miletos of the hundred overseas settlements in the sixth century BC, this is demographic illusionism. The genealogical background of the individuals involved in the complex negotiations of Mediterranean colonialism is the least interesting feature of their history. We do not need the humid vocabulary of swamping, drowning, melting and absorption.[19] It is the movements which count.

The 'most resettled land known': the example of South Italy

It may be useful to exemplify these wide-ranging observations in a particular chronological and geographical context. The southern part of the Italian peninsula in the first millennium BC lends itself to analysis of this kind. The environmental approaches of the last generation which did so much to make *Corrupting Sea* possible have also influenced archaeologists working here. Their insights can be combined with the interest in frontier history to illuminate the zone of contacts, confrontations and exchanges between Greek-speakers and others.

First, these are characteristic Mediterranean landscapes, in which study of human occupation must take account of extreme fragmentation by geology, hydrology, relief and climate.[20] There is easy access from the sea, but the mountainous interior entails a marked connectivity gradient (though the summits of the mountains, at least in summer, represent another kind of relatively easy – if specialized – communication along certain highly constrained routes). The upland and lowland zones have agrosystems which are often complementary, but which may readily be distinguished. The importance of portals between the two is particularly clear.[21]

One prominent feature of this region is the formation of local foci of super-production, niches in which intensification, specialization and experiment might be carried out because good communications by sea enabled effective redistribution. A reputation for wonderful fertility (eloquently called by the same name as aristocratic all-round excellence, *arete*, in the later tradition) was attached to certain well-drained and well-watered lowlands near the sea.[22] The territory of Siris had such a reputation by the middle of the seventh century (Archilochos 18; Athenaios 12, 253 c-e); that of Sybaris rapidly followed suit. The lowlands of Campania in the hinterland, in a broad sense, of Cumae (and especially the zone which the Romans were to know as the *ager Campanus*) are less celebrated in the Greek literary tradition, but were certainly highly productive by the second half of the sixth century. It is relevant, however, that Archilochos saw Siris as only one (admittedly preferable) possible opportunity: he contrasted lovely Siris with Thasos, for which 'all the filth of the Panhellenes' was headed, as part of the miserable but lucrative life of the sea (fragments 53-4). Thasos was of course only less developed, not less productive, as later generations saw, reading with puzzlement Archilochos' railing against the 'donkey's backbone' of Thasos, covered in wild forest. That island stands for the other part of the opportunity of the interface, a gateway to *peraiai* and interiors rich in exchangeable produce which you don't have to grow yourself.[23] And these opportunities too were naturally available through the gateways of the Italian peninsula. The establishment of cash-crop production in the landscape of Hellenic overseas settlement is one of the more radical dislocations in Mediterranean agrarian history.

Interaction, gateway-functions, points of cultural transition, of the sort already mentioned, are easy to document: Eboli in the Picentine plain or Pomarico Vecchio on the edge of the chora of Metapontion may serve as examples.[24] Sometimes the point of transition was sanctified through the establishment of a sanctuary. The zones in which these transition-points are located have been modelled as frontiers between the outsiders of Greek colonization and the indigenous societies. But the geography and social history of sanctuaries reveal a more complicated picture (Genovese 1999, with review in Carter 2001).

Here we can only mention a small selection of examples.[25] Incoronata and Francavilla Maritima, in the territories of Metapontion and Sybaris respectively, are especially important, because they have been examined in detail, and specifically because any ethnic allegiance is profoundly ambiguous.[26] It is clear that it will never be possible sensibly to classify the sanctuary at Francavilla as Greek or indigenous (see recently Papadopoulos 2003, 8-9). Next door to Metapontion, Siris was different again. At S. Maria d'Anglona is an Italic site whose inhabitants used it as a base for exploiting the terraces which slope down toward the coast. They are culturally different from other indigenous people immediately inland, such as those of Armento. This centre, like Incoronata, already sat on the frontier between the polities of the interior and the world of Mediterranean redistribution before the establishment of city-structures by the Greeks.[27] The difficulty for the researcher lies in the rapidity of change and the mutability of the divides in space. Incoronata demonstrates how rapidly communities whose members were not on the whole from outside the region might adopt aspects of the material culture of elsewhere.[28]

In this case too the settlement did not long survive the reorganization of the territory around the new centre of Siris. But, despite attempts to save something of a colonial interpretation of sites such as these, through invoking theories of hybridization or creolization, it is clear that the discourse of ethnicity is fundamentally unhelpful in analysing these data.[29] This is less the *schéma classique*, by which a dynamic Greek settlement succeeds an involuted indigenous one, than the replacement of one group exploiting the interface between interior and seaboard by another: recursivity. Here, as in so many cases, the world of the eighth and seventh centuries begins to look more and more like that of the fourth and third. The modalities of state-formation and dissolution in relation to the great Mediterranean frontier can and should be examined in a comparative perspective which relates those two periods. And that perspective must concern above all the management of the environment in relation to the world of the maritime.

In Southern Italy it is now clear, as we should always have expected *a priori*, that both the aliens, from overseas and from over land, participated throughout the Archaic period on both sides of the frontier, in both macroecological systems, and in both kinds of mobility (e.g. Greco 1999; La Torre 1991-2). The Greeks associated these places with the wealth that brought luxury: but – crucially – they modelled this as something learned by settlers from their neighbours (Nenci 1983). Above all, the milieux of the terrestrial world were not old stable societies; they too were able to respond quickly to new conditions and to participate in new economic and political frameworks.[30] They adopted and adapted elements from new arrivals in the coastlands, including Greek modes of social organization, the *oikos*, the *polis*, the *koinon*. At the same time, they made use of social relations of production (for example in the pastoral sphere) that were their own (thus Lepore 1990: 342). In Messapia, and no doubt elsewhere, we find 'Grecs insérés dans la société indigène et son système de production' (Lamboley 1996: 470). Here too, somewhat later, the expansion of agriculture into apparently unreclaimed zones at elite initiative is to be found.[31] The conditions of the interface between the maritime and interior worlds had a similarity which transcended local variations of culture, society or environment. The resemblances catalysed the process by which those involved in the interface came to regard themselves and those with whom they dealt as having something in common with others in analogous positions. The shared experience of the interface thus helped create the mirrorings through which both Greek and Italic cultures acquired self-consciousness and identity.[32] Not the least of the manifestations of potential difference was the formation and regularizing of ideas of territory on the Greek side of the divide, in part no doubt shaped by the experience of the lot and the developing notion of property, as by the expanding vocabulary of the *apoikia* and its story.[33] But this 'territorialization' was both a persuasive strategy, imposing what was in some respects only an apparent order in a chaotic and unstable world, and one which could be readily imitated.

The wandering artisan is a literary figure, but known more frequently through the product of his craft, as it can be seen at centres such as Poggio Montano in Lucania, or Murlo, deep in the interior of Italy, where the cultural symbols of a different world are prized and accommodated, but in which the expertise to produce them is not domesticated.[34] These broad types, then, track and display the transitional zones between one *koine* and another. The inland zone is not devoid of communications, but they are different from those of the maritime world.[35]

This imbrication of communities shaped the social and cultural geography of 'Megale Hellas' and neighbouring areas. But it cannot be understood without reference to the interface where ecological systems met. It was patterned by exchanges between worlds with access to the sea and worlds with access to the mountains, worlds with olive-trees and worlds with mountain pastures, worlds with allotted land and storage-facilities and worlds without, communities with a shortage of labour and ones with a surplus.[36] Centres, gateways, conduits between these worlds took on an especial importance. In the case of South Italy, the fact that some were managed by Hellenes and some by non-Hellenes is of the highest importance in understanding the patterns of movement of materials and people.[37] 'Colonization' in other words, was indeed practised by some Hellenes in South Italy; but it was also practised by many other peoples too, and it is more helpful for the historian to conjoin the elites whose power rested on this practice than to separate the ethnicities of those whose labour they controlled.[38]

The complex federal-colonial-imperial hegemonies which were built on these social relations in Magna Graecia fit well into the spectrum of disposing power, from the smallholder to the emperor, which was evoked earlier. The portfolios of the diverse hegemonies, of which the assets of the *populus Romanus*, and the *patrimonium* of the Emperor in late Republican and Imperial Rome are the ultimate example, are precociously visible here (see recently Bugno 1999, esp. 7-36 and Greco 2003, for the central case of Sybaris).

The boundary between the interior and the maritime is by no means fixed. The remoteness of Carlo Levi's 'Gagliano' in its benighted landscape of exile has become an icon of the mezzogiorno. But the terrestrial and hopelessly remote Aliano, with the same arrangement of hills, valleys and plains, when it was the *retroterra* of Siris, was close to the domain of the maritime, a participant in the ecological zone of the coastlands and their cultural and economic life. *Cristo si e fermato a Eboli* in those days perhaps, but *Demetra non si e fermata a Siri*. But, as we saw above, recursivity occurs: across the same zones in which overseas settlers had been extending their interests into the interior, communities with little or no connection with the overseas world extended their own range of interests into the coastal plains and river valleys where the foreign settlements had taken place.

The history of the gradient must be considered in the longer term. Even if no continuity can be established between the seaborne movements of the Bronze Age and those of the eighth century, the former remind us that the difference of the world of the sea was already there to be felt; and the story of the difficult interfaces between the mountain peoples and the coastlands in the age of Lucanian and Samnite ethnogenesis must be understood alongside its precursors. The aggressive occupation of the interiors by mobile communities whose milieu was the world of the mountains was as oppressive to those who experienced it as the arrival of seaborne outsiders. We need, moreover, an approach which enables us to compare the arrival of the Sabellian peoples to the southwards drive of the Lombards, as much as one which permits the collocation of the Greek *mainmise* on the coastlands with the seaborne interventions of Arabs and Normans.

The recursive competition for these privileged niches has made the history of the most favoured locations discontinuous and troubled. The colonization and de-colonization of Mediterranean islands is a particularly overheated case.[39] But some mainland coastal plains have experienced as disrupted a settlement-history. Campania is a case in point – the sequence of possessors of the Campanian plain was a *topos* already in the early Roman Empire.[40] One author even makes this a feature of Italian history in general, asserting that Italy is the most resettled land of any known, and that it owes to this the fact that at one time it had 1,197 cities (Aelian, *Var. Hist.* 9, 16). The idea is related to other claims for the accessibility of Italy and ease of communications within the peninsula, and, above all, the buoyancy of Italian demography (these last two as early as the third century BC).[41]

This demographic felicity was most visible to Greek observers in the availability of young men for military service or as mercenary soldiers in the western Mediterranean from the fifth century BC until the second.[42] In both cases the underlying process is the contestation of the resources of the ecological meeting-zone. The outcomes were of course extremely varied. The warriors might establish their own communities in favoured lowland locations, going on through piracy and trade to become participants in the world of the sea. Or they might help to win for existing coastal polities firmer dominion over the world of the interior. Both war and mercenary-service constituted forms of the transfer of resources between maritime and interior domains. We may speculate, indeed, as to whether the prosperity and procreativity of the mountainous interiors was the product of the success of such economic relations. That is an effect famous in the history of demography and first observed in the relations between Switzerland and its neighbours from the early modern period (Viazzo 1989; Bintliff 1996).

But the situation may be best pictured through a comparison. In describing the frontier constituted by the reconquest of Valencia in 1228-45, Robert Burns details how outsider settlement works in the highly fragmented Mediterranean environment, of which the south-east Spanish *huertas* and their hinterlands are such a prime example:

> ... there were as many frontiers for the settler as there were contexts. The variables diversifying the incoming population combined with the variables of the land itself in a complex dance.
>
> Burns 1989: 320-1

In this framework, we can locate aggressive exchanges across the connectivity gradient among other possible modalities: we gain a background against which to set 'hot frontiers', militarization, and the 'warlike', which will help us to understand the aggressions both of the new settlements of the outsiders and of their neighbours.[43] The variety of transitions must include confrontations which were overwhelmingly hostile, such as that between Taranto and the Messapians.

For aggression was a real and important part of the picture. These were societies in violent flux. Thucydides' Alcibiades' description of Sicily, 'the cities, with their crowds of diverse origin, abound in manpower, and readily undergo major shifts of entitlement to citizenship and recruitments of new citizens' (6, 7, 2) is apposite. The elite systems in both Italic and Greek communities proved vulnerable to pressures, as Oenotrians gave way to Lucanians, and Greek Poseidonia or Cumae and Etruscan Capua changed their character, in a sequence which has been seen to include also the attack on Rome by the Gauls in the early fourth century (Torelli 1996: 129).

The complex social realities revealed by archaeology have made it hard, then, to make cultural or – still more – ethnic allegiance a main element in historical analysis in Southern Italy of the early Iron Age.[44] It can be replaced by the degree and nature of involvement with the maritime. It has long been clear that the maritime infrastructure was one of the principal defining features of the world of the *apoikia* and the *emporion*. If there were common frontier-like societies in this world, it was because the sea provided an easy medium of communication.[45] But we can now take the crucial step of recognizing recursivity across the terrestrial-maritime gradient, and study the engagement with the maritime of communities where the Greeks came to found their new settlements.[46] Thus it can be claimed that the character of Messapian society is shaped by the maritime system and its interactions with the coast and inland (Semeraro 1997: 403-12). The fact has become clearer with new understanding of the nature of maritime networks themselves (ibid.: 409, cf. Horden and Purcell 2000: ch. 5). The new settlements founded to control and exploit the coastlands, which we have already noted, enrich the picture: in the case of Kale Akte in Sicily, the Sicilian leader Douketios founded a city which was to all intents and purposes an *apoikia*. There was no reason why Greeks or Phoenicians should have a monopoly of redistributing the product of intensifying production in these promising environmental niches; or of controlling the sea from their new coastal settlements. Other people than the Athenians could 'become maritime'.[47]

It is a fascinating, and in many ways a disturbing, picture. But it is one in which it is very hard to find a useful place for the traditional agendas of the history of 'colonization'.

Conclusion: problems of focus

The quest for common denominators such as ecology can appear unfocussed by comparison with controversies over events or institutional particularities (thus Lombardo 1999, 746-7). But ultimately it is only in the pursuit of more general comparison that relatively short-term episodes and chronologically specific modes of behaviour will make sense.

This may be illustrated with a vignette from a vigorous contemporary debate. Cash-crop production in colonial contexts in the late Medieval Mediterranean has been seen as an instructive precursor of Atlantic colonialism.[48] Sugar production in Lusignan Cyprus has long been exhibit A (Ouerfelli 2002). The monoculture of sugar-cane and the arrangements of organized transportation by which states such as Venice convoyed its produce to their marketplaces and policed its marketing are a signal instance of the specialized manipulation of Mediterranean landscapes in a context of political domination (Stöckly 1995). But we need to be sure which aspects of the Mediterranean and Atlantic cases we are comparing. The institution of economically-productive chattel-slavery, because of its importance in the Atlantic economy, has had a prominent place in the debate. Thus, in a polemic against some of those who have proposed the Mediterranean-Atlantic comparison, M.-L. Von Wartburg (1995: 130-1) has recently insisted that the evidence for the use of slaves in Cypriot sugar-monoculture is bitty and unreliable (it does exist). Slaves were used, but for other agricultural labour; while much labour in Cyprus was provided not by chattel-slaves but by serfs, the *paroikoi*, who are the pre-Latin inhabitants of the island. This is a classic problem of historical focus. Cypriote sugar can only be understood as part of a complete agro-system, and one in the sense of *Corrupting Sea*, of which the regime of connectivity is part. Unfree labour of every kind needs to be considered as part of that agrosystem. Only then will we be in a position to assess how useful comparison may be with the labour-regimes of commercial agrosystems developed by Mediterranean people in other regions. Elevating one bit of the picture to talismanic status is unhelpful. We are not *constrained* to focus only on the chattel-slaves and omit the *paroikoi*.

Yet this unhelpful selectivity has been normal in the historiography of the Greek *apoikia*. It derives in two ways from the scraps of ancient literature which bear on the subject. First, only very recently have these been intelligently interpreted against the intellectual history of the time. The poets and historians are at their most useful in giving us a view of Greek *mentalités*; but without the wider framework which *histoire des mentalités* enjoins, the individual elements in the narratives of foundation and expansion or decline make little sense.[49] Within the intellectual horizons, and as part of such narratives, certain structures and formations have a special position, which is often of the highest interest: but they do not necessarily deserve the same emphasis in our retellings or interpretations. For the ancient world, despite the invaluable insights of the literary and documentary material, it is ultimately only the archaeological record which makes explanatory overviews of economic and social questions possible.

City-history is the most conspicuous example. City-foundation in antiquity, *ktisis*, is prominent in accounts of 'colonization'. But it has been taken in a very limited and partial way. *Ktisis* certainly deserves a starring role in any history of domination. It was an exceedingly intrusive and disruptive intervention in the social and economic landscape; and it was common. Aelian, in the passage we have cited, was right to link the density of city-foundation with the appeal of a certain set of landscapes to an inherently mobile population. Because urban nucleus and *chora* were inseparable, urbanization always meant some kind of upheaval of rights and opportunities in the productive landscape. Redistribution of land, *ges anadasmos*, and the deliberate, often forced, gathering of population for new cities, *synoikismos*, are only high-profile manifestations of the wrenching innovation that went with all urbanization. Change in settlement pattern was inseparable from contestation of land. City-building may have been in certain senses civilizing, but it certainly wasn't cosy.

Ancient representations of what we label 'colonial', therefore, classified it in unexpected ways. In late Antique Antioch, the orator Libanius praised Seleucus Nicator, founder of the Hellenistic kingdom of Syria, for far exceeding, in his multiple city-foundations, the achievements of Athens and Miletos (Libanius, *Orat.* 11, 101). We should be wrong to dismiss as mere rhetoric this juxtaposition of an Archaic *apoikia*-founder, a Classical thalassocratic hegemony, and the state-building of one of Alexander's successors. The comparison seems hard to make at least in part because historians have felt (for whatever reason) that the Greeks founding *apoikiai* are somehow 'we', whereas the Seleucids establishing all those Antiochs and Laodiceas, the Romans imposing their urban network on Italy, or the Emperors of the middle and late Empire dotting the east with *-opolis* cities, from Traianopolis to Justinianopolis, are 'they'. City-naming, from the Greek *apoikiai* onwards, each new name corresponding to an attempt, however half-hearted, at the transfer of rights, opportunities and assets from old to new beneficiaries, establishes a bleak and eloquent record. Antiquity itself may be periodized as the age of jolting re-organizations of nucleated communities, every city reinvented against the will and the interests of at least some of its inhabitants. But still the exploitation which went with urbanization was only one among many: as we have seen illustrated by emporic settlement. And the repertoire of exploitations applied similarly 'at home' and 'abroad'.

Cities are a prominent, but not an essential, element in the history of Mediterranean exploitation. Their social and cultural forms may of course have important effects on the working out of the processes of domination: allotted landscapes in the Greek world were linked with citizen ideology, the wealth won from specialized production was spent on the displays of city-politics, and so on. But these are contingent features. The producers of the Roman Sahel participated less in such a system, those of Lusignan Cyprus not at all. And the act of *ktisis*, the formal establishment of a city, does not need to be the moment of creation of the landscape of domination, merely a refinement of one. The by now well-known mismatch between the records of *ktisis* and the genesis of centres as we discern it archaeologically is perfectly natural, since the records of *ktisis* are an ingredient in a world of ideology and contested memory which often stands free of the historical realities (Purcell 2004). City-foundation, therefore, is a subset of the formation of landscapes of domination, diagnosing the existence of subjection and witnessing to its exacerbation, but not co-extensive with it.

That is a major advantage, as archaeology does more to establish the comparability of the organisms of Greek landscape organization with those of the polities alongside – a comparability which poses another problem for concepts of the 'colonial'. In antiquity cultural homogeneities united even those most distinguished by the construction of ethnicity.[50] The structures of domination, enforced acculturation and exploitative extraction were strongly developed on the vertical, intra-community, axis, so that all domination was habitually seen as the inevitable authority of the ethically superior, the *chrestoi*, the *boni*, the *honestiores*, and this despite the fact that elites regularly constructed dependent labour ethnically; while their own ethnicity was complex and problematic in ways quite different from those found among modern hegemonic states (Stoler 1989). And this was natural in a world where communities were routinely mobile – a world of mass-deportations, such as those which afflicted Aeginetans or Messenians; Phokaia-style self-displacements; mass enslavements; and 'tribal' movements. Subaltern populations and dominant groups alike were both intensely mobile. The study of the interactions between exploiter and exploited in 'colonial' contexts needs not only to re-instate the exploited, but also to get beyond an essentially ethnic mode of modelling the relationship. If that mode was sometimes used by people in antiquity, it was usually as a simplifying and legitimating strategy, and there is no reason for us to adopt it too.[51]

Both the social and cultural convergence of circum-Mediterranean peoples and the similarity of the Greeks themselves to those peoples are at least in part the product of common environmental givens. And it is here that a perspective from the Middle Ages, in which conventional assertions of the cultural superiority of the colonizer were always hollower and more vulnerable, can be a salutary addition to the historian's repertoire. Recognizing that competition for control of the zone where the maritime and the terrestrially-oriented ecological systems abut is recursive helps avoid privileging one party, and it also helps counter any tendency to Mediterranean exceptionalism.[52]

Against this more complex picture of contested dominations, the discourse of colonialism contains a simple master-narrative: there are two quite readily defined entities, colonizer and colonized; there is a phase of colonial onset, followed by the colonial period itself, during which complex social, cultural and political interactions occur; and these are seen through a phase of decolonization which rounds off the process. Whatever the merits of this narrative for understanding the last half-millennium, it is very hard to apply to the ancient world. All the elements are missing. Neither colonizer nor colonized had a group identity comparable to those of the last five hundred years: the cultural labels Greek and Roman are both problematic in themselves, but they patently referred to systems which were in rapid transition during the periods of 'colonial' encounter.[53] The 'colonized' likewise were societies in the most violent of changes, as we have seen in the case of Southern Italy. Seventh-century Sybarite: seventh-century Oenotrian::fifth-century Thurian: fifth-century Lucanian is an equivalence which does not work (cf. Lepore 2000: 69).

The long-term comparison of exploitative opportunistic settlement, in fact, shows how threadbare the traditional interpretations of Mediterranean overseas settlement have become. The concept of Greek 'colonization' itself is obsolete as a term of historical analysis.[54] It is hard to dissociate 'colonialism' as a heuristic category from a taxonomic mentality which is deservedly out of fashion. M.I. Finley's attempt (1976: 174) to pronounce on what was and was not colonization in world history, arguing that it must involve both settling people and the continuing dependency of the settlers, excluded Medieval Genoa, British India, most of the twentieth-century European colonies in sub-Saharan Africa – and the ancient Greek *apoikiai*! Finley's tone was combative, his claims about definition in historiography ambitious: 'I hold ... that for most of its history the term had a specific denotation ... encompassing specific, intrinsic elements that can be enumerated and examined over a range wide enough to take in, say, ancient Bologna or Narbonne and modern Australia or Mozambique' (1976: 170). How quickly historians' taste changes! The very project here seems to have less in common with modern historical discourse than with the formalism of nineteenth-century attempts to pigeonhole *comptoirs, colonies de commerce, colonies d'exploitation, colonies de plantation, colonies de peuplement* (Leroy-Beaulieu 1874; cf. Lepore 2000: 35). Finley himself (1976: 174) was conscious of the dangers of 'word-magic' – where fascination with the implications of a particular term impedes accurate analysis. But the piece is strongly redolent of what one might call 'concept-magic' – the sub-scientific belief that the historian's task is to impose on the past a single set of generally valid analytical categories that can, once correctly isolated and set out, be applied universally. No one would currently dream of undertaking a universal definition of colonization. By its nature, History itself is a process, a dialogue – or a soliloquy – in which, whatever truth-value different camps place on the raw data, all tend to agree that generalizations, like narratives, are representations rather than descriptions, and bound to be essentially provisional. Our views are of course shaped by previous descriptions and appropriations, even when we reject them.[55] In the seventeenth and eighteenth centuries, liberal, British interest in Greek colonization was distinguished from despotic, French and Spanish preoccupation with Roman imperialism (Pagden 1995: 127-8). In the nineteenth century it was precisely this spirit of scientific classification which patterned the European colonial project, especially in the Mediterranean (Nordman 1998; Purcell 1993). We need to understand a tradition which has shaped Mediterranean historiography, but not to adopt it.

The master-narrative of 'colonialism' in antiquity is a classic instance of a problem of historical focus: it derives from a myopic reading of ancient literature, a long-sighted failure to discern the patterns which archaeology revealed, and an astigmatic preoccupation with colonial locations outside the geographical frame of discussion. The simple story of foundation and survival is extremely artificial. The colonial onset is part of the world of self-legitimating political persuasion. The legitimating narratives of the foundations of Greek *apoikiai* have been read for decades astonishingly literally. There is a new sensibility to our readings of ancient texts about hegemony (Dougherty 1993a and b; Calame 1990), though the unpicking of the 'alibis, réfoulements et négations' (Lepore 2000: 53) could go much further. Above all, these stories do not provide very good representations of what was happening in Mediterranean coastlands in the first half of the first millennium. Nothing gives the game away more effectively in the case of the ancient Mediterranean than the weird notion of pre-colonization, palpably a desperate invention to obviate the mismatch between the literary and archaeological records, ever more apparent as late twentieth-century archaeology proceeded.[56]

But the most obvious departure from the modern colonial master-narrative is what a colonialist historian would call the failure of Greek colonization. From the very first, as we have seen, recursive competition gave peoples from the interior a stake in new forms of occupation of the coastlands, so that they even came to deploy the same organizational and conceptual instruments as their Greek neighbours. They came to threaten or to dominate communities of outsiders; they took to the sea and carried competition for redistribution to the coastlands from which the outside settlers had come. And, ultimately, it was a community of Italic indigenes that established an overarching hegemony over all the coastlands of the Mediterranean.[57] Nothing comparable has occurred in the master-narrative of modern colonization – yet.

Locating overseas settlement in a general account of oppressive power-relationships enables the historian to develop resistance to the glamour of colonization, as to Mediterranean exceptionalism. It might seem that the discipline of avoiding identification with the exploiter can be taken for granted, but scholars can still write (for instance) of medieval overseas domination 'ce grand mouvement d'expansion vers l'outre-mer, qui n'est qu'un des aspects de la dynamique acquise par l'Occident à partir du XIe siècle' (Balard and Ducellier 1995: 395). The maxim should be more widely adopted: avoid colonial discourse if you can't resist identifying with the colonizer! But as important, in many ways, is speaking of these processes without adopting the equally glamorized pose of the denouncer of colonial oppression. Which is not to say that the historian can or should avoid the political choices involved; but the political urgency of the subject has, in any case, moved on. Contemporary observers and historians alike are oriented precisely toward the undirected movements of economically and politically motivated emigrants, rather than the formal colonialisms of two generations ago. Historians must find ways of addressing anxieties and uncertainties about the nature and consequences of such social changes: a more urgent task than classifying the programmes of European imperialists and comparing not very similar events in antiquity.[58]

If we want a more detached perspective, then we need a change of focus that will enable the subset of exploitations which so appealed to our imperialist forebears and which retains its fascination for their post-imperialist epigoni to be subsumed in a wider account of domination.

Notes

1. This chapter is part of a trio of inter-related investigations arising from *Corrupting Sea*, alongside Purcell 2004 and 2005. The arguments derived from the book should naturally be credited to Peregrine Horden, too, and I am also grateful to him for his remarks on a draft of this chapter. He is, however, not responsible for any errors!

2. There was not room to discuss many of these 'superstructures' in the monograph, and their absence has been regretted by reviewers: see Horden and Purcell 2005.

3. Péberthe 1999: 132-4 has a good discussion of this 'management' of Mediterranean resources, with reference to the meaning of *nemesthai*. Purcell 2005 explores some other aspects.

4. Plutarch, *Instituta Laconica* = *Moralia* 239d-e.

5. See for instance Guy 1995; Salomon 1997. It is important to recall the similarity of Greek settlement practice within the Aegean, especially in Thrace: Graham 1964: chs 5-6; 1978; 1992; Isaac 1986; the impact of overseas experience on older Greek settlements, with Malkin 1994; and the diversity of Greeks involved in the movements.

6. Plutarch, *Moralia* 831f-832a. The location is likely to be Douketios' settlement at Kale Akte, on which see further below.

7. Krebs 1997, esp. 53 on the Tariverde agrotown, with its un-Greek appearance.

8. It is essential to understand the ambitions and aspirations of the settlers, and to recognize motifs of survival, necessity, desperation, and above all 'land-hunger' for the obfuscatory and self-legitimating smokescreens that they are. In Sicily too, over-production to yield a surplus for redistribution now seems to have begun very early: Fantasia 1993; De Angelis 2000, tentatively concluding that the carrying-capacity of Greek Sicily was at least double the likely needs of its inhabitants.

9. Pashkevich 2001. I owe this reference to Alfonso Moreno.

10. Bresson 2002 is a helpful starting-point; Wilson 1997; Bresson 1993.

11. For a stimulating attack on the older schematisms in the debate on the 'causes of colonization', Lepore 2000: 41-3. Neither *emporion* nor *apoikia* – even in their relatively well-defined Greek usages – should be rashly elevated to the status of a major category in historical analysis.

12. For the earliest settlements (1209-11) in Venetian Crete, immediately alongside the coastal fortress of Candia, see Bapt 1995.

13. Lepore 1970. The Taranto conference of 1997 is perhaps the *pièce de résistance* here: see especially Corcella 1999 on the history of the frontier in modern scholarship on antiquity. For 'frontier history' in a Roman context, see the experiment of Dyson 1985.

14. This was in fact a step similar to the development of Turner's ideas in other historical contexts: see the helpful and amusing summary of Burns 1989: 307-18 and especially 315.

15. Malkin 2002 uses the idea of 'middle ground' to explore this context; for the Middle Ground as a replacement for frontier history, see Berend 2002: xiv.

16. Horden and Purcell 2000: 383-91, with bibliography; this is a topic which we intend to treat more fully in Vol. II, *Liquid Continents*.

17. Thus Finley 1976; against, Greco 2003, emphasizing how different the *apoikia* was from Roman *coloniae* and – *a fortiori* – from more recent colonizations; Lepore 2000: 17-33.

18. For reflections of the strange world of apoikic mobility in Greek thought, García Quintela 2002. For Philip II of Macedon and the analogy between demographic policy and animal husbandry: Justin 8, 5-6; Horden and Purcell 2000: 248. On mass-displacement in the ancient world, see Sordi 1994 and 1995; in the Ottoman Empire, and especially its role in the formation of the cities, above all Istanbul, see Beldiceanu and Beldiceanu-Steinherr 1995.

19. A slightly different metaphor in Balard and Ducellier 1995: 396 'des noyaux de peuplement qui lentement s'éteignent ou se fondent dans la masse indigène'.

20. Pelosi (1991: 74) is among the scholars who have recently advanced pleas for microregional understanding of South Italian environmental archaeology. Cf. Bottini 1992: 11 'la storia della Magna Grecia e ... un mosaico di microstorie'.

21. Greco 1990: 48 'una capillare organizzazione di "gateway-communities" '. Torelli 1996: 130 speaks of 'dialettica ... tra zone più inospiti ed aree più prospere della penisola', with this distinction in mind. See Morgan 1999 on 'patchwork of small networks'.

22. The later account of Philoxenos' lot in Sicily is similar (above, n. 7). Produce: viticulture (Van Der Mersch 1996); cerealiculture (Osanna 1992). For competition over the lowlands and the river-valleys which led into the interior, see Lepore 1977.

23. For settlement in the Northern Aegean, see Graham 1978 and 1992.

24. On Eboli, Cinquantaquattro 1992, cf. Cipriani 1990; on Pomarico, Barra Bagnasco 1999.

25. La Torre 2002 on the Campora shrine at Medma is now a further very significant case, with important ideas about the Sybarite *chora*.

26. On Incoronata, Pelosi 1991; La Guardia 1992; Cavagnera 1995; for Francavilla, De La Genière 1994. Thirteen per cent of the pottery is storage amphorae: Stea 1999.

27. D'Ambrosio 1992. For recent developments: Bailo Modesti and Gastaldi 1999 on the now very substantial quantities of Greek material at Pontecagnano; Durando 1998, for a very revealing provenancing of Pithekoussai amphorae.

28. See also Cantarelli 1999 for the site of Ferrocinto in the Morano-Castrovillari area, a fertile, defensible, fortified unit which cannot be easily assigned to either Sybarite or indigenous culture.

29. Thus already Torelli 1996: 128.

30. Spadea 1996: 48-50 for the wide world represented by dedications at the Lacinion.

31. On the stoutly built farmstead at Pozzo Seccato, D'Andria 1999: 110-12.

32. Greco 2003: 29-31 for the 'invention' of concepts such as Italia and Magna Graecia in the ambit of Sybaris.

33. For mutual imitation by the settler communities, cf. Malkin 2002: 155. Bartlett 1989 shows how administrative technology, and especially charters, functioned as a new instrument of domination. There are obvious parallels with Greek writing: rapidly adapted and deployed by others. For different articulation of space in Italic territories, see Greco 1999, perhaps over-emphasizing the contrast between urban Hellenic and non-urban Italic modes.

34. Inland centres in which an elite which controlled important exchanges differentiated itself sharply from the neighbourhood: see Bottini and Setari 1996 for Serra di Vaglio; Piergrossi 2002 for Poggio Montano; MacIntosh Turfa and

Steinmeyer 2002 for Murlo; for the Iberian example of Cancho Roano, see Puytison-Lagarce 1995. See now Nijboer 1998. Parallels: Jacoby 1994; Comba 1984.

35. Where the territory of Tarquinia abuts the Silva Cimina, Poggio Montano, see Piergrossi 2002, cf. Rendeli 1993; see Cinquantaquattro 2000: 62 and 64 for the unexpected Daunian links of Archaic Abella.

36. See Guzzo 1999, 431-2, on complementarities of production. See Ampolo 1999 on *ephoria agora*.

37. For new settlements on the Tyrrhenian coasts set up by people from the interiors, in a classically recursive fashion, see Greco 2003: 32; La Torre 1999: 131-3. For emporic territories, as seen in many sanctuaries, see Carter 2001 and Genovese 1999. See Costamagna 1999 for links between *emporia* such as on the Metauros and particular inland settlements, in this case Castellace. There is a clear gradient between the gateway and the redistribution point, a clear ecological interface, even if in cases like this material culture is exchanged with great fluency and speed. De Polignac has posited a *modèle culturel* involving seafaring, trade and *territorialisation* in which the cult of Hera, derived from both Samian and Argive prototypes, alludes to both exchange and intermarriage: 1998: 29. For South Etruria, see Zifferaro 1995. On similar interdependence in Southern Gaul, see Bats 1992.

38. Note the formulation of Lamboley 1996: 468: 'la fondation de Tarente ne conditionne pas l'évolution des échanges entre Grecs et Messapiens, elle confirme simplement que la colonisation grecque s'inscrit dans un mouvement d'intensification des échanges entre le monde égéen et l'Occident', cf. Torelli 1977, 1993.

39. Broodbank 2000; Genoese/Venetian parallels in Koder 1998.

40. Pliny, *Hist. Nat.* 3, 60; Campania between land and sea, with Strabo 5, 4, 3 (242); shore-to-land perspectives, Malkin 2002: 154.

41. On Italy's harbours, see Strabo 6, 4, 1 (286); the strange pseudo-Aristotelian *On Wondrous Reports* speaks of the common effort of the peoples of Italy to maintain the coastal route which Herakles had established, and to guarantee the safety of travellers on it (85), and of the demographic resources of the peninsula (94).

42. Among an extensive bibliography, note Heurgon 1957; Tagliamonte 1994; Dench 1995; Papi 1996.

43. For the contrast between weapon-rich graves of Sala Consilina and those of Francavilla, see De La Genière 1994; for a similar point made with reference to Chalkidice, see Vokotopoulou 1994: 88; for another cultural boundary, see Virgilio 1987 (Caria).

44. Thus recently De La Genière 1995. The revolution began with the recognition that it was hard to produce sensible distinctions between Greek and Phoenician overseas settlement, cf. Niemeyer 1990.

45. Compare Burns 1989: 329 on deliberate replications of frontier experience.

46. Morgan 2001: 90 speaks of a study by Anne Keenlyside of the human remains of Phanagoria in the Cimmerian Bosporus which will investigate the long-term alternation of marine-based and land-based nutrition systems.

47. On this theme see Cristofani 1989, Jannot 1995 and De Simone 1996 for the Etruscans; cf. Prontera 1996; Colonna 1993: 58 for Rome's coastal ambitions; Erdkamp 1998: 298 for army supply and coastal 'magazines'. We may note that certain maritime adventures conducted by Greeks closely resembled these later transformations of formerly interior peoples: the Achaian settlements in South Italy are a case in point. Cf. Lombardo 1999: 54-5.

48. The related view that the Crusades can be seen in this light is associated especially with Verlinden 1995, 1970, 1954. This interesting theme cannot be developed here.

49. A useful recent example is García Quintela 2002.

50. Woolf 1997, esp. 341 and Van Dommelen 1997 make similar points.

51. Hence some difficulties with the chapter of Antonaccio, this volume. For a similar plea to 'eliminate the culture paradigm' in a Roman context, see Ellis 1998, following Hodder 1978. For telling remarks on status as opposed to ethnicity in conceptualizing power relationships in *apoikiai*, see Malkin 2002: 157.

52. On this, see in more detail Purcell 2004: 13-17.

53. The implications of this tendency for the age of Greek overseas settlement have been explored above all by Morgan 1999 and 2001.

54. Osborne 1998; Purcell 1997; for an attempt to find a way out of the difficulties, see Dominguez 2002; also the overview in Lyons and Papadopoulos (eds) 2002. See also Snodgrass, this volume and Terrenato, this volume.

55. Some recent investigations along these lines: De Angelis 1998, Torelli 1999, Ellis 1998.

56. On the history of the idea of pre-colonization, a response to the categorical assertion of Georges Vallet that all Greek material in the West is subsequent to colonization, see now Gras 1999: 9-10; and against the notion itself, already Lepore 2000: 28.

57. For a suggestive account of the role of salt in the development of Rome, see Giovannini 1985.

58. This interest is explicit in the Italian conference sponsored by the Accademia dei Lincei and published as *Il fenomeno coloniale*: see especially Godart 2003 on 'flussi migratori'. Alertness to language, as in the case of the 'swamping' vocabulary discussed above, is essential.

especially Kirk, Vandiver 1993, 1995 [illegible] argument cannot be developed here.

49. A useful [illegible] example [illegible] 1998.

50. Wolf 1997 [illegible] and van Dommelen 1997 [illegible] point.

51. The [illegible] with the chapter [illegible] this volume. For a [illegible] challenge [illegible] and Ellis 1998 [illegible] following [illegible] remarks [illegible] commonly in contemporary [illegible]

On [illegible] see [illegible] detail [illegible]

53. The implications of this [illegible] for the use of Greek [illegible] employed [illegible] and [illegible]

54. [illegible] 1997 [illegible] an attempt to [illegible] of the [illegible] 2000. [illegible] this volume [illegible]

55. [illegible] De Angelis 1998 [illegible] 1995.

56. [illegible] colonization [illegible] Valley [illegible] Greek material [illegible] Western [illegible] 1998 [illegible] already [illegible] 2000: 24.

57. For a suggestive account of [illegible] the development of [illegible] 1985.

58. This [illegible] is [illegible] especially [illegible] vocabulary [illegible]

Consolidated Bibliography

Abercrombie, N., Hill, S. and Turner, B. (1980) *The Dominant Ideology Thesis* (London).

Abulafia, D. (2002) 'Introduction', in Abulafia and Berend (2002) 1-34.

Abulafia, D. and Berend, N. (2002) *Medieval Frontiers: concepts and practices* (Aldershot).

Acuto, F. (1994) 'La organización del almacenaje estatal: La ocupación Inka en el sector norte del valle Calchaquí y sus alrededores.' Unpublished thesis, Facultad de Filosofía y Letras, Universidad de Buenos Aires.

Adroher, A.M. et al. (1993) 'El yacimiento de Mas Castellar de Pontós y el comercio del cereal ibérico en la zona de *Emporion* y *Rhode*', *Arch Esp Arq* 66, 31-70.

Alcock, S. (2000) 'Heroic myths, but not for our times', in Fentress (ed.) (2000) 221-6.

Alcock, S., D'Altroy, T., Morrison, K. and Sinopoli, C. (2001) *Empires* (Cambridge).

Allcroft, A.H. and Mason, W.F. (1890) *A History of Sicily 491-289 BC* (London).

Ampolo, C. (1999) 'La frontiera dei Greci come luogo del rapporto e dello scambio: frontiera e circolazione dei beni fino al V secolo a.C.', in *Confini e frontiera* (1999) 451-64.

Antonaccio, C. (1997) 'Urbanism at Archaic Morgantina', *Acta Hyperborea* 7, 167-93.

Antonaccio, C. (1999) '*Kypara*, a Sikel nymph?', *Zeitschrift für Papyrologie und Epigraphik* 126, 177-85.

Antonaccio, C. (2001) 'Colonization and Acculturation', in Malkin (ed.) (2001) 113-57.

Antonaccio, C. (2003) 'Hybridity and the cultures within Greek culture', in C. Dougherty and L. Kurke (eds) *The Cultures within Greek Culture: contact, conflict, collaboration* (Cambridge) 57-74.

Antonaccio, C. (2004) 'Siculo-geometric and the Sikels: identity and material culture in Eastern Sicily', in Lomas (ed.) (2004).

Archibald, Z. (1998) *The Odrysian Kingdom of Thrace: Orpheus Unmasked* (Oxford).

Asheri, D. (1999) 'Processi di "decolonizzazione" in Magna Grecia: il caso di Poseidonia Lucana', in *La colonisation grecque en Méditerranée occidentale*, 361-70.

Bailo Modesti, G. and Gastaldi, P. (eds) (1999) *Prima di Pithecusa: i piu antichi materiali greci del Golfo di Salerno*, exhibition catalogue (Pontecagnano).

Balard, M. and Ducellier, A. (1995) 'Conclusions', in Balard and Ducellier (eds) (1995) 395-6.

Balard, M. and Ducellier, A. (eds) (1995) *Coloniser au Moyen Âge: méthode d'expansion et techniques de domination en Méditerranée du 11e au 16e siècle* (Paris).

Bapt, J. (1995) 'Venise en Crete: revoltes et soumissions', in Balard and Ducellier (eds) (1995) 359-66.

Barletta, B. (2001) *The Origins of the Greek Architectural Orders* (Cambridge).

Barra Bagnasco, M. (1999) 'Contributo alla lettura dei sistemi insediativi della Basilicata: il caso di Pomarico Vecchio', in S. Quilici Gigli (ed.) *La forma della città e del territorio: esperienze metodologiche e risultati a confronto: atti dell'incontro di studio, S. Maria Capua Vetere, 27-28 novembre 1998* (Rome 1999) 119-30.

Bartlett, R. (1989) 'Colonial aristocracies of the high middle ages', in Bartlett and MacKay (eds) (1989) 23-47.

Bartlett, R. and MacKay, A. (eds) (1989) *Medieval Frontier Societies* (Oxford).

Bats, M. (1992) 'Marseille, les colonies massaliètes et les relais indigènes dans le trafic le long du litoral méditerranéen gaulois (VIe-Ier s. av. J.-C.)', in M. Bats (ed.) *Marseille grecque et la Gaule: actes du Colloque international d'histoire et d'archéologie et du Ve Congrès archéologique de Gaule méridionale (Marseille, 18-23 novembre 1990)* (Aix-en-Provence) 263-78.

Bauer, B. (1992) *The Development of the Inca State* (Austin).

Bauer, B. (1996) 'Legitimization of the state in Inca myth and ritual', *American Anthropologist* 98, 327-37.

Beldiceanu, N. and Beldiceanu-Steinherr, I. (1995) 'Colonisation et deportation dans l'état ottomane (XIVe – debut XVIe siècle)', in Balard and Ducellier (eds) (1995) 172-9 and 180-5.

Bell, J. (1992) 'On capturing agency in theories about prehistory', in J-C. Gardin and C. Peebles (eds) *Representations in Archaeology* (Bloomington) 30-55.

Bell, M. (1988) 'Excavations at Morgantina. Preliminary report XII', *AJA* 92, 313-42.

Bell, M. (2000) 'Morgantina e Camarina al congresso di Gela', in *Un ponte tra l'Italia e la Grecia. Atti del simposio in honore di Antonino di Vita* (Padua) 291-7.

Berend, N. (2002) 'Preface', in Abulafia and Berend (2002) x-xiv.

Bernal, M. (1987) *Black Athena: the Afroasiatic roots of Classical civilisation* (London).

Bernard, P. (1964) 'Céramiques de la première moitié du VIIe siècle a Thasos', *BCH* 88, 77-146.

Bettini, M. (1991) *Anthropology and Roman Culture: kinship, time, images of the soul. Ancient society and history* (Baltimore).

Bhabha, H.K. (1994) *The Location of Culture* (London).

Bintliff, J. (1996) 'The mountain peoples of ancient Greece: the relevance of world-systems theory and neo-Malthusianism to their development', in E. Olshausen and H. Sonnabend (eds) *Gebirgsland als Lebensraum (Stuttgarter Kolloquium zur Historischen Geographie des Altertums, 5, 1993)* (Amsterdam) 105-41.

Birkenhead, F.W.F.S., Earl of (1978) *Rudyard Kipling* (London).

Birmingham, J. (1990) 'The archaeology of colonizations: observations from *Terra Australis*', in Descoeudres (ed.) (1990) 635-48.

Blagg, T. and Millett, M. (1990) *The Early Roman Empire in the West* (Oxford).

Blakeway, A. (1932-3) 'Prolegomena to the study of Greek commerce with Italy, Sicily and France in the eighth and seventh centuries BC', *ABSA* 33, 170-208.

Blakeway, A. (1935) ' "Demaratus". A study in some aspects of the earliest Hellenisation of Latium and Etruria', *JRS* 25, 129-49.

Blegen, C.W., Palmer, H. and Young, R.S. (1964) *Corinth XIII. The North Cemetery* (Princeton).

Blinkenberg, C. (1926) *Fibules grecques et orientales* (Copenhagen).

Boardman, J. (1964, 2nd ed. 1972; 3rd enlarged ed. 1980; 4th enlarged ed. 1999) *The Greeks Overseas: their early colonies and trade* (London).
Boardman, J. (1994) 'Settlement for trade and land in North Africa: problems of identity', in Tsetskhladze and De Angelis (eds) (1994) 137-49.
Boardman, J. (2001) *The History of Greek Vases* (London).
Bottini, A. (1992) 'La Magna Grecia in epoca preromana', *Dd'A* 3, 10, 11-20.
Bottini, A. and Setari, E. (1996) 'Una metropolis della Lucania arcaica', *Ostraka* 5, 2, 205-14.
Bourdieu, P. and Wacquant, L. (1992) *An Invitation to Reflexive Sociology* (Cambridge).
Bradley. G. (2001) 'Colonial Identities in Roman Italy', Roman Archaeology Conference (Glasgow).
Brandt, R., and Slofstra, J. (eds) (1983) *Roman and Native in the Low Countries: spheres of interaction*, BAR International Series 184 (Oxford).
Bresson, A. (1993) 'Les cités grecques et leur *emporia*', in A. Bresson and P. Rouillard (eds) *L'Emporion* (Paris) 163-226.
Bresson, A. (2002) 'Quatre emporia antiques: Abul, La Picola, Elizavetoskoie, Naucratis', *REA* 104, 475-505.
Broodbank, C. (2000) *An Island Archaeology of the Early Cyclades* (Cambridge).
Brumfiel, E.M. (1992) 'Distinguished lecture in archaeology: breaking and entering the ecosystem – gender, class and faction steal the show', *American Anthropologist* 94, 551-67.
Brumfiel, E.M. (2001) 'Aztec hearts and minds: religion and the state in the Aztec empire', in Alcock et al. (eds) (2001) 283-310.
Bryce, J. (1914) *The Ancient Roman Empire and the British Empire in India* (London).
Bugno, M. (1999) *Da Sibari a Thurii: la fine di un impero* (Naples).
Burns, R.I. (1989) 'The significance of the frontier in the Middle Ages', in Bartlett and MacKay (eds) (1989) 307-30.
Buttrey, T. et al. (eds) (1989) *Morgantina Studies* II. *The Coins* (Princeton).
Calame, C. (1990) 'Narrating the foundation of a city: the symbolic birth of Cyrene', in L. Edmunds (ed.) *Approaches to Greek Myth* (Baltimore) 275-341.
Canfora, L. (1980) *Ideologie del classicismo* (Turin).
Cantarelli, F. (1999) 'intervento' in *Atti del XXXVII Convegno Internazionale di Studi sulla Magna Grecia, Confini e frontiera nella grecità d'Occidente* (Taranto) 429-31.
Carandini, A. (ed.) (1985a) *La romanizzazione dell'Etruria: il territorio di Vulci* (Milan).
Carandini, A. (1985b) 'Schiavitù antica e moderna a confronto', in A. Carandini (ed.) *Settefinestre*, vol. 1 (Modena) 187-206.
Carter, J.C. (1998) *The Chora of Metaponto: the necropoleis* (Austin).
Carter, J.C. (2001) 'Rural sanctuaries in Calabria' (review of Genovese 1999), *JRA* 14, 462-5.
Carter, J.C. (2004) 'The Greek Identity at Metaponto', in Lomas (ed.) (2004) 363-90.
Cartledge, P. (1985) 'Rebels and Sambos in Classical Greece: a comparative view', in P.A. Cartledge and F.D. Harvey (eds) *Crux: essays in Greek history presented to G.E.M. de Ste. Croix on his 75th birthday* (London) 16-46.
Cartledge, P. (1993) *The Greeks* (Oxford).
Cartledge, P. (1994) 'The Greeks and anthropology', *Anthropology Today* 10 (1994), 3-5.

Cartledge, P. (1998a) 'The economy (economies) of ancient Greece', *Dialogos: Hellenic Studies Review* 5, 4-24.

Cartledge, P. (1998b) 'Who were the Greeks?', in P. Cartledge (ed.) *The Cambridge Illustrated History of Ancient Greece* (Cambridge) 35-53.

Cataldi, G.N. and Cataldi, S. (1983) 'Strumenti e procedure nei rapporti tra greci e indigeni', in *Forme di contatto e processi di trasformazione nelle società antiche. Atti del convegno di Cortona (24-30 maggio 1981)* (Pisa) 588-604.

Cavagnera, L. (1995) 'Ceramica protocorinzia dall'Incoronata presso Metaponto', *MEFRA* 107, 869-936.

Ceserani, G. (1999) 'The Study of Magna Graecia: classical archaeology and nationalism since 1750'. Paper delivered at the annual meeting of the American Philological Association, Dallas, Texas, December 1999.

Champion, T. (ed.) (1989) *Centre and Periphery: comparative studies in archaeology* (London).

Christ, K., and Momigliano A. (eds) (1988) *L'Antichità nell'Ottocento in Italia e Germania* (Bologna).

Cieza de León, P. (1967 [1551]) *El Señorio de los Incas, Segunda Parte de la Crónica del Perú* (Lima).

Cieza de León, P. (1984 [1553]) *Crónica del Perú. Segunda Parte,* (ed.) Francesca Cantu (Lima).

Cinquantaquattro, T. (1992) 'Dinamiche insediative nell'agro Picentino dalla protostoria all'età ellenistica', *AION* 14 [1993], 245-58.

Cinquantaquattro, T. (2000) 'Abella, un insediamento della *mesogaia* campana, note di topografia', *AION* n.s. 7, 61-85.

Cipriani, M. (1990) 'Eboli preromana. I dati archeologici: analisi e proposte di lettura', in M. Tagliente (ed.) *Italici in Magna Grecia: lingua, insediamenti e strutture* (Venosa) 119-60.

Clark, J. and Parry, W. (1990) 'Craft specialization and cultural complexity', *Research in Economic Anthropology* Vol. 12 (Greenwich, CT) 289-346.

Cobo, B. (1892 [1653]) *Historia del Nuevo Mundo* (Seville).

Cobo, B. (1979 [1653]) *History of the Inca Empire,* trans. Roland Hamilton (Austin).

Collier, G., Rosaldo R., and Wirth J. (1982) *The Inca and Aztec States, 1400-1800: anthropology and history* (New York).

Collingham, E.M. (2001) *Imperial Bodies. The Physical Experience of the Raj, c. 1800-1947* (Cambridge).

Collingwood, R.G. (1956) *The Idea of History* (New York).

Colonna, G. (1993) 'Doni di Etruschi e di altri barbari occidentali nei santuari panellenici', in A. Mastrocinque (ed.) *I grandi santuari della Grecia e l'Occidente* (Trento) 43-67.

Comba, R. (1984) 'Emigrare nel medioevo. Aspetti economico-sociali della mobiltà geografica nei secoli XI-XVI', in R. Comba, G. Piccinni and G. Pinto (eds) *Strutture familiari, epidemie, migrazioni nell' Italia medievale* (Naples) 45-74.

Confini e frontiera nella grecità d'Occidente (*Atti del trentasettesimo convegno di studi sulla Magna Grecia, Taranto, 3-6 ottobre 1997*) (1999) (Taranto: Istituto per la storia e l'archeologia della Magna Grecia).

Conkey, M. (1999) 'An end note: reframing materiality for archaeology', in E. Chilton (ed.) *Material Meanings: critical approaches to the interpretation of material culture* (Salt Lake City).

Conrad, G.W. and Demarest A.A. (1984) *Religion and Empire: The dynamics of Aztec and Inka expansionism* (Cambridge).

Coombes, A. (1994) 'The recalcitrant object: culture contact and the question of hybridity', in F. Barker, P. Hulme and M. Iversen (eds) *Colonial Discourse / Postcolonial Theory* (Manchester / New York) 89-114.

Corcella, A. (1999) 'La frontiera nella storiografia del mondo antico', in *Confini e frontiera* (1999) 43-82.

Costamagna, L. (1999) 'intervento', in *Confini e frontiera* (1999) 424-7.

Costin, C.L. (1998) 'Housewives, chosen women, skilled men: cloth production and social identity in the late Prehispanic Andes', in C. Costin and R. Wright (eds) *Craft and Social Identity*, Archeological Papers of the American Anthropological Association, No. 8, 123-44.

Cowgill, G. (1988) 'Onward and upward with collapse', in N. Yoffee and G. Cowgill (eds) *The Collapse of Ancient States and Civilizations* (Tucson) 244-76.

Cowgill, G. (1993) 'Beyond criticizing New Archaeology', *American Anthropologist* 95, 551-73.

Cramb, J.A. (1915) *Origins and Destiny of Imperial Britain* (2nd ed.) (London).

Cristofani, M. (1989) *Gli Etruschi del mare* (Milan).

Cromer, E.B., Earl of (1910): *Ancient and Modern Imperialism* (London).

Cunliffe, B. (1988) *Greeks, Romans and Barbarians: spheres of interaction* (London).

D'Altroy, T.N. (1992) *Provincial Power in the Inka Empire* (Washington DC).

D'Altroy, T.N. (2001) 'A view of the plains from the mountains: Comments on Uruk by an Andeanist', in M. Rothman (ed.) *Uruk, Mesopotamia and its Neighbours: cross-cultural interactions in the era of state formation* (Santa Fe, NM) 445-75.

D'Altroy, T.N. (2002) *The Incas* (Oxford).

D'Altroy, T.N. and Earle, T. (1985) Staple finance, wealth finance, and storage in the Inka economy, *Current Anthropology* 26,187-206.

D'Altroy, T.N. and Hastorf C. (eds) (2001) *Empire and Domestic Economy* (New York).

D'Ambrosio, I. (1992) 'Tipologie insediative ed organizzazione territoriale nell'entroterra sirite tra VIII e VI sec. a. C. Indagini su Santa Maria d'Anglona e il suo comprensorio', *AION* 14 [1993] 259-75.

D'Andria, F. (1999) 'Ricerche recenti sugli insediamenti indigeni di Puglia e Basilicata', in S. Quilici Gigli (ed.) *La forma della città e del territorio* (Rome) 103-18.

Dalrymple, W. (2002) *White Mughals: love and betrayal in eighteenth-century India* (London).

Danov, Chr. (1990) 'Characteristics of the Greek Colonization in Thrace', in Descoeudres (ed.) (1990) 151-5.

De Angelis, F. (1994) 'The foundation of Selinous: overpopulation or opportunities?', in Tsetskhladze and De Angelis (eds) (1994) 87-110.

De Angelis, F. (1998) 'Ancient past, imperial present: the British Empire in T.J. Dunbabin's *The Western Greeks*', *Antiquity* 72, 539-49.

De Angelis, F. (2000) 'Estimating the agricultural base of Greek Sicily', *PBSR* 68, 111-48.

De la Genière, J. (1994) 'L'exemple de Francavilla Marittima. La nécropole de Macchiabbate, secteur de la Temperella', in De la Genière (ed.) (1994) 153-63.

De la Genière, J. (ed.) (1994) *Nécropoles et sociétés antiques: Grèce, Italie, Languedoc: actes du colloque international du Centre de recherches archéologiques de l'Université de Lille III, Lille, 2-3 décembre 1991* (Naples).

De la Genière, J. (1995) 'Les grecs et les autres. Quelques aspects de leurs relations en Italie du Sud à l'époque archaïque', in *Les Grecs et l'Occident* (1995) 29-40.

De Polignac, F. (1995) *Cults, Territory, and the Origins of the Greek City-state* (Chicago).

De Polignac, F. (1998) 'Navigations et fondations; Héra et les Eubéens de l'Égée à l'Occident', in M. Bats and B. D'Agostino (eds) *Euboica: l'Euboea e la presenza euboica in Calcidica in Occidente (Atti del convegno internazionale di Napoli, 13-16 novembre 1996)* (Naples: Collection du Centre Jean Bérard, 16) 23-9.

De Simone, C. (1996) *I Tirreni a Lemnos: evidenza linguistica e tradizioni storiche* (Florence).

DeMarrais, E. (1997) 'Materialization, ideology, and power: the development of centralized authority among the pre-Hispanic polities of the Valle Calchaquí, Argentina'. University Microfilms (Ann Arbor).

DeMarrais, E. (2001) 'The architecture and organization of Xauxa settlements',. in D'Altroy and Hastorf (eds) (2001) 115-54.

DeMarrais, E., Castillo, L.J. and Earle, T. (1996) 'Ideology, materialization, and power strategies', *Current Anthropology* 37, 15-85.

Dench, E. (1995) *From Barbarians to New Men: Greek, Roman, and modern perceptions of peoples from the central Apennines* (Oxford).

Descoeudres, J.-P. (ed.) (1990) *Greek Colonists and Native Populations: proceedings of the First Australian Congress of Classical Archaeology held in honour of emeritus professor A.D. Trendall, Sydney, 9-14 July 1985* (Oxford).

Desideri, P. (1991) 'La romanizzazione dell'impero', in *Storia di Roma*, vol. 2.2 (Turin) 577-626.

Dietler, M. (1995) 'The cup of Gyptis: rethinking the colonial encounter in Early-Iron-Age Western Europe and the relevance of world-systems models', *Journal of European Archaeology* 3.2, 89-111.

Dietler, M. (1999) 'Consumption, cultural frontiers, and identity: anthropological approaches to Greek colonial encounters', in *Confini e frontiera* (1999) 475-501.

Dinsmoor, W.B. (1927) *The Architecture of Ancient Greece* (London).

Dinsmoor, W.B. (1950) *The Architecture of Ancient Greece* (3rd ed.) (London).

Dissanayake, E. (1995) *Homo Aestheticus* (Seattle).

Dobres, M.A. and Robb, J. (2000) *Agency in Archaeology* (London).

Dominguez, A.J. (2002) 'Greeks in Iberia: colonialism without colonization', in Lyons and Papadopoulos (eds) (2002) 65-95.

Dougherty C. (1993a) *The Poetics of Colonization: from text to city in Archaic Greece* (Oxford, New York).

Dougherty, C. (1993b) 'It's murder to found a colony', in C. Dougherty and L. Kurke (eds), *Cultural Poetics in Archaic Greece* (Cambridge) 178-98.

Dunbabin, T.J. (1937) *Contributions to the History of Sicily and South Italy in the Seventh and Sixth Centuries BC*. Unpublished thesis, Bodleian Library Oxford MS Eng. Misc. d. 1229.

Dunbabin, T.J. (1948) *The Western Greeks* (Oxford).

Dunbabin, T.J. (ed.) (1962) *Perachora II* (Oxford).

Durando, F. (1998) 'Phoenician and local amphorae from Pithekoussai: archaeometrical tests', in R. Rolle, K. Schmidt and R.F. Docter (eds) *Archäologische Studien in Kontaktzonen der antiken Welt* (Göttingen) 389-400.

Dyson, S. (1985) *The Creation of the Roman Frontier* (Princeton).

Dyson, S. (ed) (1985) *Comparative Studies in the Archaeology of Colonialism*, BAR International Series 233 (Oxford).

Earle, T. (1997) *How Chiefs Come to Power* (Stanford).

Earle, T. et al. (1987) *Archaeological Field Research in the Upper Mantaro, Peru,*

1982-83: investigations of Inka expansion and exchange, UCLA Institute of Archaeology, Monograph XXVIII (Los Angeles).

Ellis, L. (1998) ' "Terra deserta": population, politics and the [re]colonization of Dacia', in S. Shennan (ed.) *Population and Demography* (= *World Archaeology* 30 (2)) 220-37.

Erdkamp, P. (1998) *Hunger and the Sword: warfare and food supply in Roman republican wars (264-30 BC)* (Amsterdam).

Erdkamp, P. (1999), 'Agriculture, underemployment and the cost of rural labour in the Roman world', *CQ* 49, 556-72.

Espinoza Soriano, W. (1987) *Los Incas: economía, sociedad y estado en el era de Tahuantinsuyo* (Cuzco).

Fabre, G. (1981) *Libertus: recherches sur les rapports patron-affranchi à la fin de la République romaine* (Rome, Paris).

Fantasia, U. (1993) 'Grano Siciliano in Grecia', *AnnScNormPisa* 23, 9-31.

Feinman, G. and Marcus, J. (1998) *Archaic States* (Santa Fe, NM).

Fentress, E. (ed.) (2000) 'Romanization and the city: creation, transformation, and failures', *JRA*, Supplementary Series No. 38.

Finley, M.I. (1973) *The Ancient Economy. Sather Classical Lectures. v. 43* (Berkeley).

Finley, M.I. (1975) *The Use and Abuse of History* (London).

Finley, M.I. (1976) 'Colonies: an attempt at typology', *Transactions of the Royal Historical Society* 26, 167-88.

Folz, R. (1953) *Idée d'Empire en Occident du Ve au XIVe Siècle* (Paris).

Foster, R.F. (1988) *Modern Ireland, 1600-1972* (London).

Foucault, M. (1980) *Power/Knowledge: selected interviews and other writings* (New York).

Foucault, M. (1984) 'The subject and power', in B. Wallis (ed.) *Art after Modernism: rethinking representation* (New York) 417-34.

Frank A.G. and Gills B.K. (eds) (1993) *The World System: five hundred years or five thousand?* (London).

Frank, A.G. and Gills, B.K. (2000) 'The five thousand year world system in theory and praxis', in R.A. Denemark, J. Friedman, B.K. Gills and G. Modelski (eds) *World System History: the social science of long-term change* (London) 3-23.

Frankenstein, S. and Rowlands, M. (1978) 'The internal structure and regional context of Early Iron Age society in western Germany', *Bulletin of the University of London Institute of Archaeology* (15) 73-112.

Freeman, E.A. (1883) *Some Impressions of the United States* (London). Reviewed in *The Oxford Magazine* (1883) vol. 1, 18 April 1883, pp. 161-2.

Freeman, E.A. (1886) *Greater Greece and Greater Britain and George Washington, The Expander of England. Two Lectures with an Appendix* (London).

Freeman, E.A. (1891-4) *A History of Sicily from the Earliest Times*, vols I-IV (Oxford).

Freeman, P. (1996) 'British Imperialism and the Roman Empire', in Webster and Cooper (eds) (1996) 19-34.

French, S. (1975) 'The cemetery as cultural institution: the establishment of Mount Auburn and the "Rural Cemetery" movement', in D.E. Stannard (ed.) *Death in America* (Pennsylvania) 69-91.

Frézouls, E. (1983) 'Sur l'historiographie de l'impérialisme romain', *Ktema* 8, 141-62.

Friedrich, P. (1989) 'Language, ideology, and political economy', *American Anthropologist* 91, 295-312.

Gabrici, E. (1933) 'Per la storia dell'architettura dorica in Sicilia', *MA* xxxv cols 137-250.

Gandhi, L. (1998) *Postcolonial Theory, a Critical Introduction* (New York).

García Quintela, M.V. (2002) 'Anthropologie et colonisation chez Anaxagore (D-K 59 B 4 et son contexte historique et sociale)', *AncSoc* 32, 329-41.

Garcilaso de la Vega (1989 [1609]) *Royal Commentaries of the Incas and General History of Peru*, trans. H. Livermore (Austin).

Geertz, C. (1957) 'Ethos, world-view, and the analysis of sacred symbols', *Antioch Review* 17, 421-37.

Genovese, G. (1999) *I santuari rurali nella Calabria greca* (Rome).

Giardina, A., and Schiavone, A. (eds) (1981) *Società romana e produzione schiavistica* (Rome / Bari).

Giddens, A. (1984) *The Constitution of Society: outline of the theory of structuration* (Berkeley).

Giovannini, A. (1985) 'Le sel et la fortune de Rome', *Athenaeum* 63, 373-87.

Godart, L. (2003) 'I flussi migratori nel Mediterraneo tra passato e presente', in *Il fenomeno coloniale*, 9-15.

Gosden, C. (1999) *Anthropology and Archaeology: a changing relationship* (London).

Gosden, C. (2004) *Archaeology and Colonialism: cultural contact from 5000 BC to the present* (Cambridge).

Graham, A.J. (1964) *Colony and Mother City in Ancient Greece* (1st ed.; 2nd ed. 1982) (Manchester).

Graham, A.J. (1978) 'The Foundation of Thasos', *BSA* 73, 61-98.

Graham, A.J. (1982) 'The colonial expansion of Greece', *CAH* III Part 3 (2nd ed.) (Cambridge) 83-162.

Graham, A.J. (1992) 'Abdera and Teos', *JHS* 112, 44-73.

Graham, A.J. (2001) 'Thasian Controversies', in A.J. Graham *Collected Papers on Greek Colonization* (Leiden) 365-402.

Grandjean, Y. (1988) *Recherches sur l'Habitat Thasien à l'Époque Grecque* (= *Études Thasiennes* XII) (Paris).

Gras, M. (1999) 'Georges Vallet et le commerce', in *La colonisation grecque en Méditerranée occidentale*, 7-22.

Graves-Brown, P. et al. (eds) (1995) *Cultural Identity and Archaeology* (London).

Greco, E. (1990) 'Serdaoi', *AION* 12 [1991] 39-57.

Greco, E. (2003) 'La colonizzazione greca in italia meridionale. Profilo storico archeologico', in *Il fenomeno coloniale*, 17-35.

Greco, G. (1999) 'Santuari extraurbani tra periferia cittadina e periferia indigena', in *La colonisation grecque en Méditerranée occidentale*, 231-47.

Gruzinski, S. (1999) *La pensée métisse* (Paris).

Gruzinski, S., and Rouveret, A. (1976) ' "Ellos son como niños". Histoire et acculturation dans le Mexique colonial et l'Italie méridionale avant la romanisation', *MEFRA* 88, 159-219.

Guaman Poma de Ayala, F. (1936 [1615]) *Nueva corónica y buen gobierno (Codex* Péruvien Illustré), Université de Paris Travaux et Memoires de L'Institut d'Ethnologie XXIII (Paris). http://www.kb.dk/elib/mss/poma/ p. 379.

Guy, M. (1995) 'Cadastres en bandes de Metaponte à Agde: questions et méthodes', in *Sur les pas des Grecs en Occident* (= *Études Massaliètes* 4), 427-44.

Guzzo, P.G. (1999) 'intervento', in *Confini e frontiera* (1999) 431-2.

Gwynn, A. (1918) 'The character of Greek colonisation', *JHS* 38, 88-123.

Hall, C. (2000) 'Introduction: thinking the post-colonial, thinking the empire', in C. Hall (ed.) *Cultures of Empire: a reader* (Manchester), 1-33.
Hall, E. (1989) *Inventing the Barbarian: Greek self-definition through tragedy* (Oxford).
Hall, J. (1997) *Ethnic Identity in Greek Antiquity* (Cambridge).
Hall, J. (2002) *Hellenicity. Between Ethnicity and Culture* (Chicago).
Hall, J. (2003) 'Culture, cultures and acculturation', in R. Rollinger and C. Ulf (eds) *Das Archaische Griechenland: interne Entwicklungen – externe Impulse* (Berlin) 35-50.
Hasebroek, J. (1933) *Trade and Politics in the Ancient Greek World* (London).
Hastorf, C. (2001) 'Agricultural production and consumption', in D'Altroy and Hastorf (eds) (2001) 155-78.
Hastorf, C. and DeNiro, M. (1985) 'Reconstruction of prehistoric plant production and cooking practices by a new isotopic method', *Nature* 315, 489-91.
Hayashida, F. (1999) 'Style, technology and state production: Inka pottery manufacture in the Leche Valley', *Latin American Antiquity* 10 (4) 337-52.
Helms, M. (1988) *Ulysses' Sail* (Princeton).
Helms, M. (1993) *Craft and the Kingly Ideal: Art, Trade and Power* (Austin).
Heurgon, J. (1957) *Trois études sur le 'ver sacrum'* (Brussels).
Hiller von Gaertringen, F. (1934-6) 'Noch einmal das Archilochosdenkmal von Paros', *Nachrichten von der Gesellschaft der Wissenschaften zu Göttingen* (Phil.Hist.Kl. I) 41-56.
Hingley, R. (1996) 'The "legacy" of Rome: the rise, decline and fall of the theory of Romanization', in Webster and Cooper (eds) (1996) 35-48.
Hingley, R. (1997) 'Resistance and domination: social change in Roman Britain', in Mattingly (ed.) (1997) 81-100.
Hingley, R. (2000) *Roman Officers and English Gentlemen: the imperial origins of Roman archaeology* (London, New York).
Hingley, R. (ed.) (2001) *Images of Rome* (Portsmouth).
Hodder, I. (1982) *The Present Past* (London).
Hodder, I. (ed.) (1978) *The Spatial Organization of Culture* (London).
Hodge, A.T. (1960) *The Woodwork of Greek Roofs* (Cambridge).
Hodos, T. (2000) 'Wine Wares in Protohistoric Eastern Sicily', in C.J. Smith and J. Serrati (eds) *Sicily from Aeneas to Augustus. New Approaches Archaeology and History* (Edinburgh) 41-54.
Horden, P. and Purcell, N. (2000) *The Corrupting Sea: a study in Mediterranean history*, (Oxford).
Hyslop, J. (1990) *Inka Settlement Planning* (Austin).
Hyslop, J. (1993) 'Factors influencing the transmission and distribution of Inka cultural materials throughout Tawantinsuyu', in D. Rice (ed.) *Latin American Horizons* (Washington DC) 337-56.
Iannantuono, P. (1986) 'Olle geometriche daunie', in Swaddling (ed.) (1986) 335-41.
Il fenomeno coloniale dall'antichità ad oggi (Roma, 19 e 20 marzo 2002) (2003) (*Atti dei convegni lincei* 189) (Rome).
Isaac, B. (1986) *The Greek Settlements in Thrace until the Macedonian Conquest* (Leiden).
Jacoby, D. (1994) 'The migration of merchants and craftsmen: a Mediterranean perspective (12th-15th century)', in D. Cavaciocchi (ed.) (1994) *Le migrazioni in Europa, secc. XIII-XVIII* (Florence) 533-60.

Jannot, J.-R. (1995) 'Les navires étrusques, instruments d'une thalassocratie?', *CRAI*, 743-78.
Jenkyns, R. (1980) *The Victorians and Ancient Greece* (Oxford).
Jentoft-Nilsen, J. (1988) 'Two Attic Vases of Unique Shape', in J. Christiansen and T. Melander (eds) *Proceedings of the 3rd Symposium on Ancient Greek and Related Pottery* (Copenhagen) 278-83.
Jentoft-Nilsen, J. (1990) 'Two Attic Vases of South Italian Shape', in Descoeudres (ed.) (1990) 243-9.
Johnson, M. (1999) *Archaeological Theory: an introduction* (Oxford).
Johnson, P. (1972) *The Offshore Islanders* (London).
Jones, S. (1997) *The Archaeology of Ethnicity* (London).
Keay, S.J., and Terrenato, N. (eds) (2001) *Italy and the West. Comparative Issues in Romanization* (Oxford).
Klein, N.L. (1998) 'Evidence for West Greek influence on mainland Greek roof construction and the creation of the truss in the Archaic period', *Hesperia* 67, 335-74.
Koder, J. (1998) *Aigaion Pelagos (Die nordliche Ägäis)* (= *Tabula Imperii Byzantini* 10) (Vienna).
Koukouli-Chrysanthaki, Ch. (1996) *Προτοϊστορική Θάσος* (Athens).
Krebs, S.A. (1997) 'Greek colonization and agriculture in Dobrudja', in J.M. Fossey (ed.) *Antiquitates Proponticae, Circumponticae et Caucasicae II: proceedings of the first international conference on the archaeology and history of the Black Sea (McGill University, 22-24 Nov. 1994)* (Amsterdam) 47-65.
Kristiansen, K. and Rowlands, M. (eds) (1998) *Social Transformations in Archaeology: global and local perspectives* (London).
Kron, G. (2002) 'Archaeozoological evidence for the productivity of Roman livestock farming', *MBAH* 21.2, 53-73.
Kus, S. (1989) 'Sensuous human activity and the state: towards an archaeology of bread and circuses', in D. Miller, M. Rowlands, and C. Tilley (eds) *Domination and Resistance* (London) 140-54.
La colonisation grecque en Méditerranée occidentale: actes de la rencontre scientifique en hommage à Georges Vallet organisée par le Centre Jean-Bérard, l'École française de Rome, l'Istituto universitario orientale et l'Università degli studi di Napoli 'Federico II' (Rome-Naples, 15-18 novembre 1995) (= *Collection de l'École française de Rome* 251) (1999) (Rome).
La Guardia, R. (ed.) (1992) *Dall villaggio indigeno all'emporio greco. Ricerche archeologiche all'Incoronata di Metaponto* (Milan).
La Torre, G.F. (1991-2) 'Greci ed indigeni tra Lucania e Calabria in età arcaica. Nuovi dati e prospettive di ricerca lungo il versante tirrenico', *RendPontAcc* 64 [1994], 27-61.
La Torre, G.F. (1999) 'Enotri e Lucani nel territorio di Laos', in M. Barra Bagnasco, E. De Miro and A. Pinzone (eds) *Magna Grecia e Sicilia: stato degli studi e prospettive di ricerca: atti dell'Incontro di studi, Messina, 2-4 dicembre 1996* (Messina) 131-43.
La Torre, G.F. (2002) *Un tempio arcaico nel territorio dell'antica Temesa: l'edificio sacro in località Imbelli di Campora San Giovanni* (Rome).
Lamboley, J.-L. (1996) *Recherches sur les messapiens, IVe-IIe siècle avant J.-C.* (Rome).
Lawrence, A.W. (1957) *Greek Architecture* (Harmondsworth).
Leighton, R. (1989) 'Antiquarianism and prehistory in the West Mediterranean Islands', *Antiquaries Journal* 69, 183-204.

Leighton, R. (1993) *Morgantina Studies* IV. *The Protohistoric Settlement on the Cittadella.* (Princeton).

Leighton, R. (1999) *Sicily before History. An Archaeological Survey from the Palaeolithic to the Iron Age* (London).

Leone, M. (1984) 'Interpreting ideology in historical archaeology: The William Paca garden in Annapolis, Maryland', in Miller and Tilley (eds) (1984).

Lepore, E. (1970) 'Per una fenomenologia storica del rapporto città-territorio in Magna Grecia', in *Atti del VII Convegno Internazionale di Studi sulla Magna Grecia, La città e il suo territorio* (Taranto-Naples) 29-66.

Lepore, E. (1977) 'Fiumi e città nella colonizzazione greca di Occidente con speciale riguardo alla Magna Grecia', in P.-M. Duval and E. Frézouls (eds) *Thèmes de recherches sur les villes antiques d'Occident* (Paris) 267-72.

Lepore, E. (1990) 'Tavola rotonda', in M. Salvatore (ed.) *Basilicata: l'espansionismo romano* (Conv. Venosa 1987), 321-2, 324-8, 339-44.

Lepore, E. (1991) 'Conclusioni', in *La romanisation du Samnium aux IIe et Ier siècles av. J.-C.* (Naples) 261-4.

Lepore, E. (2000) *La Grande Grèce: aspects et problèmes d'une colonisation ancienne* (Naples).

Leroy-Beaulieu, P. (1874) *De la colonisation chez les peuples modernes* (Paris).

Les Grecs et l'Occident: actes du Colloque de la Villa 'Kérylos' (1991) (1995) (Rome).

Levillier, R. (1940) *Don Francisco de Toledo, supremo organizador del Perú, su vida, su obra (1512-1582)*, 3 vols (Buenos Aires).

Linderski, J. (1984) 'Si vis pacem, para bellum: concepts of defensive imperialism', in W.V. Harris (ed.) *The Imperialism of Mid-Republican Rome* (Rome) 133-64.

Lloyd, G.E.R. (2004) *Ancient Worlds, Modern Reflections: philosophical perspectives on Greek and Chinese science and culture* (Oxford).

Lomas, K. (ed.) (2004) *Greek Identity in the Western Mediterranean: papers in honour of Brian Shefton* (Leiden).

Lombardo, M. (1995) 'Food and "frontier" in the Greek colonies of southern Italy', in M. Dobson, D. Harvey and J. Wilkins (eds) *Food in Antiquity* (Exeter) 256-72.

Lombardo, M. (1998) 'Siri e Metaponto: sperienze coloniali e storia e sociale', in *Siritide e Metapontino* (1999) 45-66.

Lombardo, M. (1999) 'intervento', in *Confini e frontiera* (1999) 743-9.

Lorandi, A.M. (1992) 'El mestizaje interétnico en el noroeste Argentino', in H. Tomoeda and L. Millones (eds) *500 Años de Mestizaje en los Andes* (Osaka, Lima) 159-200.

Lucas, C. (Sir) (1912) *Greater Rome and Greater Britain* (Oxford).

Luttwak, E.N. (1976) *The Grand Strategy of the Roman Empire from the First Century AD to the Third* (Baltimore).

Lyons, C.L. (1996) *Morgantina Studies* V. *The Archaic Cemeteries* (Princeton).

Lyons, C.L. and Papadopoulos, J.K. (eds) (2002) *The Archaeology of Colonialism: issues & debates* (Los Angeles).

MacCormack, S. (2001) 'Cuzco, another Rome?', in Alcock et al. (2001) 419-35.

MacIntosh Turfa, J. and Steinmeyer, A.G. (2002) 'Interpreting early Etruscan structures: the example of Murlo', *PBSR* 70, 1-28.

Malkin, I. (1994) 'Insider and outside: colonization and the formation of the mother-city', in B. D'Agostino and D. Ridgway (eds) *APOIKIA: i più antichi insediamenti greci in Occidente: funzioni e modi dell'organizzazione politica e sociale: scritti in onore di Giorgio Buchner* (Naples) 1-9.

Malkin, I. (1998) *The Returns of Odysseus: colonization and ethnicity* (Berkeley).

Malkin, I. (ed.) (2001) *Ancient Perceptions of Greek Ethnicity* (Washington, DC).

Malkin, I. (2002) 'A colonial middle ground: Greek, Etruscan, and local elites in the Bay of Naples', in Lyons and Papadopoulos (eds) (2002), 151-81.
Manacorda, D. and Tamassia R. (1985) *Il piccone del regime* (Rome).
Mann, M. (1970) 'The social cohesion of liberal democracy', *American Sociological Review* 35 (3) 423-39.
Mann, M. (1983) 'Review of *Power: its forms, bases, and uses*', *American Journal of Sociology* 88 (5), 1030-2.
Mann, M. (1986) *The Sources of Social Power* (Cambridge).
Marchand, S.L. (1996) *Down from Olympus: archaeology and philhellenism in Germany, 1750-1970* (Princeton).
Marcus, J. (1992) *Ancient Mesoamerican Writing Systems* (Princeton).
Marx, K. (1887) *Das Kapital: Kritik der politischen Ökonomie*, trans. S. Moore and E. Aveling (London).
Matheson, S. (1995) *Polygnotos and Vase Painting in Classical Athens* (Madison).
Mattingly, D.J. (1997) 'Africa: a landscape of opportunity?', in Mattingly (ed.) (1997) 117-42.
Mattingly, D.J. (ed.) (1997) *Dialogues in Roman Imperialism: power, discourse, and discrepant experience in the Roman Empire*, *JRA* Supplementary Series, No. 23 (Portsmouth).
Mauss, M. (1990 [1950]) *The Gift,* trans. W.D. Halls (London).
Mazzei, J. (1986) 'Le trozzelle messapiche', in Swaddling (ed.) (1986) 357-65.
McGuire, R. (1992) *A Marxist Archaeology* (San Diego / London).
Menjot, D. (1995) 'Une méthode de domination: les concessions royales de terres dans les *huertas* de la basse vallée du Segura à l'époque de la reconquête', in Balard and Ducellier (eds) (1995) 161-80.
Mertens, D. (1990) 'Some principal features of West Greek colonial architecture', in Descoeudres (ed.) (1990) 373-83.
Mertens, D. (1996) 'Greek Architecture in the West', in G. Pugliese Carratelli (ed.) *The Western Greeks* (London).
Metzler, J., Millett, M., Roymans, N., and Slofstra, J. (eds) (1995) *Integration in the Early Roman West. The Role of Culture and Ideology* (*Dossiers d'archéologie du Musée National d'Histoire et d'Art*, 4) (Luxembourg).
Miller, D. and Tilley, C. (1984) *Ideology, Power and Prehistory* (Cambridge).
Millett, M. (1990) *The Romanization of Britain: an essay in archaeological interpretation.* (Cambridge).
Milton, G. (1999) *Nathaniel's Nutmeg: how one man's courage changed the course of history* (London).
Morel, J.-P. (1991) 'La romanisation du Samnium et de la Lucanie', in J. Mertens and R. Lambrechts (eds) *Comunità indigene e problemi della romanizzazione nell'Italia centro-meridionale (IVo-IIIo sec. av. C.)* (Brussels / Rome) 125-44.
Morgan, C. (1999) 'The archaeology of ethnicity in the colonial world of the eighth to sixth centuries BC: approaches and prospects', in *Confini e frontiera* (1999) 85-145.
Morgan, C. (2001) '*Ethne*, ethnicity and early Greek states, ca. 1200-480: an archaeological perspective', in Malkin (ed.) (2001) 75-112.
Morgan, C. (2003) *Early Greek States beyond the Polis* (London).
Morris, C. (1972) 'State settlements in Tawantinsuyu: A strategy of compulsory urbanism', in M. Leone (ed.) *Contemporary Archaeology* (Carbondale, IL) 393-401.
Morris, C. (1985) 'From principles of ecological complementarity to the organiza-

tion and administration of Tawantinsuyu', in S. Masuda and C. Morris (eds) *Andean Ecology and Civilization* (Tokyo) 477-90.

Morris, C. (1993) 'The wealth of a native American state: value, investment, and mobilization in the Inka economy', in J. Henderson and P. Netherly (eds) *Configurations of Power* (Ithaca) 36-50.

Morris, C. (1998) 'Inka strategies of incorporation and governance', in G. Feinman and J. Marcus (eds) *Archaic States* (Santa Fe, NM) 293-310.

Morris, C. and Thompson, D. (1985) *Huánuco Pampa: an Inca city and its hinterland* (London).

Morris, I. (1994a) 'Archaeologies of Greece', in I. Morris (ed.) *Classical Greece. Ancient Histories and Modern Archaeologies* (Cambridge).

Morris, I. (1994b) 'The Athenian economy twenty years after *The Ancient Economy*', *Classical Philology* 89, 351-66.

Morris, I. et al. (forthcoming) 'Stanford University Excavations on the Acropolis of Monte Polizzo, Sicily, III: Preliminary Report on the 2002 Season', to appear in *MAAR*.

Morris, S. (1992) *Daidalos and the Origins of Greek Art* (Princeton).

Munzi, M. (2001) *L'epica del ritorno* (Rome).

Murra, J. (1972) 'El "control vertical" de un máximo de pisos ecológicos en la economía de las sociedades Andinas', in I. Ortiz de Zúñiga (ed.) *Visita de la Provincia de Huánuco y la Selva Central*, 2 (Huánuco, Peru) 427-76.

Murra, J. (1980 [1956]) *The Economic Organization of the Inca State* (Greenwich, CT).

Murra, J. and Morris C. (1976) 'Dynastic oral tradition, administrative records, and archaeology in the Andes', *World Archaeology* 7 (3) 270-7.

Najdenova, V. (1990) 'Rock shrines in Thrace', in V. Velkov and P. Petrov (eds) *Studies in Settlement Life in Ancient Thrace* (Sofia) 85-100.

Neils, J. (1995) 'The Euthymides Krater from Morgantina', *AJA* 99, 427-44.

Nenci, G. (1983) 'Truphe e colonizzazione', in *Modes de Contact et Processus de Transformation dans les Sociétés Anciennes* (Pisa / Rome) 1019-31.

Niebuhr, B.G. (1812) *Römische Geschichte* (Berlin).

Niemeyer, H.-G. (1990), 'The Phoenicians in the Mediterranean: a non-Greek model for expansion and settlement in antiquity', in Descoeudres (ed.) (1990) 469-89.

Nijboer, A.J. (1998) *From Household Production to Workshops: archaeological evidence for economic transformation, pre-monetary exchange and urbanisation in central Italy from 800 to 400* BC (Groningen).

Nordman, D. (1998) 'La Méditerranée dans la pensée géographique française (vers 1800-vers 1950)', in C. Guillot, D. Lombard and R. Ptak (eds) *From the Mediterranean to the China Sea* (Wiesbaden) 1-20.

Noyes, A. (1957) *The Accusing Ghost or Justice for Casement* (London).

Orsi, P. (1895) 'Siracusa – Gli scavi nella necropoli del Fusco a Siracusa nel giugno, novembre e dicembre del 1893', *Notizie degli Scavi*, 109-92.

Ortner, S. (1984) 'Theory in anthropology since the sixties', *Comparative Studies in Society and History* 26 (1) 126-66.

Osanna, M. (1992) *Chorai coloniali da Taranto a Locri: documentazione archeologica e ricostruzione storica* (Rome).

Osborne, R. (1998) 'Early Greek Colonization? The nature of Greek settlement in the West', in N. Fisher & H. van Wees (eds) *Archaic Greece: new approaches and new evidence* (London) 251-70.

Ouerfelli, M. (2002) 'Les migrations liées aux plantations et à la production du sucre dans la Méditerranée à la fin du Moyen Âge', in Balard and Ducellier (eds) *Migrations et Diasporas* (Paris) 485-500.

Owen, S. (2000a) 'A theory of Greek colonisation: EIA Thrace and initial Greek contacts'. PhD Thesis, University of Cambridge.

Owen, S. (2000b) 'New light on Thracian Thasos: a reinterpretation of the "cave of Pan" ', *JHS* 120, 139-43.

Owen, S. (2003) 'Of Dogs and Men: Archilochos, archaeology and the Greek settlement of Thasos', *PCPS* 49, 1-18.

Pace, B. (1938) *Arte e civiltà della Sicilia antica* vol. II (4 vols, 1935-49) (Milan).

Pagden, A. (1995) *Lords of All the World: ideologies of empire in Spain, Britain and France c. 1500-c. 1800* (New Haven, CT).

Panciera, S. (ed.) (1982) *Epigrafia e ordine senatorio. Tituli 4-5* (Rome).

Papadopoulos, J.K. (2001) 'Magna Achaea: Akhaian Late Geometric and Archaic Pottery in South Italy and Sicily', *Hesperia* 70, 373-460.

Papadopoulos, J.K. (2003) *La dea di Sibari e il santuario ritrovato. Studi sui rinvenimenti del Timpone Motta di Francavilla Marittima*, II 1 *The Archaic Votive Metal Objects* (= *Boll. D'Arte supp.*) (Rome).

Papi, R. (1996) 'Produzione metallurgica e mobilità nel mondo italico', in L. Del Tutto Palma (ed.) *La tavola di Agnone nel contesto italico: Convegno di studi, Agnone 13-15 aprile 1994* (Florence) 89-128.

Pare, C. (1993) 'La dimension européenne du commerce grec à la fin de la période archaïque et pendant le début de la période classique', in Actes of Colloquium: *Vix et les éphémères principautés celtiques*, at Châtillon-sur-Seine 27-9 October 1993, 261-86.

Pashkevich, G.A. (2001) 'Archaeobotanical Studies on the Northern Coast of the Black Sea', *EurAnt* 7, 511-67.

Patroni, G. (1896) 'La fibula nella necropoli siracusana del Fusco', *BPI* XXII, 30-49.

Payne, H. (ed.) (1940) *Perachora I* (Oxford).

Pease, F. (1982) 'The formation of Tawantinsuyu: mechanisms of colonization and relationships with ethnic groups', in Collier, Rosaldo and Wirth (eds) (1982) 173-98.

Péberthe, C. (1999) 'Thasos, l'Empire d'Athènes et les emporia de Thrace', *ZPE* 126, 121-54.

Pelosi, A. (1991) 'Dinamiche territoriali del VII secolo a.C. nell'area Sirite-Metapontina', *Dd'A* 3, 9, 49-74.

Perry, W.C. (1908) *Sicily in Fable, History, Art and Song* (London).

Piergrossi, A. (2002) 'Una communità di frontiera: Poggio Montano', *ArchClass* 53, 1-64.

Pinney, T. (ed.) (1990) *The Letters of Rudyard Kipling*, Vol. 2, *1890-1899* (London).

Pinney, T. (ed.) (1999) *The Letters of Rudyard Kipling*, Vol. 4, *1911-1919* (London).

Pouilloux, J. (1954) *Recherches sur l'histoire et les cultes de Thasos* (= *Études Thasiennes* III) (Paris).

Pouilloux, J. (1964) 'Archiloque et Thasos', *Fond.Hardt* x, 3-27.

Prontera, F. (1996) 'Sulla geografica nautica e sulla rappresentazione litoranea della Magna Grecia', in Prontera (ed.) (1996) 281-98.

Prontera, F., (ed.) (1996) *La Magna Grecia e il mare. Studi di storia marittima* (Taranto).

Purcell, N. (1993) 'Continuity and change: the Mediterranean from antiquity to the present', *Der altsprachliche Unterricht* 2, *Das Mittelmeer*, 16-28.

Purcell, N. (1997) Review of G.R. Tsetskhladze and F. De Angelis (eds) *The*

Archaeology of Greek Colonisation. Essays dedicated to Sir John Boardman, Oxford 1994, *Antiquity* 71, 500-2.
Purcell, N. (2004) 'The boundless sea of unlikeness? On defining the Mediterranean', *MHR* 18.2 (December 2003 [2004]) 9-29.
Purcell, N. (2005) 'The ancient Mediterranean: the view from the customs-house', in W.V. Harris (ed.) *Rethinking the Mediterranean* (Oxford) 200-32.
Purcell, N. and Horden, P. (2005) 'Four years of corruption', in W.V. Harris (ed.) *Rethinking the Mediterranean* (Oxford) 348-75.
Puytison-Lagarce, E. du (1995) 'Recherches sur la période orientalisante en Étrurie et dans le midi ibérique', *CRAI*, 569-604.
Racine, P. (1995) 'Hommes d'affaires et artisans d'Italie interieure en Mediterranée orientale vers 1250-vers 1350', in Balard and Ducellier (eds) (1995) 142-60.
Rappaport, R. (1971) 'The sacred in human evolution', *Annual Review of Ecology and Systematics* 2, 23-44.
Reece, R. (1988) *My Roman Britain* (Cirencester).
Rendeli, M. (1993) *Città aperte: ambiente e paesaggio rurale organizzato nell'Etruria meridionale costiera durante l'età orientalizzante e arcaica*, on *colonizzazione interna* (Rome).
Ridgway, B.S. (1977) *The Archaic Style in Greek Sculpture* (Princeton).
Ridgway, D. (1992) *The First Western Greeks* (Cambridge).
Rostworowski, M. (1999) *History of the Inca Realm* (Cambridge).
Rowe, J.H. (1946) 'Inca culture at the time of the Spanish conquest', *Handbook of South American Indians* (Bureau of American ethnology, Bulletin 143) Vol. 2 (Washington DC) 183-330.
Rowe, J.H. (1982) 'Inca policies and institutions relating to the cultural unification of the empire', in Collier, Rosaldo and Wirth (eds) (1982) 93-118.
Rowlands, M. (1987) ' "Europe in prehistory": a unique form of primitive capitalism?', *Culture and History* 1, 63-78.
Rowlands, M. (1998) 'The Archaeology of Colonialism', in Kristiansen and Rowlands (eds) (1998), 327-33.
Rowlands, M., Larsen, M. and Kristiansen, K. (eds) (1987) *Centre and Periphery in the Ancient World* (Cambridge).
Ruskin, J. (1870) 'Inaugural', in J. Ruskin, *Lectures on Art delivered before the University of Oxford in Hilary Term, 1870* (Oxford).
Rutherford, A. (ed.) (1964) *Kipling's Mind and Art* (Edinburgh).
Said, E.W. (1978) *Orientalism* (1st ed.) (New York).
Said, E.W. (1993) *Culture and Imperialism* (London).
Salomon, N. (1997) *Le cleruchie d'Atene: caratteri e funzione* (Pisa).
Santillán, F. de (1879) 'Relación del orígen, descendencia, política y gobierno de los Incas [1563]', Biblioteca de Cultura Peruana, serie 1, No. 2 (Paris) 117-185.
Saprykin, S.J. (1994) *Ancient Farms and Land Plots in the Khora of Khersonesos Taurike (Research in the Herakleian Peninsula 1974-1990)* (Amsterdam).
Scott, J.C. (1985) *Weapons of the Weak: everyday forms of peasant resistance* (New Haven, CT).
Scott, J.C. (1998) *Seeing Like a State: how certain schemes to improve the human condition have failed. Yale Agrarian Studies* (New Haven, CT).
Semeraro, G. (1997) *En neusi: ceramica greca e società nel Salento arcaico* (Bari).
Shaw, B. (2004) 'A Peculiar Island: Maghrib and Mediterranean', *MHR* 18/2 (December 2003 [2004]), 93-125.

Shepherd, G. (1993) 'Death and religion in Archaic Greek Sicily: a study in colonial relationships'. Unpublished Ph.D. thesis, University of Cambridge.
Shepherd, G. (1995) 'The pride of most colonials: burial and religion in the Sicilian colonies', *Acta Hyperborea* 6, 51-82.
Shepherd, G. (1999) 'Fibulae and females: intermarriage in the Western Greek colonies and the evidence from cemeteries', in G.R. Tsetskhladze (ed.) *Ancient Greeks West and East* (= Mnemosyne supp. 196) (Leiden) 267-300.
Shoe, L.T. (1952) *Profiles of Western Greek Mouldings*, Papers and Monographs of the American Academy, 14 (Rome).
Siritide e Metapontino: storia di due territori coloniali: Atti Conv. Policoro 1991, 1999 (Rome).
Sjöqvist, E. (1958) 'Excavations at Serra Orlando (Morgantina): Preliminary Report II', *AJA* 62, 155-64.
Sjöqvist, E. (1960) 'Excavations at Serra Orlando 1959: Preliminary Report IV', *AJA* 64,125-35.
Sjöqvist, E. (1973) *Sicily and the Greeks. Studies in the Interrelationship between the Indigenous Populations and the Greek Colonists* (Ann Arbor).
Slofstra, J. (1983) 'An anthropological approach to the study of Romanization processes', in Brandt and Slofstra (eds) (1983) 71-140.
Smyth, W.H. (1824) *Memoir Descriptive of the Resources, Inhabitants, and Hydrography, of Sicily and its Islands, Interspersed with Antiquarian and other Notices* (London).
Snodgrass, A. (1994) 'The nature and standing of the early western colonies', in Tsetskhladze and De Angelis (eds) (1994) 1-10.
Solovyov, S.L. (1999) *Ancient Berezan* (Leiden).
Sordi, M. (ed.) (1994) *Emigrazione e immigrazione nel mondo antico* (Milan).
Sordi, M. (ed.) (1995) *Coercizione e mobilità umana nel mondo antico* (Milan).
Spadea, R. (1996) *Il Tesoro di Hera: scoperte nel Santuario di Hera Lacinia a Capo Colonna di Crotone* (Rome).
Spatafora, F. and Vassallo, S. (eds) (2002) *Sicani, elimi e greci: storie di contatti e terre di frontiera* (Palermo).
Stea, G. (1999) 'Forme della presenza greca sull'arco ionico della Basilicata: tra *emporìa* e *apoikìai*', in M. Castoldi (ed.) *Koina. Miscellanea di studi archeologici in onore di P. Orlandini* (Milan) 49-71.
Stöckly, D. (1995) 'Le transport maritime d'état à Chypre. Complément des techniques coloniales vénitiens (XIIIe-XIVe siècle): l'exemple du sucre', in Balard and Ducellier (eds) (1995) 131-41 and 153-6.
Stoler, A. (1989) 'Rethinking colonial categories: European communities and the boundaries of rule', *Comparative Studies in Society and History* 31, 134-61.
Stubbings, J.M. (1962) 'Ivories', in T.J. Dunbabin (ed.) *Perachora II* (Oxford).
Sundwall, J. (1943) *Die älteren italischen Fibeln* (Berlin).
Swaddling, J. (ed.) (1986) *Italian Iron Age Artefacts in the British Museum* (London).
Symonds, R. (1991) *Oxford and Empire* (Oxford).
Tagliamonte, G. (1994) *I figli di Marte: mobilità, mercenari e mercenariato italici in Magna Grecia e Sicilia* (Rome).
Taylor, T. (1989) 'Iron and Iron Age in the Carpatho-Balkan Region: Aspects of Social and Technological Change 1700-400 BC', in M.-L.S. Sørensen and R. Thomas (eds) (1989) *The Bronze Age – Iron Age Transition in Europe*, BAR International Series S483 (Oxford) 68-92.
Terrenato, N. (1998a) 'The Romanization of Italy: global acculturation or cultural

bricolage?', in C. Forcey, J. Hawthorne, and R. Witcher (eds) *TRAC 97* (Oxford) 20-7.

Terrenato, N. (1998b) 'Tam firmum municipium. The Romanization of Volaterrae and its cultural implications', *JRS* 88, 94-114.

Terrenato, N. (2001) 'A tale of three cities', in S.J. Keay and N. Terrenato (eds) *Italy and the West. Comparative issues in Romanization* (Oxford).

Terrenato, N. (2002a) 'Ancestor cults: the perception of ancient Rome in Italian culture', in Hingley (ed.) (2001) 71-89.

Terrenato, N. (2002b), 'The innocents and the skeptics. Classical Archaeology and Antiquity', *Antiquity* 76, 1104-11.

Terrenato, N. (forthcoming) 'The Versatile Clans', paper given at a Conference on State Formation in the Mediterranean and Beyond (D.C. Haggis and N. Terrenato (eds), forthcoming).

Thomas, N. (1991) *Entangled Objects: exchange, colonialism and material culture in the Pacific* (Cambridge, MA).

Thomas, N. (1994) *Colonialism's Culture. Anthropology, Travel and Government* (Cambridge).

Torelli, M. (1977) 'Il santuario greco di Gravisca', in *Lazio arcaico e mondo greco* (= *PdelP* 32) 398-458.

Torelli, M. (1993) 'Gli aromi e il sale. Afrodite ed Eracle nell'*emporia* dell'Italia', in A. Mastrocinque (ed.) *Ercole in Occidente* (Trento) 91-117.

Torelli, M. (1996) 'Per un'archeologia dell'*Oinotría*', in S. Bianco et al. (eds) *I Greci in Occidente. Greci, Enotri e Lucani nella Basilicata meridionale* (Naples) 122-31.

Torelli, M. (1999) *Tota Italia* (Oxford).

Trendall, A.D. (1989) *Red Figure Vases of South Italy and Sicily* (London).

Trendall, A.D. (1990) 'On the Divergence of South Italian from Attic Red-figure Vase-painting', in Descoeudres (ed.) (1990) 217-30.

Triantafyllidou-Baladié, Y. (1981) 'Dominations étrangères et transformations de l'agriculture crétoise entre le XVIe et le XIXe siècle', *Greek Review of Social Research* (Athens) 180-90.

Trigger, B.G. (1984) 'Alternative Archaeologies: nationalist, colonialist, imperialist', *Man* n.s. 19, 354-70.

Trigger, B.G. (1993) 'The state-church reconsidered', in J. Henderson and P. Netherly (eds) *Configurations of Power* (Ithaca) 74-111.

Tsantsanoglou, K. (2003) 'Archilochus fighting in Thasos: Frr 93a & 94 from the Sosthenes inscription', *Hellenika* 53, 235-55.

Tsetskhladze G. and De Angelis, F. (eds) (1994) *The Archaeology of Greek Colonisation. Essays dedicated to Sir John Boardman.* Oxford University Committee for Archaeology, Monograph 40 (Oxford).

Turner, F.J. (1921) *The Frontier in American History* (New York).

Turner, V. (1981) 'Social Dramas and Stories about Them', in W.J.T. Mitchell (ed.) *On Narrative* (Chicago / London) 137-64.

Van Der Mersch, C. (1996) 'Vigne, vin et économie dans l'Italie du sud grecque à l'époque archaïque', *Ostraka* 5, 155-85.

Van Dommelen P. (1997) 'Colonial constructs: colonialism and archaeology in the Mediterranean world', *World Archaeology* 28 (3) 305-23.

Van Dommelen, P. (1998) *On Colonial Grounds: a comparative study of colonialism and rural settlement in first millennium* BC *west central Sardinia* (Leiden).

Van Dommelen, P. (2002) 'Ambiguous matters: colonialism and local identities in Punic Sardinia', in Lyons and Papadopoulos (eds) (2002) 121-47.

Vasunia, P. (2003) 'Hellenism and empire: reading Edward Said', *Parallax* 9, 88-97.
Venturi, L. (1984) *Settecento Riformatore* (Turin).
Verlinden, C. (1954) *Précédents mediévaux de la colonie en Amérique* (México).
Verlinden, C. (1970) *The Beginnings of Modern Colonization: eleven essays with an introduction* (Ithaca).
Verlinden, C. (1995) 'The transfer of colonial techniques from the Mediterranean to the Atlantic', in F. Fernandez-Armesto (ed.) *An Expanding World*: Vol. 2 *The European Opportunity* (Brookfield VT) 225-54.
Vernant, J.P. (1983) *Myth and Thought Among the Greeks* (London / Boston).
Viazzo, P. (1989) *Upland Communities: environment, population and social structure in the Alps since the sixteenth century* (Cambridge).
Virgilio, B. (1987) 'Conflittualità e coesistenza tra greci e non-greci, e il caso di Alicarnasso del V secolo a. C.', in *Studi ellenistici* II (Pisa) 115-27.
Vokotopoulou, J. (1994) 'Anciennes nécropoles de la Chalcidique', in De la Genière (ed.) (1994) 79-98.
Von Wartburg, M.-L. (1995) 'Production du sucre de canne a Chypre: un chapitre de technologie medievale', in Balard and Ducellier (eds) (1995) 126-31.
Wailes, B. and Zoll, A. (1996) 'Civilization, barbarism and nationalism in European archaeology', in M. Díaz-Andreu and T. Champion (eds) *Nationalism and Archaeology in Europe* (London) 21-38.
Wallerstein, I. (1974) *The Modern World System I* (New York).
Wallerstein, I. (1980) *The Modern World System II* (New York).
Wallerstein, I. (1991) *Unthinking Social Science: the limits of nineteenth century paradigms* (Cambridge).
Webster, J. and Cooper, N.J. (eds) (1996) *Roman Imperialism: post-colonial perspectives*, Leicester Archaeological Monographs 3 (Leicester).
Weill, N. (1985) *La plastique archaique de Thasos I* (= *Études Thasiennes* XI) (Paris).
White, R. (1991) *The Middle Ground: Indians, empires, and republics in the Great Lakes region, 1650-1815* (Cambridge).
Whittaker, C.R. (1997) 'Imperialism and culture: the Roman initiative', in Mattingly (ed.) (1997) 143-63.
Wiessner, P. (1983) 'Style and information in Kalahari San projectile points', *American Antiquity* 49, 253-76.
Wiessner, P. (1990) 'Is there a unity to style?', in M. Conkey and C. Hastorf (eds) *The Uses of Style in Archaeology* (Cambridge) 105-12.
Wilson, J.-P. (1997) 'The nature of Greek overseas settlements in the archaic period: *emporion* or *apoikia*?', in L. Mitchell and P.J. Rhodes (eds) *The Development of the Polis in Archaic Greece* (London) 199-207.
Wilson, P. (1988) *The Domestication of the Human Species* (New Haven, CT).
Winter, F.E. (1976) 'Tradition and Innovation in Doric Design I: Western Greek Temples', *AJA* 80, 139-45.
Wolf, E.R. (1999) *Envisioning Power: ideologies of dominance and crisis* (Berkeley).
Woodhead, A.G., (1962) *The Greeks in the West* (London).
Woodruff, P. (1953) *The Men who Ruled India*: Vol. 1, *The Founders* (London).
Woodruff, P. (1954) *The Men who Ruled India*: Vol. 2, *The Guardians* (London).
Woolf, G. (1989) 'Core-Periphery Relations', *JRS* 79, 236-9.
Woolf, G. (1993) 'European social development and Roman imperialism', in P.

Brun, S. van der Leeuw and C.R. Whittaker (eds) *Frontières d'empire: nature et signification des frontières romaines* (Nemours) 13-20.
Woolf, G. (1997) 'Beyond Romans and natives', *World Archaeology* 28 (3) 339-50.
Woolf, G. (1998) *Becoming Roman: the origins of provincial civilization in Gaul* (Cambridge).
Woolley, L. (1938) 'Excavations at Al Mina, Sueidia: i, the archaeological report', *JHS* 58, 1-30.
Woolley, L. (1953) *A Forgotten Kingdom being a record of the results obtained from the excavations of two mounds, Atchana and Al Mina, in the Turkish Hatay* (London).
Wrong, D. (1997 [1979]) *Power: its forms, bases and uses* (Oxford).
Wylie, A. (2002) 'The reaction against analogy', in *Thinking from Things: essays in the philosophy of archaeology* (Berkeley / London) 136-53.
Zanker, P. (1988) *The Power of Images in the Age of Augustus*, trans. A. Shapiro (Ann Arbor).
Zhivkova, L. (1986) *Liudmila Zhivkova: her many worlds, new culture and beauty, concepts and actions*, Collected Speeches (Sofia).
Zifferero, A. (1995) 'Economia, divinità e frontiere: sul ruolo di alcuni santuari di confine in Etruria meridionale', *Ostraka* 4, 2, 333-50.
Zuidema, R.T. (1964) *The Ceque System of Cuzco* (Leiden).
Zuidema, R.T. (1983) 'Hierarchy and space in Incaic social organization', *Ethnohistory* 30, 49-75.

Index

www.ingramcontent.com/pod-product-compliance
Lightning Source LLC
Chambersburg PA
CBHW070547100726
47907CB00004B/1301

* 9 7 8 0 7 1 5 6 3 2 9 8 7 *